THE FLAG
My Story: Kidnapped by Red China

A True Story By

Steve E. Kiba

ISBN: 1-4033-2904-4 (e-book)
ISBN: 1-4033-2905-2 (Paperback)
ISBN: 1-4033-2906-0 (Dustjacket)

Library of Congress Control Number: 2002105679

This book is printed on acid free paper.

Printed in the United States of America
Bloomington, IN

1stBooks - rev. 9/24/02

Table Of Contents

June 29, 2001
Jackson Hole, Wyoming

It was the last night of a Writers' Conference sponsored by the University of Wyoming. My wife and I were attending a barbecue supper in the pool area of the Snow King Resort in Jackson Hole, Wyoming. Sitting at our table were several other couples. Among them were Mr. & Mrs. Thomas Barnes from Austin, Texas. Linda Cummins from Glencoe, California, sat on my right, and her son John Bryan was next to her.

After a short period of general conversation, I learned that Mr. Barnes had been in Korea during that conflict and had assisted in the repatriation of POWs after the cease fire was declared. This reminded me of my own combat experience in Korea with the 581st AR Squadron and the missions we flew into enemy territory in unarmed SA-16 amphibious aircraft. But most of all, I remembered the incident of one of our other aircraft, a B-29 that was shot down; I was very familiar with the subsequent tragic story of its crew. Colonel Arnold, our Wing Commander, was aboard, and his presence increased the size of the crew to 14 members. I told the group at the table a short version of their story.

A/1C Alvin Hart, the Tail Gunner, was killed when their B-29 was attacked by numerous MIG fighters. The others managed to bail out before the plane exploded, and they were all captured by the North Koreans.

The North Koreans quickly turned them over to some Chinese Communists in the area rather than transporting them to a Prisoner of War camp in Korea; the Communists violated the rules set forth by the Geneva Convention in the treatment of POWs and carried them across the border into Manchuria. After a short imprisonment there, they were again moved, this time to Peking, China, where they were later tried as spies and sentenced to prison terms of up to 15 years. The trials and the sentences were unjust because they were not spies; they were just American airmen doing their duty in time of war. When they were captured, they should have been treated as prisoners of war and sent to a regular POW camp. They should have been released shortly after the cease fire in July 1953, but they were not; their captivity and brutal treatment continued two years and three months beyond that date.

From the time they were captured in January 1953, until they were released in August 1955, they were kept mostly in solitary confinement, on starvation diets, without proper sanitary facilities or adequate clothing, and they were tortured both physically and mentally in ways that no civilized person would think of. That they survived such a long period of cruel treatment is incomprehensible.

Ultimately, it took efforts by the United States Congress, President Eisenhower, Secretary of United Nations Dag Hammarskjold, Secretary of State John Foster Dulles, U. S. Ambassador Henry Cabot Lodge, and pressure by the British government and other nations of the world to obtain their freedom.

As I related the story of this unfortunate crew, I noticed that the young man sitting at the table was listening very attentively. After we finished eating and went our separate ways, he searched for me in the crowd. He introduced himself as John Bryan Cummins and told me that his generation "had no clue as to how they got what they had, in the way of freedom, material things, and opportunity." He said that they were a "spoiled bunch" who took everything for granted and that the story I had just related (about the B-29 crew) should also be told to "his generation."

On the way home to Abernathy, Texas, I thought about his suggestion, and I decided he had a good point. I had just finished a novel and was set to begin compiling a book of my short stories, but I put it all aside to concentrate on this new project. Since the B-29 crew was in my squadron during the war, I had personal knowledge of the matter. In addition, I knew most of the crew members. I had numerous newspaper and magazine clippings that I had kept in a scrapbook concerning their ordeal and the unfolding drama of their negotiated release. I believed I was in a good position to write a true and interesting account of their experience.

I began trying to arrange interviews with all of the surviving members of the crew. I spoke with Eugene Vaadi, the Aircraft Commander, who now lives in Florida. I also spoke with Colonel

Arnold, who was our Wing Commander; he too lives in Florida. Then I contacted the Radio Operator, Steve Kiba, who resides in South Carolina. I made tentative arrangements for interviews, and I was able to schedule them and make travel reservations for early September 2001. The plan was for me to meet with Steve Kiba first, then drive down to Florida to see the other two.

Steve and his wife Darlene were gracious enough to invite me to stay with them while I was doing my interviewing. I accepted their invitation, and it was an ideal situation; we were able to visit at length while we were not working.

Everything went well until the second day when, in the process of our work, I came to a greater understanding of the separate plights of each individual crew member and how it would affect what I wanted to write. First, the crew members were essentially "kidnaped" by the Red Chinese, then separated and put into solitary confinement. They were kept apart and in isolation for most of the duration of their false imprisonment; therefore, each one of them had his own particular story to tell, and that fact presented the feasible probability that enough material existed for eleven books—one for each prisoner— not just the one I had in mind. Second, Eugene Vaadi called, and he was having second thoughts about an interview. After talking with him, I realized that my proposed interview would bring up many unpleasant memories that would be too painful for him to discuss, so we cancelled it. However, he gave me permission to use the information I had already gathered that pertained to him, plus some of the things we had discussed personally. Third, in my conversations with Colonel Arnold, Eugene Vaadi, and Steve Kiba, I learned that three of the crew were deceased, two had written their own books, and the others, for various reasons, did not want to talk about the experience. Fourth, in the midst of my interview with Steve, I learned that he had kept notes, a kind of diary, and he had already put his story in manuscript form.

This broader knowledge led me to a logical conclusion: the book I wanted to write for the Bryan Cummins generation was embodied in the individual stories of each crew member. Wallace Brown had already written his book, THE ENDLESS HOURS, published in 1961. Two of the other members were in the process of writing their own books. Steve Kiba had his unpublished manuscript, so it seemed to me that my most reasonable course was to work with Steve in getting his story published. I presented this idea to him, and he agreed.

A couple of days later I left and drove down to Florida where I met with Colonel John Arnold. We had a fine visit, and during the interview he gave me some printed material regarding his imprisonment. He had a twinkle in his eyes when he quoted poetry to me that he wrote during his imprisonment. It was clear by his demonstration that he confounded the Communist interrogators at times by interjecting his poetry in response to their rigorous questioning. I already knew about the extensive torture he went through, but he explained it again for me, and I marveled that at 89 years of age he could talk about it in a matter-of-fact way, yet with just enough defiance to show the steel of his character—a trait that was surely instrumental in his survival during those horrible years of imprisonment. We reminisced about our past experiences when we flew together on the amphibious SA-16 that I was assigned to, and very soon he grew tired. I was appreciative of the time he gave me, but I realized it was time to leave. I took some pictures, thanked him, and left. I came home the next day, September 9, 2001—two days before the September 11 tragedy in New York City.

When I got home, I began work immediately on Steve's book. I had trouble putting it in the computer because I got very interested in his riveting story; I often found myself reading rather than working. It is the story of a man falsely accused and unjustly treated. His diary-like account of the conflict with his Chinese captors and the brutal treatment he received from them expresses his rage, sometimes graphically, sometimes in subtle ways. From the moment of his capture until his release two years and eight months later, his anger and frustration grow in intensity daily, sometimes to a point where he has desperate thoughts, but never to the point of hopelessness. Indeed, it is his fighting spirit that sustains him. In spite of the torture, inhumane treatment, and prolonged interrogation sessions imposed on him, he rallies his courage, his hope, by frequent and deliberate confrontations with guards and other prison officials. He continually shows his contempt for the Communist Chinese by his steadfast refusal to cooperate with them in their indoctrination sessions and by ignoring, to the extent he can, their inhumane prison rules; the depth of that contempt is revealed by his adamant refusal to capitalize the word "communist" anywhere in his written story.

After reading Steve's story and Wallace Brown's book, THE ENDLESS HOURS, plus interviewing and visiting with other crew members, I have concluded that their survival was a remarkable feat of great self-discipline, determination, and personal faith. And I agree with the young man, John Bryan Cummins, who said their story should be told to his generation.

So, Mr. John Bryan Cummins, here is the story you asked for. The tragedy in New York City more than two months **after** our meeting proved beyond a doubt that you were right to be concerned about your nation and your generation. May the heroic story of Steve Kiba and his fellow crew members inspire you and your peers as it has many of us in earlier generations.

·Truman Dayon Godwin

Dedication:

This book is dedicated to all who took part in World War II, the Korean War, the Cold War, and the Vietnam War, but with even greater appreciation to the thousands of selfless men and women who gave their lives in order to keep America and the West free, and to the thousands of unfortunate American servicemen who were "left behind" to languish and suffer a slow agonizing existence in a dismal foreign communist hellhole.

I should like to make a special dedication to my dear friend Alvin Dale Hart, our Tail Gunner, who sacrificed his life during our night of terror, and to Henry Weese and Paul Van Voorhis, both of whom failed to return from our horrible nightmare, thus joining the thousands of "living dead" in the communist gulag system.

Steve E. Kiba

JOHN 15:13

Greater love hath no man than this, that a man lay down his life for his friends.

Scofield Reference Bible

Introduction
By John H. Noble

Let's imagine that you were somewhere in trouble and desperately needed help. Worse yet, you were not even sure that anyone was ever coming who would be willing to help. You probably would be wishing that you had a thousand voices to join you in calling for help.

Here is the account of a few who feel just like that. They have been left behind in the hands of the Communists. No captor is kind and good to his captives, and the Communists hold the record in making you feel it. It is bad enough to live like an animal and to be kicked around like one; but, when you are told by your captors that they don't even believe in a superior being, then you are in trouble.

While reading these pages, I was carried right back to "Vorkuta," the dreaded Soviet slave camp in the Arctic, where I spent 9½ years seeking to exist from one day to another. The hardships of nature were hard enough to endure: food was not sufficient and clothing was not adequate, but this was not the worst of camp life. To know when to fear and whom to trust was a much bigger problem. Yet, worst of all is the thought that no one cares or knows about you back home. This thought drove many a prisoner out of his mind, and it might just do the same to you if you were over there.

For 9½ years, I wondered if anyone in the outside world was willing to help me or even cared about me. The Soviet officers often laughed at me and said, "If your government cared about you, they would get you out of here!"

In these pages, Steve Kiba has given America and the world a detailed account of exactly what goes on and always will go on when one falls into the clutches of the "Reds," unless we begin to learn and heed the message.

Here is another document which should cause every freedom loving individual to see the need to take a stand against the Communists and their sympathizers.

Most important of all is the plea of those "left behind." Today there are still so many Americans from World War II in Russian slave camps; there are several thousand still in Red China from the Korean

Conflict, and many, many more from recent years in Vietnam and elsewhere. These helpless, voiceless, "abandoned ones" are pleading with you through this account to help them call for "help." They are asking you to raise your voice loud and clear, first of all in prayer to Our Father in Heaven and then to everyone who has a heart and the will to stand up for what is right.

God knows and cares. He uses our hearts and hands to do the work. The question is—do you care?

J.H.N.

Preface

While languishing in a cold, damp Red Chinese political prison, I often thought of writing about my experiences if I were ever released. There were three reasons which caused me to hesitate in writing my story immediately upon being "deported" from Red China. First, U. S. Government officials and agencies "advised" us to keep silent about fellow American countrymen whom we had seen in Red Chinese prisons and who had not been "deported" with us. Second, we were admonished to forget a three week period and all incidents which had occurred during this particular time. We were led to believe that to write or talk about this episode would be most harmful to the individuals concerned and most embarrassing for their superiors and the agency for which they worked. Third, having been instilled with ultra-patriotism by my impoverished but proud immigrant parents, I was extremely reluctant to do anything that might be detrimental or harmful to my government or to my fellow countrymen who had been held over by the ruthless, vile communists.

After returning to the United States, I immediately set about recording my recent nightmarish experiences in Red China; but, for the aforementioned reasons, I had no intention of going public with my story at that time. I arranged my notes in book form and had them typed. The manuscript was completed in 1959, and I put it into a closet and tried to forget about that horrible nightmare in hell. I endeavored to push from my mind the stark reality that there were still fellow Americans, four of whom I knew personally, languishing in that hellhole over there and still living and enduring moment by moment that same horrendous nightmare to which we had been subjected. But try as I would, I just couldn't forget them! How could I? The agonies of that frightful nightmare had been burned indelibly onto my mind.

I struggled with my conscience for several years. It kept urging me to speak out against the unbelievable thing that the Air Force and U. S. Government had asked us to do. Their admonitions kept running through my mind. Finally, I decided to heed my conscience and to do what was morally right: I decided to speak out on behalf of the voiceless American captives who had been abandoned.

I maintain that every American must hear and know the real truth—that the communists *did* hold over American servicemen and civilians, even after the Korean Armistice had been signed and after they had vehemently claimed that they had released them all. I know this to be a fact, for I was one of those whom they held over.

The communists do not provide (nor have they ever provided) a complete and accurate list of the prisoners-of-war whom they hold in captivity. For eighteen months (twelve months after the signing of the Korean Armistice), I was not on any official list, and it was only through a freak twist of fate that I and the other members of our B-29 crew were finally listed as prisoners. Had it not been for this odd twist of fate, our B-29 crew could very well still be wasting away in solitary confinement in filthy, stifling, six-by-ten cells in some political prison in Peking along with the many other American and U. N. servicemen from the Korean War who, to this very day, have not been accounted for, and who, it appears, have been abandoned and forgotten by the United States—its government and its people.

Red China saw in Colonel Arnold (our Wing Commander) and our crew a bargaining chip to be used in its negotiations to gain admission into the United Nations and to force the return of Formosa (Taiwan) to Red Chinese control.

It was Red China's eagerness to interrogate and to torture and torment Colonel Arnold that saved most of our crew from being transported to Siberia. Had he not accompanied us on our routine leaflet-drop mission that night, our entire crew would most assuredly have joined the thousands of other American servicemen "left behind" after World War II and the Korean War to endure a never-ending existence of pain, anguish, misery, and disillusionment in some god-forsaken Soviet gulag. Even so, I believe that two of our crew (the radar men) did make the frightful train ride into that frigid, frozen hell-on-earth.

The story which you are about to read basically chronicles our crew's sojourn into hell, but unfortunately it is also the sad story of the thousands of voiceless, abandoned, and "all but forgotten" American servicemen and civilians who unquestioningly volunteered to carry out our government's efforts—feeble and wavering as they were—to halt the persistent onslaught of raw communist aggression.

I decided to make our story public so that the caring American people might know that there are indeed American countrymen suffering and enduring physical and mental abuses at the hands of the cruel, sadistic, and inhumane communists. Also, I pray to God Almighty that our story opens the eyes of all Americans (especially the elected and appointed officials in Washington, D. C.) to the startling fact that a cease-fire or treaty with the wily communists does not automatically guarantee the release of all captives being held by them. It didn't in 1953! Nor did it in 1973!

In this story I endeavor to convey the feelings of loneliness, frustration, anguish, disillusionment, fear, and abandonment which a captive experiences in his solitary cell thousands of miles away from home. I also describe several interrogation-indoctrination sessions and the maltreatment at the hands of the Red Chinese jailers. These sessions and our mistreatment (physical, emotional, and mental) were mild compared to what those "left behind" had to endure and are likely still enduring.

This story is not a pleasant one; in fact, it is downright horrendous. It is not meant to entertain you; it is meant to show you the harsh realities of living under communism or socialism.

May this frightful story touch the heart and conscience of each and every caring, sensitive fellow American and inspire people to vow never again to allow our calloused, insensitive, overpaid government officials (vegetating in their plush D. C. offices) to abandon and then forget a single American who might have the misfortune of being taken captive while in the service of our great nation—THE UNITED STATES OF AMERICA!

S.E.K.

Those On Board Stardust Four Zero

1. Colonel John Knox Arnold, Commander of the 581st Air Resupply & Communications Wing (Now deceased).
2. Major William E. Baumer, Instructor Pilot from the 91st Strategic Reconnaissance Squadron.
3. Captain Eugene Vaadi, Aircraft Commander, 581st AR Squadron.
4. Captain Elmer F. Llewellyn, Navigator, 581st AR Squadron.
5. 2nd Lieutenant Wallace L. Brown, Pilot, 581st AR Squadron.
6. 1st Lieutenant John W. Buck, Bombardier, 581st AR Squadron.
7. A/1C Steve E. Kiba, Radio Operator, 581st AR Squadron.
8. T/Sgt. Howard W. Brown, Flight Engineer, 581st AR Squadron (Now deceased).
9. A/2C Harry M. Benjamin, Left Scanner, 581st AR Squadron (Now deceased).
10. A/2C John W. Thompson, Right Scanner, 581st AR Squadron.
11. A/2C Daniel C. Schmidt, Central Fire Control (CFC) Scanner, 581st AR Squadron (Now deceased).
12. A/1C Alvin D. Hart, Tail Gunner, 581st AR Squadron (Killed in Action when the plane was shot down).
13. 2nd Lieutenant Henry D. Weese, Radar Operator, 581st AR Squadron. (Was seen bailing out. Red Chinese said he was killed in the crash, but they have given no proof).
14. 1st Lieutenant Paul E. Van Voorhis, Radar Operator, 581st AR Squadron. (Was seen bailing out. Red Chinese said he was killed in the crash, but they have given no proof).

PART I

JUMP INTO HELL

Steve E. Kiba

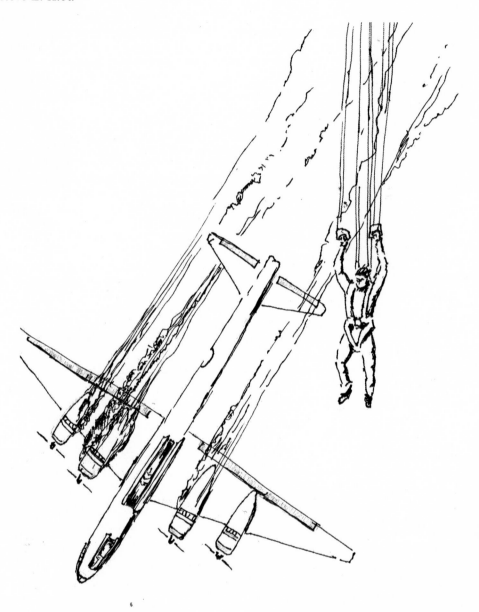

We arrived at Yokota Air Force Base, Japan, on December 18, 1952. Our mission was to fly routine leaflet-drops over North Korea. According to our Wing Commander, these would be "milk runs." My job was that of Radio Operator on Captain Eugene Vaadi's crew.

Our *first* mission, however, was on January 12, 1953. It was a dark, gloomy afternoon; dark black clouds clung almost motionless near the horizon. Shortly before takeoff it began to rain.

At 5:25 P.M. we boarded our aircraft and took our respective positions. Shortly, our B-29 was winging its way across the rough Japanese Sea. As our bomber approached the Korean coastline, the heavy rain subsided. While we proceeded inland toward our targets, the clouds disappeared and the stars came out, making it easier for the enemy to spot our plane. In our briefing we were promised heavy cloud covering over the target areas. At 24,000 feet, the outside temperature was 50 degrees below zero, and a thin covering of ice was forming on the wings. Suddenly we were blinded by enemy searchlights below as our B-29 became focused in their beams.

We evaded the searchlights and continued on course. A few minutes later the persistent beams of light again scanned the clear sky. Then the monstrously large white eyes focused continuously on our plane. The inside of the plane, usually dark, now was light as day. Hoping to get to the safety of a lower altitude, and to the "deck" if possible, Captain Vaadi put the bomber into a nosedive. Reaching the deck would have afforded us sanctuary from the enemy's jet fighters, but such a maneuver was dangerous in the mountainous terrain we were in. Before we could reach the deck or before we were diving for any length of time, all HELL broke loose! Our B-29 was unarmed except for tail guns, so we were in a perilous situation. We could see the red flashes of the tracers from the Red Chinese and Russian M I G 15's. Twenty millimeter rockets were whizzing all around our helpless B-29. One engine after another burst into flames as the rockets found their marks. We could see the red flashes of ground fire beneath us, and whitish-gray puffs of smoke appeared as bursts of flak exploded beneath us. The explosions gradually got closer and closer. Suddenly an ear-piercing blast, followed by a jolt, sent loose objects flying through the burning plane.

I looked across my cramped space toward Captain Elmer Llewellyn, our Navigator, and saw a dark crimson liquid trickling from behind his right ear. There was a hole about the size of a silver dollar in his four-inch Plexiglas window. I heard Major Bill Baumer, our Instructor Pilot who was sitting on the floor over the nose wheelwell, tell Captain Llewellyn that he was badly hurt.

To my right and about two feet beyond my seat, the forward bomb-bay was being gulped up by a greedy mass of orange-red flames. I felt a gust of cold air sweep through the aircraft, heard the shrill whistle of the cold night wind, then SILENCE; it seemed the world itself had ground to a halt. The silence was broken by a di-di-dit, dah-dad-dah, di-di-dit, Morse code for SOS, and a frantic voice shouting, "Mayday! Mayday! Mayday!" The crew members all over the plane were performing their emergency duties and preparing to bail out. Just before being hit, we had made our leaflet drop on our fifth target.

The remaining leaflet bombs were dropped simultaneously to clear the aft bomb-bay, which was a means of escape for the men in the rear section. Three engines were afire, and the forward bomb-bay was also full of flames. Red and white flames were trailing the plane, and molten metal was falling off and slowly burning itself out on its way to the frozen earth below.

Captain Llewellyn put on his chest pack and walked to the twisted bulkhead door leading into the forward bomb-bay. He saw the gaping inferno and turned toward me, tapped me on the shoulder, and said something, but I couldn't hear him because of the noise and confusion. I assumed he was telling me not to exit thought the bomb-bay, so I nodded my head and continued to send my distress message. I then locked the key in its "SEND" position and pushed the detonator button on the IFF (Identification Friend or Foe) set. By this time, the flames were creeping into the navigator and radio compartments. I sat for a few seconds folding and unfolding my microphone cord as if nothing had happened and I had all the time in the world. Llewellyn walked to the nose wheelwell and followed Colonel John Arnold, our Wing Commander, Major Baumer, and First Lieutenant John Buck, our Bombardier, out into the cold, cold night.

After neatly laying aside my hand mike and snapping on my chest pack, I swiveled in my seat and looked at the shattered bulkhead door, then at the blazing bomb-bay which was my bailout exit. I stood up and walked to the nose wheelwell. I stood there for a few seconds watching Technical Sergeant Howard Brown, our Flight Engineer. I smiled at him; then I climbed down the wheelwell ladder and dropped into the frigid ocean of darkness that surrounded us.

As I fell through space, I had the strange sensation that my chest pack was pulling away from me. Tumbling haphazardly through the icy air, I mechanically pulled the ripcord. Instantly, the canopy popped out with a tremendous force. When the parachute was fully open, I scanned the sky for a last glimpse of the burning plane. I did not see the abandoned aircraft, but far below me I saw a parachute make two wide sweeps and disappear.

A few minutes later I realized what had happened, but I refused to believe the facts. I kept thinking it was a bad dream and I would wake up back at Yokota.

The piercing cold wind penetrated my thin summer clothing. The cold air rushed up my pants legs; I desperately tried to zip them tighter, but I was unable to do so. My gloves were in the bottom pocket of my flight fatigues. I tried to unzip the pocket to reach them, but by this time my fingers were too numbed by the icy air. I put my hands into the pockets of my flight jacket and let the fierce wind carry me along.

I scanned the sky around me. Above me and to my right, I saw another parachutist. The MIGs were everywhere. Several planes were making passes and firing rockets at us as they whizzed by. It seemed as if I would never reach the ground.

As I continued to descend, I looked downward, and I saw scattered lights that appeared to be on the ground. A few minutes later I sensed my nearness to the terrain below that grew ever closer. Peering into the darkness, I made out the outline of hills against the horizon. Suddenly, there was a snapping of branches, and I found myself sitting on a frozen hillside deep inside North Korea.

The shroud lines of my parachute were entangled in a small bush, and the canopy was flapping noisily in the stiff breeze. After rubbing my hands vigorously to restore circulation, I was able to remove my

Steve E. Kiba

gloves from my pocket. While still in the chute harness, I struggled with the snap. With great effort I finally managed to free myself. I hid the chute as best I could; then I removed my Mae West (inflatable life jacket) and hid it also.

After a close survey of my surroundings, I saw that I was about 200 yards from the summit of the hill. It was covered with scattered patches of dirty snow and a few withered bushes. In the moonlight I could see a train station a few hundred yards down in the valley, and steel rail tracks ran beside it and curved out around the hill. I saw the lonely light of a locomotive, creeping along lazily, headed south, and I toyed with the idea of hitching a ride.

I was sure that the North Korean Army had already begun searching for us, and I figured that by hopping the train I could get completely out of the particular geographical area they would be concentrating on. It was possible I could get close enough to our lines to sneak across to safety. I really wanted to hightail it, but I just couldn't get the two wounded crew members out of my mind. My conscience told me that it was my responsibility to find them and help them if I could. Yet, my better judgment urged me to flee, so I was forced into an inner struggle to resolve the conflict. My conscience and sincere loyalty to my fellow crew members, created by a long history of working together with them, won the struggle, and I decided to stay and look for them. I sat down on the ground and watched the train until it merged with the blackness of the night and became as invisible and remote as the opportunity I'd had to evade capture. I remained there, sitting, collecting my wits, and watching the train station lights blink on and off, for what seemed like hours. Finally, I arose and just stood there on the hillside listening to the howling wind.

About fifteen minutes later I heard another train. It was also traveling south. Again I considered the possibility of hopping it, but my conscience was still adamant that I remain and look for my wounded friends. After the train disappeared from sight, I started walking slowly up the hill toward unknown trials and destinations.

My mind was active, and I wondered where the others might be. It was now 11:30 P.M., and everything was quiet except for the occasional howling of a dog and the crunching of snow under my feet.

The Big Dipper was visible overhead, and I frequently checked my bearing with it. I walked, slid, and crawled mile after mile up and down the steep, rocky North Korean hills, periodically taking cover behind a boulder from the stinging wind. I contemplated building a fire, but with what? I had no matches. In my haste to exit the burning aircraft, I failed to pick up my survival gear.

I continued my search for the wounded men until daybreak, and then I took cover under a rock ledge to avoid possible capture. The ledge offered little comfort from the sub-zero temperature.

In a valley below my position of refuge, there was a shabby straw house with a thatched roof. Next to the house was a chicken coop. On the other side of the road there stood a large, yellow wooden house. Bluish smoke curled slowly skyward from their chimneys. This made me even more aware of the extreme bitter cold that was relentlessly sapping my strength.

I sat under the ledge thinking about my fellow crew members, especially the ones I knew were wounded. I decided I must continue my search for them, so I left my icy sanctuary and crawled up the hillside. From my position above, I saw men—enemy soldiers or scouts, I was sure—combing the area. I heard a shout and hastily retreated to my hiding place under the rock ledge.

Very soon I heard the stomping of feet and voices chattering rapidly in an unrecognizable language. I remained motionless, almost afraid to breathe. Finally, I heard the footfalls and voices fade away, and I felt relieved, at least for a short while. I took the prudent course and remained in hiding while I watched the movement of men in the valley below. This observation made it very clear that the enemy was everywhere.

About eight o'clock in the morning I noticed a plane resembling a C-47 circling to the south of me. The plane circled at an altitude of approximately 100 feet for three hours; then it headed north. During that time I heard searchers on the ridge above me again, and the valley below was still a beehive of search activity.

The enemy search parties climbed into their jeeps and weapons carriers and left the area around noon. I thought about leaving my hiding place, but I was too afraid. I was getting colder by the minute and my extremities ached. I kept moving my toes and fingers. I pounded my arms, legs, and chest. The gradual loss of feeling in my extremities made me feel exhausted and drowsy, but I forced myself to stay awake.

By late afternoon the bitter cold was getting the best of me. My face, hands, arms, and legs were now completely numb. I was also starting to lose feeling in my chest. My hands and face swelled up and turned bluish-black. I tried to open my Escape and Evasion kit, but I was unable to do so. Using my teeth, I tried again and succeeded. I took out a map of Korea and studied it to determine the best way to get to safety in the south.

Driven by hunger, fatigue, and the indescribable cold, I left the sanctuary of the rock ledge and ventured into the ravine. I was convinced that I would freeze to death if I didn't find adequate shelter.

I started moving slowly down the hollow and headed toward the straw house. I had absolutely no feeling in my legs. After taking only a couple of steps, I fell. I attempted to get to my feet, but I couldn't, so I rolled and slid the rest of the way down the hillside. Once I reached the bottom, I struggled to get back on my feet. Finally, after much exertion, I succeeded.

Unsure whether or not I could trust the inhabitants of the straw house, I stood in the yard staring at the door. Several minutes later the door opened and an elderly couple came out. They walked toward me, looked me over carefully, and then smiled. The old man tugged at his right earlobe. As they got closer, they smiled again and then turned onto a path and headed up the valley.

Assuming that the old man had given me the correct pre-arranged signal, I thought that all of the inhabitants of the house were with the underground. I wobbled over to the door and knocked. A middle-aged woman opened the door and let me in.

As I shuffled into the house, I saw a concrete structure where a fire was burning. The woman stared at my swollen, discolored hands and face and shook her head in disbelief. She quickly filled an aluminum washbasin with hot coals and placed it on a bed board near the concrete structure. I held my hands over the hot coals. All the while, her little boy watched me. I smiled at him, and he smiled back. I tried to give the woman and her child articles (fountain pen, watch, needles, thread, etc.) from my Escape and Evasion kit, but she refused them. Neither would she let the child touch anything I offered. She seemed extremely upset over the articles.

Although the woman showed only kindness at first, within a short time her terror of the communists overcame her Christian charity. While I was occupied warming myself and trying to make friends with her small boy, she slipped out of the house. It was perhaps five or ten minutes before I sensed her absence. I quickly realized that I had made a terrible mistake in trusting her. I was about to leave the house and head for the woods. Just as I reached the door, it flew open and the women and eight local Korean militiamen dressed in blue cotton padded uniforms rushed into the house.

I reached for my .45 pistol, but they grabbed my arms and forced them up behind my back. They relieved me of the pistol, my E & E kit, and then they searched me. They just glared at me as they examined the contents of the E & E kit. I tried to get them to read the blood chit, and one of them read aloud the Korean writing on it, after which they all laughed about it.

A few minutes later eight more militiamen arrived, and my .45 pistol was given to one of the newcomers who, by his actions and air of authority, appeared to be their leader. He, too, took the blood chit and read it aloud; then he and his comrades laughed hysterically. (In brief, the blood chit stated that I was a United Nations airman, and the United States Government would pay a reward to anyone who helped me get back to my unit so that I might continue my fight against communist aggression.)

I stood there filled with deathly fear while my captors kept up a constant chatter. I was still weak from my long exposure to the bitter cold; I was hungry, thirsty, and exhausted, so my comprehension of what was happening to me was beyond my scope at that moment. It all seemed like a hellish nightmare.

Just then another militiaman entered the house carrying a large strand of rope. He came to me and started to tie my hands behind my back, but his leader motioned him away. Instead, they grasped my arms and led me out of the straw house.

We headed down the valley. Their leader still had my .45 pistol, and most of the time he held it to my left temple. As we walked down the valley, more and more people joined us. Soon the crowd accompanying me numbered several hundred. An old woman came up to me and shoved two dirty buns into my hands and motioned for me to eat them. I was still too scared to be ravenously hungry, but I didn't want to offend the woman. I took a small bite out of one of the buns. I started to chew the bread and almost gagged on it. Somehow I managed to swallow it. The woman had a broad smile on her face and kept urging me to eat more. I forced myself to eat several more bites. The woman, seeming pleased, finally disappeared into the huge crowd. After she left, my escorts took the rest of the buns away from me.

A few minutes later a small boy came out of the crowd and offered me a cigarette. I tried to explain to him that I didn't smoke, but he didn't understand and continued to offer it to me. The leader of the enemy group repeatedly caressed my temple with the barrel end of my pistol and insisted that I take the cigarette. Therefore, I took it. The boy lit it, and I took a puff or two and almost choked on it. The leader, the "boss," took the cigarette from me and finished it.

After walking for about an hour or so, we came to a crossroad where Red Chinese soldiers were waiting for us. The Korean militiamen handed me over to the Red Chinese, and they threw me into a jeep. We quickly departed, and I wondered where they were taking me. Up to that point, they had not been conversant, so it was no surprise that they did not reveal our destination to me.

After a long bumpy ride, the jeep pulled up to a small stone building. Two of the soldiers jerked me from the jeep and shoved me through the mob that had gathered around the stone building. Once inside the building, they shoved me into a filthy room on the right. The room had two boards situated about three feet off the concrete floor; these boards were used as beds, and someone was lying on one of them. A potbellied coal stove occupied the center of the room, and a single, barred window was on one wall. Five or six Red Chinese soldiers with rifles, an officer, and a young lad dressed in black were standing around the stove. The young lad spoke English and served as an interpreter.

They searched me and took my identification card and dog tags. The interpreter questioned me briefly. He boasted that they had already picked up thirteen airmen from our B-29, two of them as they touched the ground. He indicated that two were wounded and the others were in good shape. Then he told me to lie down. I obeyed his command and lay down on the other board, but I was too unnerved to sleep. Weird thoughts kept fleeting through my mind.

I had been lying on the board for only a short time when the interpreter said, "Follow me. Someone wants to take your picture."

When the other man got up from his bed board, I saw that it was Airman Second Class Harry Benjamin, the Left Scanner on our crew. The soldiers escorted us out into a courtyard where a young boy with a box camera snapped our picture. I took out my comb and ran it through my hair. Benjamin borrowed my comb and did the same, after which the young squirt snapped another picture. Then we were taken back to the room.

A few minutes later I had to use the latrine. I told the interpreter, and he had two guards escort me outside. We forced our way through a multitude of human bodies that were gathered in the courtyard and all around the outside walls. We passed through the gates and went to an outhouse several yards outside the building where they had us confined. By this time I had concluded that the building was their jail.

Many of the men, women, and children in the crowd followed us to the outhouse, which had no door. Whatever one had to do was done in full view of everyone. I was embarrassed. I stood over the slit trench for what seemed like hours trying to relieve myself. The curious mob kept staring at me, pointing, chattering, and laughing. Finally I was able to urinate, and the guards pushed and shoved me through the unsympathetic mob and back into the jailhouse. On the way back, I saw Second Lieutenant Wally Brown, our Co-pilot, sitting outside of the room in which Benjamin and I were being detained. We managed to exchange nods as the guards hurriedly pushed me through the door and into the room.

About six o'clock in the evening the Red Chinese threw Benjamin and me into an American weapons carrier. Three of our crew were already in the vehicle. Howard Brown and Wally Brown were sitting in front of us. Eugene Vaadi, our Aircraft Commander, was sitting next to Benjamin.   There were also twelve armed guards on the weapons carrier.

We rode through a small town not far from the jailhouse. About an hour later we entered another town and stopped in front of a large U-shaped building. They pulled us one at a time from the vehicle and carried us into the building. Once inside they put us in separate rooms.

My room was large, but dirty. There was a whole row of bed boards with pads and blankets on them. I had not been in the room for more than ten minutes when a group of natives filed in to examine me. The group consisted of men, women, teenagers, and children. They looked at me as if they had never seen an American. Some stared at me as they might have visually examined a wild animal. Many who were unable to restrain their curiosity felt the material of my flight jacket. Several of the young girls ran their fingers through my long, wavy hair, looked at each other, and giggled. My swollen, discolored hands and face caught the attention of most of them there; some shook their heads, while others laughed sadistically. This procession and examination continued for several hours. During that time I was brought a small piece of dry bread and some warm water.

Around nine o'clock that night I was blindfolded. A soldier slung me over his shoulders—like a sack of potatoes—and carried me outside. I felt twinges of body pain when he flung me into the back of a truck. A driver started the engine, engaged the gears, and started us off on an uncomfortable journey that lasted for about an hour. When we arrived at our destination, they removed me from the truck, carried me piggyback into a building, up a flight of stairs, and dropped me onto a straw mat.

When my captors left the room, I pulled off the blindfold. I was pleasantly surprised to find myself next to a radiator. Hoping to warm my hands, I reached out and touched it, but it was ice cold. There was no glass in the windows, only paper, which did little to keep out the frigid air. An extremely low wattage light bulb hung from the ceiling, and it gave off scarcely any heat or light.

After surveying my luxurious suite, I lay down on the cold straw mat and tried to sleep. Having only a very thin pad for cover, I was just too damn cold. I could only lie there, shivering, thinking, and trying to figure out everything that had happened.

At seven o'clock the next morning (January 14, 1953), the guard ordered me to sit up. Shaking continuously from the intense cold, I sat on the hard straw mat waiting for—I didn't know what.

Two hours later a soldier placed a small bowl of rotten potato peels and a set of wooden chopsticks on the filthy floor. I picked them up and for several minutes stared at the unappetizing contents of the bowl. I attempted to use the chopsticks, but my hands were too numb. Frustrated, I threw the chopsticks across the room and used my fingers. I took a couple of bites and gagged. I shoved the garbage aside.

At ten o'clock an English speaking soldier dressed in an olive-drab colored padded uniform paid me a visit. He spoke perfect English, and he even knew all of our G. I. slang. He was about five nine and had a round, chubby face. He first asked me some general questions, and then he provided me some information regarding the other crew members. He, too, mentioned that two men from our B-29 were captured immediately upon reaching the ground. He talked to me for about 45 minutes and then told me he had to interview the other members of the crew. Before he left, I told him I needed to use the latrine. He escorted me to the ground floor where he asked two guards to take me to the outhouse.

After we reached the primitive toilet, I held my breath as long as I could and breathed as little as possible because of its awful odor. I stood over the slit trench, and even in sub-zero temperatures the foul stench from the trench was overpowering. After I had urinated, the guards hustled me back to the icebox that served as a jail.

At five o'clock that afternoon, chow—rotten potato peels and wormy rice—was served. I tried to use the chopsticks again, but every time I got the garbage to my mouth, it would fall off. In anger, I broke the chopsticks and used my fingers. Smelling and looking at the crap made me sick, so I closed my eyes and tried holding my breath. Each bite caused me to gag. I was able to force down only a couple of bites. The rest I pushed aside.

After chow, I sat on the dirty straw mat and listened to Benjamin walk below. Occasionally I could hear the guard hack and spit on the floor. The Red Chinese had a filthy habit of spitting on the floor and then rubbing it in with their foot.

I was extremely cold and could see my breath as I exhaled. I sat on the mat shaking violently. Unable to control my shivers, I decided to try to move around. While I was doing so, I saw plastered on the walls Red Chinese newspapers containing political cartoons lashing out at the American Government.

Time passed slowly, and every minute seemed like years. Finally, at 9:00 P. M. the guard ordered me to lie down and go to sleep. I did lie down, but it took forever to go to sleep; my shaking from the biting cold kept waking me.

Early the next morning, after another restless night of tossing and turning, I was aroused to again face the uncertainty of my future. Sometime in the late morning, a Red Chinese soldier came into my room. He was taller than average, stout, and dressed like the others. His English was poor. He began asking me generic questions, like name, rank, serial number, and outfit. He insisted that I was from the 581st Air Resupply and Communications Wing and that I was a no good liar. I feigned ignorance to any information about the ARC Wing. This infuriated him. He lost his temper and yelled all kinds of obscenities at me. Finally, in a furious rage, he stormed out of the room. I sat on the mat shaking and wondering whether I was really a prisoner or merely having one hellish nightmare.

Occasionally I could hear Benjamin singing below. Hoping to attract his attention, I pounded on the icy radiator. After hearing someone tap back, I started sending a message. I received an answer, but I couldn't identify the "fist" (distinguishing characteristics in the way the different radio operators press down on the key when sending Morse code). I assumed that Benjamin had forgotten much of his Morse code. Off and on throughout the morning, I continued to tap messages and kept getting undecipherable answers. That afternoon two Red Chinese men came into the room. One had a blow torch, and I realized that what I thought was someone answering me was in reality the Red Chinese pounding on the radiator trying to thaw it out. They put the torch to the cold radiator and banged on it in an effort to thaw it. They worked on it for 30 minutes and then left. I didn't notice any change in the temperature of the room; it was still ice cold, as was the radiator.

That night I lay down and tried again to sleep. I was dead tired, but I still couldn't sleep. I was just too damn cold, and every little noise disturbed me. The uncertainty of our situation really grated on my nerves. Shortly after I "retired," I heard someone coming up the stairs. Several people came into my room. One, dressed in white and apparently a doctor, asked me why I wasn't eating. He took my temperature and checked my pulse. Then they went back downstairs, and I was left alone with my thoughts and fears.

The next afternoon at two o'clock, January 16, 1953, the obnoxious soldier entered my room and interrogated me. He kept insisting that I was in Red China, and he threatened me with all sorts of torture if I didn't confess. He pointed out that they had ways of making a man talk. He boasted that before he was through with me I would be most willing to cooperate. Finally, the jerk left. As he walked out the door and down the stairs, I shouted, "Shove it up your bung (rectum, anus) you no good bastard!"

Later, as I was forcing down my wormy rice and rotten potato peelings, the friendly soldier came in and informed me that shortly I would be taking a long train ride and that my conditions would improve greatly. I asked him when we would be leaving and if they were moving us to a Prisoner of War camp. I asked him if we were being taken to Red China and if he would be going with us. He confirmed that Red China was our destination. He said he would very much like to accompany us but that he had to stay in Korea. He said that he did not know where in Red China they were taking us and that he did not know if the whole crew was being moved. It was a little after 5:00 P.M, and he said that they ate supper at this time every day. He added that if you were late it was tough luck and you did not get any supper. Then the good-natured soldier left, and I finished what I wanted of the garbage.

Within the hour several Red Chinese men entered, clamped leg irons around my ankles, clamped handcuffs on my wrists, covered my eyes with a black blindfold, picked me up and carried me down the stairs, and threw me into a jeep. We rode for 45 bumpy minutes before the ride came to an end. The rough road left my blindfold in disarray, so with limited vision I was able to see the U-shaped building where we stopped. They took me out of the jeep and carried me into the building and into a large room where they removed the blindfold. Again, I was subjected to hours of searching scrutiny and sadistic taunting by curious mobs of natives.

At 9:00 P. M. they took me to the basement of the building. A young man in uniform and another in black were assigned to guard me. Both men were heavily armed.

There were blackout curtains on the windows. About an hour later, I heard sirens and trampling of feet rushing to the basement. Occasionally the lights would dim and then go out, so candles were lit. The air raid lasted about half an hour.

At 11:30 P. M. we left the warm building and walked down bomb-beaten back alleys toward the train station. Twenty minutes later we drew near a long flight of steps alongside the station. We stopped. The guard in black went on ahead to see if the way were clear. Momentarily he returned. We climbed the steps and then passed in front of the station, which was overflowing with civilians and soldiers. We finally reached our coach and climbed aboard. The car was already filled with soldiers. We took seats close to the center of the car.

The seats were wooden, and there was scarcely any leg room. When the train was completely filled with passengers, we started our long, slow journey northward. The train kept starting and stopping, always in jerks. It was a long, tiresome journey. The seats became harder and harder and harder, and the leg room seemed to grow shorter and shorter and shorter. I was not permitted to budge. My legs were cramping, and my tail bone was sore.

Throughout the entire trip, my breathing was stifled by the smell of the Red Chinese soldiers. You could almost see the garlic fumes coming from their nostrils. The terrible smell of their bodies and clothing, mixed with the garlic smell, was nauseating, almost unbearable. In addition, they assailed my ears with loud voices and created an unintelligible babble by everyone talking at once. One fellow took out a harmonica and started playing. Many of his comrades began singing as loud as they could.

The train continued to snake its way north. The shade was pulled down over my window, but I could see around the side and under the bottom of it. Sometimes I could see snow on the ground outside. The leg irons and handcuffs cut into my ankles and wrists and made my journey even more unbearable. A number of passengers were munching on tangerines, which made me drool. It seemed as if the trip would never end.

At twelve noon on January 17, 1953, after a long and arduous ride, the "Korean Express" finally came to a stop in front of a station somewhere in Manchuria. After all the passengers had gotten off, the guards placed a blindfold over my eyes and hauled me out into the cold, cold day. Suddenly, the guards began to run, dragging me along behind them. I heard behind us a patter of feet that came closer and closer. The guards dragged me down a flight of steps in a zigzag pattern. We were chased for about 15 minutes; then the audible footsteps of our pursuers faded out. We stopped and the guard dressed in black left. I lifted the blindfold and saw that we were in an alley and that there were large buildings all around us. Suddenly the soldier realized that I had lifted the blindfold and was looking around. He quickly put it back in place. In a few minutes the other guard returned. They led me out into the main street and threw me into the back of an American weapons carrier.

We traveled away from town on a fairly good highway for about an hour. The weapons carrier turned off the main highway and went down a bumpy road for a short distance. Finally we arrived at a prison compound, and the vehicle came to a halt. My escorts checked my blindfold and then carried me into the prison. I was thrown into a cell where my blindfold, handcuffs, and leg irons were removed. Before they left, they searched me thoroughly and took everything I had except my comb.

I surveyed my new quarters. The door was about three inches thick with a half-inch slit. The guard used the slit to continuously spy on me. There were no windows. A single, dim, low-power light bulb furnished the only light in the cell. There were no furnishings except for an old metal cot, and there was nothing on it: no mattress, no cover, and no pillow. I quickly figured out that the cells in the structure were constructed in such a way that there were spaces between the walls of individual cells, and fires were built in those spaces to heat the cells. Consequently, it was hot in my cell, damn hot. I named the prison the "Hotbox." It was like living inside an oven, hot and stuffy. I could hardly breathe, and I felt as though I would suffocate. The intense heat caused my entire body to ache. I experienced the sensation that long, sharp needles were being jabbed into every part of my body.

Bedtime was still hours away, but I was exhausted. I lay down on the springs of the cot, and in spite of my discomfort, I was asleep in a matter of minutes. My fatigue caused me to fall into a deep sleep.

At five o'clock that evening the cell door flew open with a loud bang. Startled, I jumped to my feet and rubbed my weary eyes. I had been aroused from the first good sleep I'd had since before my unfortunate capture. Little did I suspect that it would be the last for quite some time.

A guard placed a small bowl of wormy steamed rice, a small bowl of cabbage-less cabbage soup, and a spoon on the floor just inside the door of my cell. I hurried over, picked up the bowls and spoon, and returned to the cot. I picked out the maggots and threw them away; then I hastily gulped down the slop. The meal was terrible, but I was so hungry I finished it anyway. When I was through, the guard removed the bowls and the spoon. The rest of the evening I sat on the edge of the cot. I kept wondering why they brought us to Red China.

At 9:00 P. M. the guard ordered me to lie down. I told him that I needed to use the john. He escorted me to a toilet located at the end of the hall. It was a dirty, crude, barbaric place with slit trenches.

Bright and early the next morning, January 18, 1953, the guard pounded on the door to awaken me. I sat up and waited to learn what was next. Thirty minutes later the caretaker brought in a pan containing scarcely a quarter inch of warm water. This was the first "wash" water since my capture. He also gave me a bar of soap, a toothbrush, a tube of toothpaste, a small, green tin cup, and a hand towel with Chinese characters on it. I washed my hands and face, brushed my teeth, and started to sponge bathe the rest of my body. Suddenly the caretaker rushed in and explained in an angry tone that bathing was against the rules. He removed the pan and slammed the door behind him when he left.

18

I sat down on the metal springs of the cot. In spite of the acute pain that racked my whole body, I had to struggle to stay awake. The cell seemed even hotter than it was the day before. I was terribly uncomfortable from the profuse sweating caused by the excessive heat. In an effort to make it more bearable, I stripped down to my underclothes, but even this didn't help much. My eyelids got heavier and heavier, and my head kept dropping against my chest. Suddenly the door flew open, and I jumped as if I'd been shot. I had dozed off, and the loud noise of the door being opened gave me a jolt. I stared at the door and saw that it was breakfast time; I got the "Hotbox Special," cabbage juice and wormy rice. I was so hungry that I didn't even bother to pick out the worms.

After gulping down the meager portion, I spent the long morning hours just sitting and thinking about different things and wondering why I was in this mess. The inactivity of sitting on the edge of the cot made me drowsier by the minute. I kept dozing off, and the alert "eyeball" just outside my cell kept pounding his fist on the door to wake me up.

At 2:00 P. M. the lights went off. I took advantage of the situation, threw my clothes in a corner, lay down on them, and went to sleep. After awhile the guard shined a flashlight through the peephole to check on me. He couldn't see me anywhere, so he opened the door, came into the cell, and flashed his light all around. When he found me asleep in the corner, he shined his light in my face. I looked up and glared at him. He delivered a swift kick to my upper thigh, just missing my groin, and ordered me back to the edge of the cot. I obeyed him; but after he left, I put my clothes behind the cot, curled up on them, and went back to sleep.

About five o'clock the lights came back on. The guard couldn't see me, so he opened the door and looked around for a short time. Without disturbing me, he closed the door quietly and left. Within a few minutes he returned, accompanied by a prison official. The prison official chattered angrily, pointed his finger at me threateningly, and motioned for me to sit on the edge of the cot. He strongly indicated that I was not to sleep. I couldn't understand all his gibberish, but I think he was trying to explain that it was against prison rules to sleep during the day and that violators would be severely punished. Finally, they left and slammed the door behind them. A few minutes later the caretaker opened the door and set my slop on the floor.

I soon learned that only two meager meals per day were served at the Hotbox. During my brief time there no one spoke English to me. My discomfort and pain were aggravated by the guard's continual watchfulness; the most obvious things I could see from anywhere in the cell were his eyeballs staring at me through the invasive slit in the door.

Later that evening I was sitting on the edge of the cot staring first at the walls and then at the door. I reacted with a start when the door was suddenly jerked open. Several Red Chinese soldiers entered. One was carrying leg irons and handcuffs. He attached the hardware to my ankles and wrists and then blindfolded me. Their cruelty was becoming repetitive: they again hauled me out of the building and threw me into an American jeep. I felt the jeep surge into motion, and I made a somewhat desperate mental note that I was off on another bumpy ride to another unknown destination.

PART II

WELCOME TO THE PEANUT PALACE

After leaving the Hotbox, we traveled about ten minutes on a bumpy road. The jeep then pulled onto a smooth highway, and I soon sensed that we were headed back toward town. In about an hour the jeep came to a halt. They pulled me from the jeep and took me into a building, down a flight of stairs, and into a basement. They shoved me into a cell, removed the blindfold, and searched me again. This time they did a thorough job. They even took my comb, which really infuriated me.

After they left, I looked around my new "castle." There were no windows. There was a small opening about six inches by eight inches in the three inch thick door through which they watched me and handed in slop. Several boards nailed together served as my bed. A straw mat, a cotton pad, and a thin blanket were on the board. On the other side of the cell there was another board which left very little place for me to walk or move around for exercise. A small, open-topped earthenware jar was included in the meager furnishings; it was, of course, a crude vessel for me to use as a urinal. It remained in the cell at all times, except when I took it out to be emptied. The floor was made of red tile, and a single, bare light bulb hung from the ceiling. It was extremely cold in my new prison quarters, and there was no heating equipment, not even any physical evidence to suggest that the room could possibly be heated.

It was about 10:30 P. M., so I lay down on my "Chinese orthopedic" mattress and covered myself as best I could. It was extremely difficult to keep the blanket on myself because of the handcuffs and leg irons. I spent a restless night and continuously shivered from the intense cold. I estimated that the temperature in the cell was about 25 degrees.

The next morning (January 19, 1953), I was awakened at seven and taken outside to empty my jar. I had to walk down the hall, turn right or left, and walk down another hall to the toilets. There were five cells in my stall; as far as I could see, there were similar stalls on each side of mine, thus accounting for 15 cells in that part of the basement. I was billeted in cell number seven.

That evening several Red Chinese soldiers came into my cell and took away my Air Force B-15 jacket, my lightweight summer flight suit, my fatigue jacket, and my fatigue pants. They replaced those garments with a padded jacket and padded trousers. There were no buttons on the jacket, and the sleeves were too long. The trousers were also many sizes too large and had no buttons except for one at the top. The crotch was down near my knees, and the fly stood wide open. I rolled up the jacket sleeves and the trouser legs and harbored the sarcastic attitude that I really looked sharp in my new wardrobe.

Sometime between eight and nine o'clock, I was given a small bowl of very watery gruel, a tiny bun, and about 15 half-peanuts, unsalted of course. Between twelve noon and one o'clock, I received two tiny buns and 15 half-peanuts. For supper, between six and seven o'clock, I got two small buns, 15 half-peanuts, and sometimes watery soup. The Redchink bastard who brought the chow always asked me if I wanted more. I always said yes, but I never got more. I was given one cup of boiled water daily, unless I was being punished. If they thought I was being uncooperative in the interrogation room, the boiled water was withheld and my food ration was reduced. If I happened to be out of my cell when a meal was served or the water doled out, I simply didn't get to eat or drink, and this was a frequent occurrence. Consequently, I went days on end without as much as a crumb of bread or a drop of water. At first this "backdoor" rationing of my food and water didn't bother me too much, but I soon lost 50 pounds. I called this place the "Peanut Palace."

At the Peanut Palace the guards, armed with machine pistols, changed shifts every two hours. The door was bolted and padlocked from the outside, and the guard stationed outside in the hall did not carry a key to the lock.

Shortly after we arrived, interrogations really began in earnest. I was interrogated every day. The sessions lasted anywhere from six hours to 24 hours. When the sessions lasted for any length of time, the interrogation was done by teams. A team would work for four to six hours. During the sessions I had to stand about 15 feet from the interrogator's desk. A guard armed with a rifle stood behind me. Whenever I failed to give an answer that pleased the interrogator, the guard would jab me in the back with the barrel of his rifle.

I was in leg irons and handcuffs almost the whole time I was there. Because the chain connecting my leg irons was only about six inches long, I could only take very small steps. Going up stairs was extremely difficult, and most of my interrogations were conducted on the third floor. The guard would help me up the steps and along to the interrogation room by poking the barrel of his rifle in the small of my back. If I got back to the cell before boardtime (bedtime), I was supposed to stand at attention or walk.

On January 20, after I had eaten a meager breakfast, a guard armed with a rifle took me from my cell and escorted me to the third floor and into a large room. Three sinister-looking characters were seated behind desks. The one seated in the middle was wearing an official-looking uniform; the other two were wearing padded, olive drab clothing. The man in the middle was the interrogator; the man seated on his right was the recorder, and the man on the interrogator's left was the interpreter. Neither rank nor insignia was visible on any of them.

The interpreter, whom I named "Tongue," yelled for me to stand at attention. I told him that I WAS at attention and that it was their damned over-sized Red Chinese padded clothes that gave the appearance that I was at ease.

Tongue told the interrogator what I had said. The interrogator rattled off something in Chinese; and the gung-ho guard, standing directly behind me, jabbed me in the back with the barrel of his rifle. Tongue screamed in a loud, exasperated voice, "What you name?"

I told him my name was Kiba.

"Kiba, you shall show more respect for the officers of the People's Liberation Army!"

I responded that I didn't see any officers or insignia or rank.

He said, "You a wise guy. We know how to take care of you kind. When we get through with you, you show more respect."

Again, I felt a sharp jab in the back.

Tongue was now wild-eyed and angry. He said, "This the 'judge,' and you on trial."

Once again the guard delivered a painful jab to the small of my back. Almost simultaneously my three adversaries picked up their cups and took a long slurp of tea.

The inquisition continued with the interrogator ordering me to cooperate fully and telling me that it would be most harmful for me if I didn't. He called me a "no good bastard" and accused me of lying.

He told me that the Red Chinese abhor liars, and then he advised me to change my "incorrect" attitude at once. Tongue asked me if I understood what the "judge" had said. I didn't answer and looked at them with a "shit-eating" grin on my face.

"Do you realize you situation?" Tongue screamed. "It is very serious! You must realize that."

The guard, a consistent player in their stupid game, gave me another sharp jab with his rifle barrel.

Acting dazed, I asked Tongue what he had just said and told him my mind was wandering. As I expected, this provoked them to further anger. Tongue said the "judge" called me a "smart-ass" and warned me to start answering correctly or it would be my end.

"Are you threatening me?" I asked defiantly.

"We do more than threaten if you do not start to cooperate. Now answer correctly. What you outfit?"

Since they already knew that we were somehow connected to the 91st, I answered that I was in the 91st.

"You lie," Tongue said. "You cheat the 'judge.' You no damn good! You must change you attitude. If you continue to lie, it be most harmful for you. What you outfit?"

After repeating this question several times more, the Redchink pigs started asking all kinds of personal history questions. This grueling inquisition went on for ten long, weary hours before Tongue finally said, "The 'judge' is very lenient and sees that you tired. He will permit you to go back to you cell and think over all that we have asked you. The next time we talk to you, you must cooperate, or the 'judge' be angry. Now go."

The raunchy guard escorted me back to my cell. I immediately sat my tired, aching body on the board. This annoyed the guard, and he made me get up and walk. I took several steps and sat back down. My defiance made the guard very angry; so when I asked him about my supper and my hot water, he laughed and told me supper and water had already been served. Then he ordered me to get up and walk. I just laughed at him and remained seated. He yelled obscenities at me and walked away from the door.

Finally, at 9:00 P. M., I was told to lie down. I was sleepy, tired, disgusted, and hungry. Unable to make myself comfortable because of the leg irons and handcuffs, I lay on the hard board and tried my best to go to sleep. That was not an easy thing to do, regardless of how exhausted I was. The leg irons pressed against my ankles, and my feet swelled up and ached so bad that I got very little sleep. The pain was indescribably excruciating when I got up and walked, and it grew in intensity while I was forced to stand in the interrogation room for hours. In addition, the pain in my back, caused by the severe blows from the guard's rifle barrel, was so extreme it monopolized my mind and emptied it of any pleasant or hopeful thoughts that would make my life more bearable. I was miserable.

One morning as I was leaving the cell to empty my little brown jar, I stumbled, dropped the jar, and spilled the contents all over myself. My angry guard yelled abuses at me and shoved me back into my cell. My clothes eventually dried, but the pungent odor of urine lingered on.

Later, I noticed that there were several cuts on my left hand and that there was a chunk of flesh torn from my right thumb. I had not noticed the cuts before, but a stinging sensation caused by the urine spill brought them to my attention. A few days after I first noticed the wounds, my thumb became infected. The infection spread rapidly, and shortly extended up into my wrist. A faint red line appeared running up my arm from my wrist.

Living, if that's what you call it, at the Peanut Palace was no picnic. They grilled us hour after hour asking us the same questions repeatedly. I would be safe in saying that a question would be asked 500 times a day. They cursed us, insulted us, jabbed us in the back, flattered us, and tried every conceivable means to extort information from us.

The first four or five days I was questioned on personal history and seemingly unimportant military information. After the fifth day, the nature of the interrogations changed; the line of questioning was altered, and it became more serious.

My last painful trip to the third floor resulted in an extremely long and tedious session with major emphasis on one particular question. The entire session was interspersed with threats and attempts to cause me to lose faith and trust in my country and its leaders.

Q: What is the story?

A: I don't have a story.

Q: Talk! What is the story?

A: I have no story. Even if I did, I wouldn't tell it to you.

Q: What is the story?

A: What story?

Interrogator's Answer: You fabricated story.

My answer: I have no fabricated story.

Q: What is you story?

A: No story.

Q: Do you want to live?

A: I don't give a damn.

Interrogator: If you do, you better come across with that story.

A: What friggin' story?

Interrogator: You story!!!

A: Blast you, I told you I had no story!!! What the hell you want me to do, make one up?

Interrogator: Do not swear at us. No, we do not want you to make one up. We only want you to tell us you story, and we want the truth. Now are you going to tell us the story you were to fabricate and use on us?

A: Tell you what?

Interrogator: You story. Now tell us!!!

A: What story?

Interrogator: You story. The crew's story.

A: My story. The crew's story. Man, what are you talking about? I have no story, and the crew has no story. How can I tell you something I don't know?

Interrogator: Tell us, or we shoot you.

A: Go ahead. I don't care. I wish the hell you would.

My answer was truthful. There were many times I wished that they would go ahead and kill me and put me out of my misery. Many times I was at the point where I just didn't give a damn anymore.

Interrogator: We have many ways to make you answer. Sooner or later you will tell us what we want to know.

Several hours later, I was still standing; or rather I was weaving back and forth on my wobbly, aching legs. My head felt twice its normal size, my tongue was swollen, my throat and mouth were dry, and it even took great effort for me to talk. When I opened my mouth, my throat burned. All I could think of was a good, cool glass of water, but I knew I wouldn't get it. Their questions hit my eardrums like a huge sledgehammer, and the room seemed to be spinning like a top. I struggled to control my inner self and to maintain my physical being. I had not had a drink for five or six days, and my tormentors were sipping tea in front of me. The interrogation continued.

Q: What is the story?

"No story," I said for about the hundredth time in a weak voice that had grown fainter and which through its ragged, mournful sound reflected the pain I was being forced to endure.

"Lousy no-good Yankee, what is you story?" The interrogator screamed.

"No story."

"You no-good, rotten son-of-a-bitch! How ignorant do you think we are? Now what is you story?"

"No story."

"Rotten, no-good Yankee! If you do not tell us, we are going to shoot you."

"No story."

"You no good. You lie. You no-good bastard. You cheat. You are big liar. I warn you again that we Chinese do not like liars. You better take my warning and tell us. If you do not, then it will be most harmful for you. Now tell us!"

"Tell you what?"

"What we just asked you."

"What was it you asked?"

"You better change you attitude, or we will finish you now."

"I wish you would."

"We will do it nice and slow. We will not let you off easy by shooting you. You are the type we like to drag it out on. With you attitude you will get no mercy. Do you understand what I mean?"

"Yes."

"Well, are you going to tell us, or are we going to have to get rough?"

"I can't tell you what I don't know."

"You know! You know! We know that you know. Do you value you life?"

"What life?"

"You life. You are young and intelligent. If you use you head, you can go a long way with us. If you cooperate and help us to punish you capitalistic bosses, you will be doing the world a big favor. You will do youself a great favor. You are smart enough to see that you have been exploited by you warmongering bosses. You do the dirty work, and they reap the profits. Do you call this justice? Are you truly satisfied with you form of government? Now will you be smart and help us?"

I said wearily, "I'm just a capitalist at heart, and I'm satisfied with my government."

"You are a naive kid! You have been thoroughly poisoned by those Imperialistic-Capitalistic Warmongers. You are rotten clean through, but we do not give up easy. After we are through with you, you will have a different attitude. What do you think?"

"I think you're a bunch of no-good pigs, and I don't think you can change my attitude."

"Time will tell. We have all the time we need to work on you. Now tell us you story."

"No story."

"You are very stubborn, but you will tell us before we finish with you. You will tell us what story you had made up to use on us. The others have already told us, so why do you resist?"

The interrogators paused for a prolonged sip of tea and then resumed their barrage of questions. Now they began directing their questions toward a variety of topics, such as survival training, survival and communications gear, and the organizational structure of various Air Force wings. Four hours later they switched back to the original line of questioning and for the next six hours the interrogator kept screaming this question at me in Chinese and the interpreter in English (always using "you" instead of "your"): "What is you story?"

My throat was raw, and I could barely respond. My eyes were bleary and bloodshot, and I ached all over. I was so exhausted that I felt nauseated. Everything was spinning before me, and I could barely hold myself up. When I felt myself on the verge of fainting, I fought to remain conscious. Just as I reached the point of passing out, I experienced a sensation similar to a severe electrical shock surging through my entire body, and I would be jolted back to the horrible reality of my situation. I was hanging on through sheer willpower. I was determined not to fall. I was also determined that I was not going to beg for mercy, or even a sip of water. I decided I would die before I'd let them break my spirit.

The interpreter finally said, "Well, we let you go back to you cold cell and hard board. While you there, stop and think of all those fat-cat businessmen in nice warm houses and sleep under white sheets tonight and have breakfast of bacon and eggs. While you on you board, you think of white sheets. When you bite you tongue and cheeks eating peanuts and bun, you think of bacon and eggs. Why should you take all the knocks? Do you owe them anything? If you ever get back, will they treat you any different? Ho-ho-ho! You are naive kid. Now you go back and think. You have nothing else to do but think. Ha-ha-ha!"

My legs were wobbling from standing so long. I was led back down to my cold, damp dungeon. After the door locked behind me, I lay down on the hard, cold board. The board seemed harder than usual, but it still felt good after being upstairs all day and half the night. Pain in my legs and feet kept me awake. I lay there the rest of the night shivering and trying to remember what I had said upstairs. I spent the long, sleepless hours mentally attempting to anticipate their next questions and wondering how I could avoid answering them.

I realized that their brutal treatment of me and the cruel, senseless, intensive interrogation sessions that they subjected me to were having its effect on me; I was growing weaker with each hour, and I was acutely aware of my depression. All of these factors were beginning to produce a feeling of disillusionment that I struggled with all my strength to oppose.

The next morning I sat alone in my cold, damp cell waiting for my usual "slop" they called a meal. The minutes passed like hours. It was Sunday, February 1, 1953. My 21st birthday was only four days away. Breakfast never did arrive. Instead, three Red Chinese soldiers appeared in my cell. They examined my handcuffs and leg irons and

31

then led me from the cell to the second floor. They let me sit down, and we began to wait—for what?

At eleven o'clock they put a pair of blacked-out goggles over my eyes and took me outside where I was loaded into the back seat of a sedan. We rode for approximately 20 minutes and ended up at a railroad station. They removed me from the car and carried me into a coach. After they seated me and removed the goggles, I saw the coach was empty except for three uniformed guards with machine pistols. I was impressed that they considered me important enough to give me an entire railroad car to myself and then honor me with such a powerful security force.

The train departed the station about 30 minutes later, and I started another journey to another unknown destination. Around one o'clock the three guards and I had a meal of sausage and bread. Compared to the garbage at the Peanut Palace, the meal was "cuisine extraordinaire."

The train snaked northwest for many hours then turned and headed southwest. The seats were just as hard as the ones on the first train, and the trip was a long one. I shifted restlessly from one position to another. All the while, I kept wondering where I was being taken, and why. I considered the possibilities, but they were so filled with unpleasant ramifications that I finally forced the thoughts from my mind.

In the late afternoon a man dressed in black came through the coach and gave us some hot water to drink. That evening we ate more sausage and bread for our supper. I slept on and off; and when I wasn't sleeping, I tried to look out the shaded window.

At two o'clock the next morning we finally arrived at our destination. The guards took me from the coach and hustled me into a car. After a long bumpy ride, which lasted about an hour, the car bounce across a set of several railroad tracks and shortly afterwards came to a stop. We ended up on the outskirts of a very large city. I was carried into the prison. We passed through a round room into a cellblock. I was put into a cell, and they searched me again.

It was a small cell, about six by ten. The only things in the cell were a bed board, a pad, and a blanket. The bed board rested on sawhorses about eight inches above the concrete floor. In the outside wall there was a window with six half-inch rusty steel bars, two rusty crosspieces, and chicken wire. In the wall facing the hallway, there was a hardwood door three inches thick. At eye level on the door, there was a narrow "observation slit" the guard used to watch me. After making this quick survey of my new surrounding, I lay down on the board and tried to sleep.

The next morning I made a closer examination of the cell. I saw that the walls were white and a small light bulb lighted my cell and an adjacent one. The thick, heavy door was painted black.

At eight o'clock the caretaker opened the door and set a small, silver mess kit on the floor. It contained a small bowl of rice gruel and a tiny bun. For lunch I was served a small portion of vegetables, a small bowl of steamed rice, and a small bowl of soup. The supper menu was the same. I decided the food here was going to be better, and the portions larger, than at the Peanut Palace. I later named this place the Wagon Wheel due to its construction, which featured cellblocks extending outward, like spokes, from a central point.

My brief stay at the Wagon Wheel was mostly uneventful, with the exception of one very embarrassing and unpleasant experience. On the second evening after I arrived, I began getting sick. My stomach was aching and cramping up in awful spasms. I indicated to the guard, whom I had dubbed "Eyeball," that I was sick and had to go to the toilet. He just stared at me, like a dummy, through the slit in the door. I was in pain and actually felt miserable all over. I clinched my fist, gritted my teeth, bit my lips, and strained with every ounce of my being to hold back. I kept trying to make Eyeball understand the urgency of my call, but my efforts were of no avail.

Finally, after ignoring me for an eternity, he opened the door. I hobbled out of the cell as fast as I could, but the damned leg irons made it impossible to hurry. Yet, I fought fiercely to hold back, even as I struggled to get my pants down. I silently cursed the handcuffs that prevented me from achieving that goal. I was both outraged with the circumstances of my predicament and angry at the guard for not helping. As I felt the warm semi-liquid soak my pants and run down my legs, I silently cursed my tormentors and their cruel ways. When the foul, pungent odor struck the guard's nose, the Redchink bastard wrinkled his nose in revulsion, then shouted curses and obscenities at me. He physically urged me back to my cell with rude shoves, while he continued to castigate me with a babbling stream of Chinese words. When we got back to the cell, he hurriedly pushed me inside, closed the door, and locked it. He glued his beady eyes to the observation slit and watched me wallow in my own excrement.

PART III

THE HOTEL

Steve E. Kiba

On the night of February 4, 1953, I was moved to a prison in the heart of the city. So far I had been unable to get anyone to tell me where I was, and during my long, idle hours I considered the matter. What I knew about Far East geography was little help in making a certain determination. I only knew that I was in a large city, and I was surrounded by and tortured by Red Chinese sadists. It wasn't a big leap to figure out that I was probably in Red China somewhere, but that was as far as I could take it. As they removed my blindfold at the new prison, I saw my greeting committee. It consisted of a short female, an officer, and several other nondescript characters dressed in black. The female read me the prison rules.

She said, "You must obey the guards. You must not talk. You must not whistle. You must not talk with the guards. You must not look out the window. You must not write on the walls. You must not move about except when told to do so. Do you understand?"

"I guess so," I said.

The officer (who turned out to be the warden) looked at my right hand and said something to the girl. She asked me about my hand and told me a doctor would come to examine it. Then the handcuffs and leg irons were removed, and my welcoming committee left the cell. My wrists and ankles had painful raw marks where the cuffs and irons had dug into the flesh.

My new cell was ten feet square. There was a window with seven iron bars in the outside wall. Wooden pickets extended from the bottom to more than half way up the exterior side of the window, making it difficult for me to see out. There was a kang (bed, usually a board that serves as a bed) in the unheated room that took up most of the space. It was mounted on sawhorses two feet above the concrete floor. There was a straw mat on it and three cruddy, filthy pads that looked and smelled as if they had never been washed. Those three elements formed the crude contraption that was my bed. Sitting on the kang, I could look up and over the window pickets and see the high perimeter wall.

In one corner of the cell, there was a five gallon bucket, which I was told to use as a toilet. The bucket smelled as if it hadn't been emptied or washed for several weeks. Hanging from the ceiling was a thick electric cord with a light bulb attached at the end. The cell door here was similar to the cell doors at my previous prisons: thick, very thick; but, instead of an observation slit, this one had a gate-like aperture. The covering over the aperture could be opened or closed at the whim of the guard on duty. When anyone looked in to observe me, I could see part of the face—something minor, I suppose, but it was less eerie than seeing two eyeballs in a slit.

After making the short survey of the cell, I laid my weary body down on the kang and went to sleep.

The guard came into my cell at six o'clock the next morning. He showed me how he wanted the pads folded; then he arranged one pad for me to sit on, one to lean against, and one to cover myself with. Then he made me walk and exercise for about five minutes.

At seven o'clock the caretaker brought in a pan with a fourth of an inch of warm water in it. I washed my hands and face and brushed my teeth, after which I stripped down to my waist. I noticed that the front of my T-shirt had a large splotch of dried blood on it. The stain had no definite shape, but I noticed that it looked similar to a map of Africa. I checked over my upper body to see if there were any wounds, but I found none. The discovery worried me enough to prompt an examination of my sweatshirt. All I found was a tiny spot on the inside. Back at the Hotbox, I had stripped down to my underclothes; but, in the dimly lit cell, I didn't notice the dried blood on my T-shirt.

I laid the T-shirt and sweatshirt on the kang and started to give myself a sponge bath. The guard saw what I was doing and rushed back inside my cell. He started to remove the washbasin but stopped momentarily when he saw my T-shirt. With my T-shirt and the washbasin in hand, he left hurriedly and returned a few minutes later with the warden. The warden was holding my shirt, and he had an inquisitive look on his face. He said nothing to me while he examined me thoroughly to find the wound that caused the blood. Finally, both the guard and the warden left; the warden carried my bloody shirt with him.

To pass the time, I checked the walls for writing, crude pictures, or code that some poor prisoner might have left. I found nothing, so I defied their damned prison rules by starting a calendar and scratching my name on the walls in several places.

I was really hungry, so I asked the guard about food. He explained in sign language that it wouldn't be long and gave me a cup of boiled water from the thermos he had. I drank the water and sat staring at the wall, the half-covered window, and the guard's opening in the door.

Finally, about eleven o'clock, chow was brought in. I was given a small bowl of watery millet gruel which I hastily and greedily devoured. My greed was from starvation, and my haste was from fear that it might be taken from me before I could finish it. I suddenly realized that my pride and dignity had been reduced to an almost animalistic, groveling level, and I was ashamed. I silently swore to continue to stand strong against their cruelties until I could stand no longer and to maintain dignity, courage, and strength to the utmost of my ability. I also realized that to do that I would have to subdue those feelings and emotions that were created when my powerful survival instinct was challenged. This was not determination without a cause. So many times since I had been taken captive, raunchy guards bedeviled me by coming back in only a few minutes after they had served me slop and screaming abuses at me for being so slow. Sometimes they would snatch the bowl from my grasp and take it away. In anger, I would scream profanities at them. Then the cruel, sadistic, Redchink bastards would laugh at me hysterically. I always waited anxiously and with anticipation for a little nourishment to get into my belly and temporarily quell the constant hunger pangs I felt, but instead I was allowed only enough to tease my stomach.

After I had gulped down my meager meal, the guard removed the bowl. I sat on my board and stared off into space as if I were in a trance. I was roused back to reality by the creaking of the door. An old white haired, white whiskered man wearing a dingy white gown entered. He was accompanied by a female interpreter, very short in stature. They asked to see my hand. I stuck it out, and the "doctor" held it in his soft, wrinkled hand. After he examined it, he punctured the infected thumb with a dull, dirty pocket knife. He squeezed and pressed on the infected area and drained as much of the pus as he could. He applied some powder to it, and then both he and the woman left.

I re-positioned myself on the kang, leaned back against one of the pads, and continued my daydreaming about better times and places.

Several hours later the guard asked me to walk around in the cell. I took about four steps one way, turned, and took four more in the other direction. I did this for about five minutes and grew wobbly from my sick and weakened condition. I felt as if I were going to fall from the exertion, so I sat down. The guard was very displeased. He scolded me severely, but I didn't understand a word because he was speaking in Mandarin. However, from the tone of his voice and the gestures he made, I assumed his words were derogatory, maybe even obscene. I ignored him.

They brought my evening meal at seven o'clock. It consisted of a bowl of cabbage-less cabbage soup and four tiny buns. I quickly ate two buns and drank the soup. I hid the other two buns with the intention of saving them for early morning. An hour or so later I felt really hungry, so I decided to eat part of a bun and save the rest. I took a couple of bites from one of them. Before I knew it, I had eaten the whole bun. In another hour or so, hunger pains were again gnawing at my stomach. I took out the last bun and gobbled it down. There was a distinct fear lurking somewhere deep within me that, if I tried to save food, the guard would take it away from me.

Never in my life had I ever expected to get so hungry. Even after I ate the last bun, I was still ravenously hungry. But with all my food gone, and faced with my stark surroundings, there was nothing left for me to do, nothing there to occupy my mind and fill the time. So I sat and stared at the wall until I was finally taken out to empty my bucket.

Right after dark on February 6, 1953, I was escorted from my cell, out of the cellblock, through the courtyard of the prison, and through the gates. We walked across a basketball court and into a stone building. I soon learned their purpose: my interrogations were resumed. When I first recognized this, I gave myself some positive reinforcement. I thought, "Oh well, at least they gave me a day off on my birthday."

The interrogations followed almost the identical pattern as those at the Peanut Palace. One slight difference was that all three characters behind the desk wore official-looking uniforms. The Red Chinese flag and a picture of Mao Tse-tung were on the wall behind the desk. The sessions took place at all hours, day or night, and lasted from a couple of hours to 24 hours. Mostly, they were long, ranging from 18 to 24 hours, with only a 30 minute break between sessions. As a result, there were many weeks when I was getting only a few hours sleep. Sometimes the sessions were split, and I would be grilled for a few hours several times throughout the day or night.

There was always a stool in the center of the room, but most of the time I had to stand. A guard stood next to me with his machine pistol pointed at my temple. The weapon was loaded and cocked.

When I was worked over during the night, I had to stay awake during the day; however, most of the time I would be taken in for another extended session the next day. As was the case at the Peanut Palace, the interrogators would have either a pot of tea or boiled water or a bottle of brandy on the desk in front of them. Intermittently during the session, they intentionally sipped and slurped their drinks to remind us of our deprived state. After 18 to 20 hours of grueling questions, they would say, "You look thirsty. Would you like a drink?"

I would answer, "Yes."

They would laugh and say, "When you start cooperating, we will give you a drink."

I would answer defiantly, "Shove it up your bung!"

On one certain occasion, the jerk in the middle position behind the desk was wearing a nice, new, fur-collared leather jacket. He looked even more sinister and evil than any other interrogator I'd had.

"What is your name?" he asked.

"Kiba," I said.

"We have been told about you. We have some questions for you, and we expect cooperation, or else. Do you understand?"

I remained silent.

"Do you understand?" he repeated.

"Yes."

"Then why do you not act like it?"

"I do."

"What have you been thinking about?"

"About how lucky I am."

"What do you mean? Do you really think you are lucky?"

"Yes. I think I'll be going home soon, and I'm lucky to be an American."

He frowned and said, "You still cling to your capitalistic ways even after you have been fooled, used, and betrayed. All the American Imperialists want is to use you. If it were up to them, you would never get home. Only the people can help you. What do you think of us, your treatment, and the things that have been discussed with you?"

"I think you're a bunch of no-good pigs! My treatment is lousy. As for your communist bullshit, you can jam it up your ying-yang!"

He was almost exploding with anger. His black eyes bored into me as he said, "You keep that attitude, and you will *never* go home. You are being treated very well. Now let us get down to business."

The Red Chinese "judges" were extremely irritated at my lack of concern for my personal safety and at my failure to show proper respect. Also, they believed that I knew much more than I was telling them, so they really got down to business. For the next eight hours they asked question after question about our Wing Commander

Colonel Arnold, the Air Resupply and Communications Wing, and its mission. As a lowly Airman 1st Class, I actually had very limited knowledge about those topics, so I was unable to give them what they considered to be the "right" answers; I believed that they knew that. Still, they accused me of lying and withholding vital information and insisted that I tell them the truth.

On this occasion, as well as others, the interrogator became extremely frustrated and continually accused me of giving them "incorrect" answers. He jumped up from behind the desk and rushed toward me with a pistol in his hand. The guard jumped back away from us, and the madman held his pistol against my head and squeezed the trigger. I was terrified, and the sound of the hammer striking metal resounded in my ears. The madman and his accomplices laughed hysterically. After doing this several times, he screamed in my ear that I change my "incorrect" attitude and cooperate or die. I was shaking all over.

During this period of time, the little female interpreter made visits to my cell. She would stand a few feet from my board.

"How are you today?" she would ask.

"Feel like hell," I would answer.

She generally stood around for about 30 minutes and just stared at me. Then she would leave. She came in every day for a month, and with each visit I became more keenly aware of my sexual hunger. She was about four feet tall and rather cute. Each day she looked cuter.

One day while the little seductress was standing in my cell, I happened to shift my position on the kang. My movement caused the contraption to make a loud squeaking sound. The guard immediately ran down the hall, jerked open the door, rushed in, and shoved his burp gun under my nose. He was so upset that his whole body was shaking. The little girl hastily explained what had happened and ordered him to leave. The guard walked out, but he left the door open. The girl ordered him to close it, which he did, reluctantly. However, he remained standing just outside the door and glared at me through his "observation gate." She ordered him to make his rounds.

I waited until the nosy guard had gotten half way down the corridor, then I made the bed board squeak again. The guard disobeyed the orders that the girl had given him and rushed back to my cell. He barged in and stuck his gun under my nose again. The girl took charge once more and sent him on his way.

I caused the kang to squeak several more times, and each time I had the same results. The guard was so dumb he kept taking the bait, and I eventually got tired of playing the stupid game.

It so happened that each time the girl visited me, this same guard was on duty. I continued to harass him until the fact that I was humiliating him finally penetrated his very small brain. Eventually he was transferred, and I pulled the same trick on his replacement. It always worked, and I concluded that brains were not a requirement for Red Chinese guards.

One morning a gung-ho Redchink guard tried to make me sit at attention facing the door. He came into my cell and forced me to sit the way he wanted me to.

Disliking force, I resumed my normal position after he left the cell. Of course this irritated him. He rushed back into the cell, pointed his burp gun at my head, and ordered me to sit at attention.

I obeyed.

But, as he turned to leave, I resumed a more comfortable position. The uneducated Neanderthal brute became enraged and ran to report my disobedience to the prison officials. An officer came down the corridor and looked into my cell but did not say anything to me. When the guard appeared at the opening again, I laughed at him. My defiance so irritated him that he showed me his weapon and indicated that he was going to shoot me. Of course I knew he wouldn't. The record of my captivity proved to me that the Red Chinese considered me and the other members of our crew much too important to permit a lowly guard to wreak his own vengeance; the guard understood that, even if he were otherwise stupid.

Later that afternoon I became violently ill. I felt hot all over and was sweating profusely. In addition, my stomach cramped and my body ached all over. To put it mildly, I felt like hell. I believed I had a severe case of influenza.

All of a sudden, I had an extreme urge to go. I rushed to the "honey bucket" (a bucket for use as a toilet) and just barely got my pants down in time. I thanked God that I wasn't in handcuffs and leg irons at that particular moment. Within the next few hours, I made 14 frantic trips to the honey bucket. It was all I could do to hold myself up. Finally, I got too weak to get up and down, so I just remained sitting on the rusty, cruddy rim of the bucket. Oh God, I felt miserable. All I wanted to do was lie down and to be left alone for awhile.

But there was to be no peace for me. That evening a guard entered my cell and motioned for me to follow him. I did not move from my half-prone position and just stared at him. He began berating me with his abusive language and ended up calling me every foul name he could think of. Still, I refused to budge, and the defiant look in my eyes said, "To hell with you."

He called for reinforcements. Another guard showed up, and the two of them jerked me off my kang and shoved me from the cell and down the hallway. I was half-carried and half-dragged toward the interrogation area. As we neared the gate, I heard a swishing sound and the thud of leather striking flesh. I heard someone whimpering and moaning. I glanced to my right and saw a figure down on his knees. Next to him was a guard brandishing a leather belt. The guard was pounding the figure with the buckle end with all his might. As I drew nearer, the savage guard stopped his beating, jerked the man to his feet, and pushed him back into the shadows.

In the interrogation room, I caught hell for giving the guards a rough time. I tried to explain that I was sick and didn't intend to irritate anyone. My explanation was either not understood or was simply ignored. They subjected me to a long lecture on my past behavior and attitude, and I was informed that any future misbehavior would result in severe punishment. After the reprimand, my interrogation began. For the next 17 agonizing hours, I went through what seemed like an eternity in hell.

By the time I got back to my cell, the evening meal had already been doled out. Again, I was too late. My stomach kept growling and rumbling. Its noises reminded me that it had been over thirty hours since my last meal—watery millet gruel. Not only was I famished, but I was also utterly exhausted—physically, mentally, and emotionally. "Miserable" was not really an adequate word to describe my feelings and condition. I ached from head to toe. I realized that each day I was growing more and more depressed. At that moment, I believed that I was about as low as a man could get. All I wanted to do was roll over and die.

As I lay on the uncomfortable board, pain and hunger kept me from falling asleep. Since I couldn't get to sleep, I could not shut off my mind. I thought, "Oh God, I'm grateful that you spared my life during the vicious attack on our plane. But I just don't know how much longer I can take this abuse. Just look at me! I'm weak, helpless, disillusioned. I feel so alone and abandoned. What's the use in hanging in there any longer? What difference does it make? Who really cares? Lord, why don't you just let them kill me and put me out of my misery? I would almost rather be dead than have to endure further pain and suffering at the hands of these godless barbarians. Oh God, I don't know what I'm saying. You alone can help me. Give me strength, Lord. Give me the strength and wisdom to do what is right. Help me to resist the temptation of taking the easy way out of my predicament. I don't want to give these inhumane barbarians the satisfaction of crushing my spirit as they have my body. But I can't do it on my own. Lord, I need You. Guide and direct my every word. Help me to control my foul language and thoughts. I try not to hate them for what they are doing to our bodies and our minds, but You know that I do hate them. Thank You for listening, Lord."

After those thoughts ran through my mind, a calm, peaceful feeling came over me, and I soon dozed off.

I slept for about an hour, and they returned to my cell. I was again hauled off to the dreaded interrogation room.

I was ordered to stand in the center of the room next to the stool. The interrogator screamed that my attitude was "incorrect," and he vowed to change it.

A huge Redchink, a monster of a man, came over to me, grasped my arms, and forced them behind my back. He squeezed my arms together close enough to place a pair of rusty clamps around my wrists. Thus bound, I was forced to stand for an immeasurable period of time while they watched and delighted in my discomfort.

Because of their speaking position, I had come to think of all interpreters as one huge "tongue." Now, this tongue looked down at me and feigned his concern. The pain in my shoulders and upper arms was excruciating, and I knew he didn't care; he was actually even satisfied.

Tongue said, "If you cooperate, the clamps will be removed."

Of course, they weren't removed. I withstood another long session bound up in manacles and suffering such unbearable pain that I have little memory of everything that happened, what I said or didn't say, or how long the interrogation lasted. I do remember that the clamps were used on numerous subsequent occasions in an effort to correct my "bad attitude." Such was life at the "Hotel."

A few days after my first experience with the clamp torture during interrogation, I was sitting on my board waiting for my unappetizing bowl of cabbage-less cabbage soup, and I kept feeling something crawling around my crotch. Since my oversized padded pants had no buttons, the fly stayed open all the time. I reached down and pulled something from the hair around my genitals. I examined it and saw that it was a crab. I immediately thought, "It isn't enough that I have to struggle against these godless, sadistic barbarians! Now I've got parasites to deal with!"

That night, and many nights to follow, I tossed and turned and scratched continuously. My new companions were running a foot race. I didn't get much sleep. The next morning I was more tired than when I went to bed the night before. To make matters worse, I had run out of soap and toothpaste.

When the old caretaker came around, I told him about the crabs and that I needed more soap and toothpaste. He laughed and looked at me as if it were nothing unusual to have crabs. Every time I saw the guard and the old man, I asked them for soap, toothpaste, and something to get rid of my crabs. Their answers were always the same: "You in prison, not hotel." Therefore, I spent my idle moments searching for and picking off the little beasts and squashing them between my thumbnails. Blood, *my blood,* would squirt all over.

The guards and prison officials didn't like seeing me pick the crabs off myself, but I paid little attention to their protests. They were the largest crabs that I had ever seen, and they grew fatter and bolder everyday. After a few days I noticed that I also had head lice. Before too long, I had them in my eyebrows, under my arms, and in the hair on my arms.

47

When I entered the interrogation room one day, I noticed I had a new crew of "screws." The interrogator was a baby-faced guy. The interpreter—Tongue—was a cute little Redchink girl, and the stenographer resembled Jerry Lewis. Every time I looked at Jerry or the girl, I'd burst out laughing. Toward the end of the session, I was given a lecture.

"Kiba, you are young and intelligent, and if you help us, we will help you. But if you continue to mistrust us and lie to us each time you open your mouth, we cannot help you. A smart man like you could really go places with us. We need men like you, men who are strong willed and who stick up for what they believe in. Men who do not give up easily even though they are wrong, as you are. You support your filthy Capitalists, and you know that they have exploited you and used you like a chess player uses a pawn.

"What were you with the capitalists? I will tell you! You are a mere airman first class risking your life for 'peanuts.' And what are you now? You are an unfortunate prisoner trying to protect the interests of your damn capitalist bosses for a measly $2.50 a day while they earn thousands. Why, even the officers on your crew make up to 20 times more than you enlisted men do. Is this fair? Do they suffer any more than you? A mere $2.50 a day for what you are enduring! Why, this is utterly ridiculous. Not only that, Kiba, you are a prisoner 24 hours a day. Your suffering is not limited to a 9 to 5 day. So, your paltry $2.50 a day comes to about ten and a half cents per hour. Think about that, Kiba. Are you satisfied with only $2.50 a day, only ten and a half cents per hour for what you are enduring? Do you think it is right for you to do all the dangerous work and endure all the pain and suffering while they get rich? Do you call this democracy? Do you call this equality? Of course you do not! Then why do you put up with it? Do you really and truly think you are fortunate to be part of such unjust tyranny? Only a fool would risk his life for 'peanuts.' Do you want to die for such an insignificant reason? Your capitalist slave-drivers do not give a damn whether you live or die. All they are interested in is reaping their blood money. They are brave as long as they are sitting in their nice plush offices. They force young fellows like you to do their dirty work. You do not appear to be the type to put up with the petty trash handed out by some stupid sergeant or some chicken-shit second 'Louie' fresh out of ROTC. But that is all over now.

"Look Kiba, do not be a fool! You are young and have great opportunities. We know that you have been fooled and used by your superiors, and we sympathize with you. It is not too late; you still have a chance, and this is your ONLY chance. We will re-educate you or else. Do not be melodramatic. This is not the movies, and you are no hero. Be realistic. You must change your attitude.

"Don't laugh when we are talking to you! Now go back to your cold cell and think. Think of the grand opportunities we are offering you. Think of how fortunate you are to be here in The People's Republic of China."

"Fortunate?" I laughed. "I'm about the most unfortunate person I can think of. Here I am cooped up like an animal, parasite infested, out of toilet articles, and being starved on watery millet gruel and cabbage to boot. Do you call it being lucky to have to look at you ugly, yellow-bellied agots (West Virginia slang word for a slow witted person) everyday?"

"Do not contradict us! If we say you are fortunate, then you are fortunate. We know what is best for you, and we would not do anything to harm you, unless, of course, you fail to cooperate and not allow us to re-educate you. Cooperate and you will receive soap, toothpaste, and medication to rid you of your unwelcome guests. Now go back and seriously consider what we have proposed to you."

On my way back to my cell, I followed directions and thought, but not the way I was instructed. "Consider helping them," I mused. "I'd rather die. They treat me worse than a dog, and yet they want me to cooperate. I say to hell with them and their friggin' communism."

Once back in my cruddy cell, I went over in my mind what they had told me. When I recalled their threats and their so-called opportunities, it made me feel good to know that I was getting under their skin by laughing at them. I had more respect for my crabs than I did for those mangy, Redchink bastards.

My "thinking," as they suggested, did not yield the results they anticipated, and I found that my mind was not subject to the "re-education" they were proposing. In fact, my thoughts turned more toward reality and retribution. I believed that someone should inform them that a hungry, chained, crab-infested man is not likely to embrace communism. Besides, they were liars; I earned more than $2.50 a day. I was really a capitalist earning $6.55 a day, including my flight pay. Why, that was 27 cents per hour. And that did not take into account my monthly room and board and medical services that were part of my military "package." But they were right about one thing: being a prisoner of war was not an eight hour per day job. My fears, anxieties, pain, hunger, and thirst knew no time limitations.

But the money issue was petty compared to my physical condition. I was gradually growing weaker. I would no sooner get over a cold when I would catch another one. My eyes were red and watery, and my nose ran constantly. I didn't have a handkerchief, so I was constantly wiping my nose on the sleeve of my jacket. My lips were dried and cracked, and my stomach cramped constantly from the lack of food. After eating the small amount they grudgingly gave to me, my stomach burned as if it contained the fires of Hell. I became so hungry I bit my lips, tongue, and the insides of my cheeks in an attempt to get the small amount of food I received to my stomach more quickly. I could hardly hold my spoon. By the time I got the spoon to my mouth, the crap they gave me might spill or fall off. Almost every night I would wake up with my mouth watering and with excruciating pain in the pit of my stomach. I involuntarily kept the parasites they refused to treat, and it seemed as if they were on motorcycles the way they moved around. Racked with pain and hunger and tormented by parasites, I had difficulty sleeping. When I eventually fell asleep, I would often dream of American food and just as often have horrible nightmares.

Though I fell away from the church after I had joined the Air Force, I still considered myself a Christian. I still believed in God, and I would pray daily. But I harbored an impression that my prayers were not penetrating the thick prison walls. My hatred against my tormentors was still as strong as ever. In fact, it grew stronger each day in spite of my asking God to help me control it and eventually eliminate it.

Perhaps I was just too impatient. I think I had expectations that God would jump at my command. Consequently, I continued to suffer bouts of extreme depression. I was so miserable that there were many times when I actually wanted them to kill me. I was disgusted and disillusioned with the whole **damned** world. My head ached as if it were going to burst into pieces. Day by day the pain increased in frequency and intensity. My ears rang constantly. I would hear a steady tone for awhile, then a variety of tones, and then Morse code. Over time, the noises increased in volume and intensity.

And my nerves were extremely raw. To make matters worse, the Chinese prisoners would sing and play games throughout the day, and this scraped on my nerves like a file on the edge of a thin metal. I tried to get the noise stopped by pounding on the wall and yelling for them to be quiet, but that was useless. When I indulged myself in such a manner, the guard remonstrated, sometimes even threatened me, but he never stopped the noise. I often reached the point of feeling that I could endure it no longer, and it was all I could do to suppress the urge to scream. I don't know how many times my mind was completely filled with one single thought: "How could I go on?"

I learned to calm myself somewhat by tapping out code on the wall or on the edge of my board. This practice infuriated the guards. Although it soothed my nerves, it evidently grated on theirs. Consequently, when they told me to stop, I would tap more vigorously and for a prolonged period of time. Another way I found to relieve my stress was by using my old, padded cap as a basketball. I spent hours tossing it against the wall pretending I was shooting baskets, and that diversion also irritated the guards. I never understood how or why those things helped, I just accepted it; I was thankful for whatever made my life less miserable.

On the afternoon of March 6, 1953, I noticed that the guards were wearing black armbands. I heard the public address speakers blasting away, and I understood enough to figure out that Stalin was dead. I asked the guard why he was wearing the armband, but he refused to answer me.

The next morning the soldiers still wore their armbands, and the squawk box was still blasting away. I asked another guard about the armband, and I asked him if Stalin were dead. He shook his head "yes." I asked several other guards the same question that morning, and each one gave me an affirmative nod.

That afternoon I was taken from my cell, across the prison yard, through the gates, and across the basketball court to a building. On the way I noticed that there were large buildings all around, and I saw a building with a grey-colored dome. I also could see enough to know that I was in a very large city, so these facts caused me to guess that I was in Peking. The domed building was about 500 yards down the street from the prison.

I also noticed that there was a guard with a burp gun on the wall just outside my cell. Whenever I was on the way to be interrogated, the guard tried to hide. As I entered the room where I was to be "quizzed" again, I saw Babyface, Jerry Lewis, and the cute girl—all familiar faces from previous interrogations. I was escorted to the center of the room and made to stand next to a stool.

Before my "screws" had a chance to begin the session, I asked them about Stalin. They denied that he was dead and wondered where I got my information. They accused me of spreading malicious propaganda. They said I was irresponsible, insubordinate, obnoxious, repugnant, contemptible, and—worst of all—unwilling to cooperate.

After that excoriating opening, they proceeded with another intensive interrogation. They bombarded me with innumerable questions about the new IFF (Identification Friend or Foe) and ECM (Electronic Counter Measures), the number and types of planes in our Air Resupply Squadron, and about certain "unusual" squadrons.

In this session, as well as in many, many others, the Red Chinese tried to force me to admit that the 581st ARC Wing was involved in training, dropping, and supplying espionage agents. They kept insinuating that we were directly associated with a highly secretive non-military agency. To them, the fact that we had three extra men on board our plane when it was shot down gave credence to their accusation. Although that assumption was preposterous, I underwent long, unpleasant hours of fielding questions regarding the extra men and their purpose for being on the flight with us. On that particular day, I was interrogated for over 24 hours.

At the next interrogation, the "screws" called me up to their desk and showed me various articles recovered from our ill-fated plane. Included among them were a Far East Radio Facility Chart, part of a Q-Z Signal book (Radio Operator's book of shorthand signals), a D.

F. map of the Manila area, part of a D. F. map of the Northwest United States, and a flyleaf of a maintenance book. The American map was torn, and Mountain Home, Idaho, was circled in red.

I denied that these articles were from our plane, but the interrogator pointed out that my name was in the Q-Z Signal book. I turned pale and felt sick to my stomach when I first saw the charts, books, and maps. The sight of them struck me like a sledgehammer blow, and I felt as if the whole world had caved in on me. I felt completely lost, and my mind was numbed. The appearance of these familiar articles in the intolerable setting of an interrogation room was by far the worst blow to my morale that I had suffered. I thought if they had all that material they could possibly have the radio flimsy and the authentication sheet which contained the frequencies, coded call sign, and keys which I was doing my best to withhold. If they did have those other folders, they were doing a good job in concealing it.

They expressed their anger with me for lying and failing to show proper respect. The secretary took notes, as he or she had done in every previous session, and I learned on that particular day that each session had obviously been very accurately recorded, probably word for word.

After I had given several answers that did not agree with my prior answers, the interrogator screamed at me with bulging eyes and said, "Well, you had better be more careful of what you say and quit lying. Even your lies are inconsistent. Let me give you an example. On March 1, 1953, you said there were eight squadrons in the ARC Wing. On March 4, 1953, you said 15; On March 5, you said five; yesterday you said there were 16, and today you say seven. Now, just how many damned squadrons are there?"

"I really don't know," I said, with a nervous giggle.

The interrogator said, "Back in February you said you did not know your plane number, and today we proved that you did. Then the first week or so after you were downed, you denied being in the 581st. You denied having any C-119s or SA-16s in the ARC Wing. We could show a hundred instances where you lied. We believe that you lie just for the pleasure of lying. We warn you for the last time that you had better start telling us the truth and start right now. We hate liars! If you continue to lie, we will have to punish you. Besides, what good is it doing you to lie? Right here in this folder we have the answers to all the questions we have been asking you. We know all about the 581st and the 91st. We know all about you and the others. We are asking you these questions simply to test your willingness to cooperate. Now, what was your pickup signal?"

"I had none."

"You filthy liar! What was it?"

I remained silent.

"Stand up," he said. "Maybe you can think better standing on your aching feet and legs. If they hurt badly enough, you might remember so you can sit down and get off of them. Did you receive any survival training while at Clark?" (Clark AFB in the Philippines).

"No," I said.

"Why do you lie?" screamed the interrogator.

"I don't lie."

"We know that survival lectures were given on jungle survival for the Far East area. What were the lectures about?"

Of course, I realized the implication in the question, that we had taken survival training not only for the jungles in Pacific islands, but also for survival in mainland Red China as well.

"I never attended any such lectures," I said.

"But you must have. Everyone in the AR Squadron was supposed to attend those lectures.

What were they about?"

"I just told you that I never attended any such lectures."

"Why didn't you?" His questions were all delivered in a squeaky, high-pitched voice that was almost a scream.

"Why didn't I what?" I grinned.

"Attend the lectures."

"What lectures?"

"The survival lectures." He was getting angrier by the minute.

"What survival lectures?"

"The survival lectures at Clark Field."

"Oh, the survival lectures at Clark."

"Yes."

"What about them?" I asked and gave him a puzzled look.

"You said that you didn't attend them. Would you mind telling us why you failed to attend those lectures?"

"No, I don't mind."

"Then tell us!" He shouted.

"Tell you what?"

"Tell us why you didn't attend the survival lectures at Clark Field."

"Did I say that I didn't attend them?"

"Yes. Why didn't you go to them?"

"I just didn't go."

"Were you supposed to?"

"To what?"

"To go."

"Go where?"

"To the lectures!" He was screaming again.

"Oh, that. Yes."

"And you just didn't go. What did they do to you for not going to the lectures?"

"Nothing," I said. I was growing weary of the games they were playing, and I was sure that no matter what I told them, they wouldn't believe me. However, I had no choice but to continue to endure their abuse.

"Nothing? You lie! In the United States Air Force you cannot skip lectures or other training classes. We know that they are very strict with the airmen, and you expect us to believe the propaganda you're giving us? You also told us earlier what you did all day at Clark. Kiba, you are nothing but a propagandist. We could make a good communist out of you. We will give you reading material later, and we will re-educate you."

"Do you think you can?" I laughed defiantly.

"We can, and if you cooperate, we will make it easier for you. We will give you more water and more to eat. We will give you soap and toothpaste and medicine to kill your little pests. But no! You have to be melodramatic. So you starve, thirst, and are pestered by crabs, and you must stand on your aching feet and legs. We see that they hurt you very much. But, if you cooperate, we well let you sit. Are you hungry? Thirsty? You should be. Wouldn't you like to have more water? Wouldn't you like to get enough to eat? Wouldn't it be nice to lie down on a full stomach? So why do you resist? You are no hero, so why try to act like one? Do you think the Capitalistic-Imperialistic Warmongers care that you are starving? That your throat is parched? Do they care for the poor condition of your feet and legs and that you must stand on them for hours and hours?"

He stopped his questioning long enough to pour himself a cup of tea and take a sip. I forced myself to look away and ignore the yearning for a drink that his action created in me. Instead, I tried to enjoy the few moments of silence the break afforded me.

After taking a few sips and purposefully reveling in them by licking his lips, he resumed the questioning. He said, "No one knows that you are alive. Furthermore, no one cares. While they chew on their steaks and sip their cocktails, do they think of the boys on the front lines or in prison camps? Hah! They do not give it a thought. So why starve? Why suffer needlessly? Tell us the truth, and we will feed you and make your life easier."

"I would, but if you were to give me an extra kernel of rice, it would upset your whole economy," I said. I laughed again.

He did not like my flippancy in regard to questions he considered serious. His anger was evident in his flashing eyes and the jabbing way he pointed his finger at me.

"You hard-headed, stupid Yankee! You are too stupid to see what is good for you. You have the wrong attitude. When you are sitting alone in your cold, damp cell suffering from hunger pangs and life-threatening thirst, just remember that every man has his price and every man can be broken. You think this over, and we will see if you change your attitude. Remember, no one knows you are alive or where you are. They don't give a damn whether you live or die."

The rigid prison rules I had to live by and the brutal treatment by my captors made the time drag by oh so slowly. Every minute seemed like an eternity, and there was no respite. I even dreaded to get up in the morning because I knew what lay ahead. My dread of facing the interrogators was even worse, for I feared I would say something that would be harmful to my fellow crew members or useful to the enemy in some way that I could not anticipate. And I dreaded sitting in the dirty cell staring at the blank wall and listening to the noisy Chinese prisoners passing the time as best they knew how.

Sometimes late at night I would be jarred awake—if I were lucky enough to be asleep—by blood-curdling screams. Those outbursts caused me to surmise that someone was being flogged or undergoing some kind of physical torture and I couldn't help but have empathy for the poor unknown souls being subjected to such cruelty.

One night, right after I had fallen asleep after undergoing a tedious 28 hour interrogation session, my cell door flew open and a guard jerked me to my feet and hustled me back to the interrogation area. He led me into the room and instructed me to remain standing next to the stool. The guard then stood next to me on the right and held a pistol pointed at my temple. Another session began.

"What is the date?" asked the interpreter.

I noticed that I had a new interrogation team. The "Mole" was the interrogator; "Bluebeard" was the secretary, and the interpreter had his right hand inside his jacket.

I thought, "This joker must think he's Napoleon."

I mocked him by placing my hand inside my padded jacket in the Napoleonic pose most people are familiar with. Then I answered him with a grin.

"Today's the twentieth," I said.

"What are you laughing at?" Snapped Napoleon.

"You," I answered.

"You wise guy!" He snorted.

I imitated him by taking my hand from my chest and putting it back again and snorted as near as he did as I could.

"Cut the comedy," he ordered. Then he said, "Now let's get down to business. What are the activities of Captain Veedee?" He mispronounced my Aircraft Commander's name (Vaadi: Vay'-di).

"I don't know," I said.

For about the next two hours Napoleon kept shouting this same question, and each time I gave him the same answer. The interrogation continued for another 12 hours with Napoleon and his substitute interpreters screaming at the top of their lungs, "What are the activities of Captain Veedee?"

When the session finally ended, I was half-carried, half-dragged back to my cell. I was totally exhausted both physically and mentally when I collapsed on the hard board.

I finally reached a point where I questioned my own motives. Why did I put up with my harsh, inhumane treatment and the long interrogations? If I felt so bitter toward my sadistic, barbaric captors and the way they were treating me, why didn't I try to escape? Then I answered my own questions, as I understood my reasons for my behavior: Even though I often thought about—*longed for*—an escape, I realized I was so starved I could never even make it to the outside prison wall. Not only that, my cell door was bolted and padlocked, and several guards roamed the hallway of the cellblock carrying loaded burp guns, while another "roaming" guard looked into my cell approximately every 30 seconds. I was monitored so closely that practically every movement I made was seen by someone. So there was no substantial opportunity to execute any kind of escape, even if I could have thought of one. And there were no tools to aid me in any way; I had only my fingernails to dig through the two foot thick cement wall.

There were also armed guards strategically posted in guard towers on top of the outside prison walls. Even if I could have, by some freak stroke of fortune, managed to get out of the prison compound, I still would have had to cross the entire countryside of Red China which, in essence, was a gigantic prison for our B-29 crew. Realistically, I believed it was impossible for a Caucasian such as me to successfully engineer an escape and get through the masses of Red Chinese people that I would certainly encounter in the attempt.

In thinking about all options, which were almost non-existent, I considered making a sudden lunge for a guard and trying to disarm him. The problem with that idea was that they always stayed far enough away so that they could shoot me dead quite easily if I tried it. In the interrogation room, the interrogators were also armed, and usually one guard always held a cocked pistol to my head. A second guard with a burp gun stood just outside the door. I could see no heroics in getting certain death attempting to escape under impossible circumstances.

During my stay at the Hotel, I had many weird dreams, or rather nightmares. Almost every night I would dream that I was home on leave, and after two weeks the U. S. Government would order me to return to Red China. Naturally, I would refuse. All of my friends and relatives would try to persuade me to return, saying that it was my responsibility to go back, that it was for my own good and for the good of the entire nation. I would plead with them not to send me back, but they just laughed at me. I'd then wake up in a cold sweat and an empty feeling.

At all times when I was awake, I felt completely alone and lost. I was relatively certain that no one knew my location or whether I was alive or dead. Still, I could not shake the terrible feeling that I had been completely abandoned, left in a communist hell by my government, and forsaken by family and friends. I tried my best to keep my dreams in perspective, to maintain a sane and logical interpretation of why I was having them, and to refrain from fruitless speculation on their meaning. It was a difficult thing to do.

On April 4, 1953, I was escorted to the interrogation building for my last session at the Hotel.

"Well, how does our wise guy feel this evening?" said the fat-faced interpreter. He snickered at his own question.

"That's a stupid question. How the hell do you expect me to feel? Well, I'll tell you. I'm fed up with your communist bull. You starve me and treat me like an animal. You deprive me of the basic necessities of hygiene and health and let your Red Chinese crabs eat away at my body. I say again, how in the hell do you expect me to feel? I tell you the truth, I feel like you're a bunch of no-good, yellow-bellied, pig-faced, squint-eyed agots; and you're not even a good excuse for human beings."

"Well, Mister Wise Guy, are you through?

"Hell, I'm just getting started!"

"And you just finished," broke in the pig-faced interpreter. "After we treat you so well, you still think badly of us. We will give you soap and toothpaste when you change your *incorrect attitude* toward us and start cooperating with us. What do you say to that?"

"Go bug yourselves. I'll never change my attitude toward you, and I'll be damned if I'll cooperate with you. Before I'll do that, I'll do without your friggin' laundry soap."

"Your belligerent attitude will get you nowhere. Since I am your friend, I will give you some good advice. Kiba, if you do not change your *incorrect attitude*, it will be most harmful for you. You will close the door forever."

"You say that you are my friend. Are you really?"

"Of course I am your friend."

"Then why don't you let me go home? You keep asking me what you can do for me, but you never do anything. I told you that you could send me home, but I'm still here. I ask about other crew members, but you never tell me anything about them except to brag about capturing two as they touched down. Now you are trying to extort information from me by not providing me the necessary articles to keep myself clean. And that's not enough for you! You even have the nerve to act as if I stink. Do you truthfully expect me to change my attitude toward you? Do you actually expect me to believe that you rotten communists are my friends?"

"Of course we are your friends. Especially me."

"You are even more stupid than I figured you to be."

"Kiba, just what do you think your chances of ever going home are?" He laughed.

I said, "I believe I'll be home by July or August. I think that the war will be over in July."

"You are not a prisoner-of-war. Your case is different, and it is up to us to decide when you go home—or if you will *ever* go home. As we've told you over and over, it depends on your attitude. If you don't change it and if you refuse to cooperate with us and if you continue to resist our efforts to re-educate you, you will be here for a hell of a long time. Just think how easy it would be for you to cooperate. If you did, your treatment would improve drastically, and your chances of getting to go home would be a hundred percent better. Don't continue being a fool. This is real life, not the cinema. If you are not smart, there will not be a happy ending for you. Think only of yourself. Forget the others. Let them worry about themselves. You owe allegiance to no one. Join us and we will make your life very pleasant. Now doesn't that sound tempting?"

"Sounds like a bunch of bull to me. You're going about it the wrong way. You should offer me the love and affection and services of a beautiful woman. You should serve me steak and eggs for breakfast. You should provide me with a good, soft bed, and then you just might start to convince me, but I doubt it. As I have said before, I'm a man of principles."

"Hah! Man of principles! You're a wise guy, nothing but a fanatic. The Capitalistic-Imperialistic Wall Street Warmongers have poisoned your mind. They have saturated your brain with useless trash. Time is running out for you. You are now at the crossroads. You have two ways to go—the right way or the wrong. The right way is to cooperate and join us. To do that you must confess your crimes against the People's Republic. You must repent and express regret for your reactionary deeds and thoughts. You must show willingness to shed old ties and cast aside your current beliefs and ideologies. And you *must* allow yourself to become re-educated. If you select this road, you will get ahead and amount to something someday. Our way offers you tremendous opportunities. Remember, **communism** is the **way**; our **Glorious Chairman Mao** is the **light**. The other way is the way of your decadent American Warmongers, the Capitalists and the Imperialists. If you take that road, you are headed for self-destruction. It is a road that leads to nothing good for you. If you insist on taking it, it will be your end. You will **NEVER** go home again. The door will close forever. Remember, time is running out for you. But you have great potential, that is, if you come along with us. You are young, so grab this opportunity. Be smart for once in your life, Kiba. Be smart!"

I said, "I'm not very intelligent, but I'm not stupid enough to fall for your line."

"Damn you, Kiba! You are hopeless. Your mind is thoroughly poisoned. You are no damn good."

Endeavoring to impress upon me the virtues of Marxism-Leninism, the joker went on and on and on with his malicious commie propaganda. I surmised that he and his comrades thought that if they continued to bombard me with that silly crap, I would eventually start to believe that it was the truth.

About six hours later the political indoctrination session switched to a bonafide interrogation. The continuous grilling lasted many tedious hours before the interrogator finally said, "We see that you are exhausted, so we will permit you to return to your cell. While you are there, please think about and consider the fantastic advantages that we offer you. We sincerely think that soon you will come to your senses and perceive things our way. Then you will willingly aid us in our efforts and struggles to stop American aggression against the peace-loving people of the Democratic Republic of Korea and the People's Republic of China. We certainly hope so, for if you do not, we will be forced to kill you. It would be a shame to have to shoot such a young man as you. Now go!"

The guards escorted me back to my cell. Upon entering, I collapsed on my board and lay there pondering the seemingly hopeless situation.

PART IV

THE SPIDER WEB

Steve E. Kiba

The following day, April 5, 1953, nothing unusual happened. When I was taken out to empty the honey bucket that night, I noticed about fifteen armed guards milling around in the latrine. I figured that something was about to happen.

I was returned to my cell where I lay down and tried to go to sleep. About an hour later, the warden and five armed guards came to my cell and woke me up. The warden had me pick up my belongings—my worn toothbrush and my tin cup—after which they handcuffed, chained, and blindfolded me. One of the guards carried me piggy-back to the outside of the prison where I was shoved into the back seat of a car.

We rode for almost an hour, and it was an unpleasant bumpy ride. Near the end of the trip, we crossed what I believed were seven railroad tracks, and almost immediately after that we came to a stop. I was pretty sure that we had arrived at some new prison.

Sure enough, I was removed from the car and taken piggy-back into this new, unknown place and dropped painfully onto a concrete floor. Someone jerked me up and searched me even before they removed the blindfold or my manacles. When they finally slipped off the blindfold, I saw a ratty looking male officer and a piggish looking female officer. The Rat read the prison rules in Mandarin, and the Pig translated them for me.

Essentially, the rules were the same as in the other prisons I had occupied: prisoners were forbidden to talk, whistle, sing, look out windows, move around in the cell without the guard's permission, talk to the guards, use the toilet without the guard's permission, write on walls, and destroy or burn prison property. Of course I realized from past experience that other "rules" would be added as time passed.

Then holding up a circular card, the pig-faced officer said: "In your cell there is a round card, green on one side and black on the other. The green side is to let the guard know that you have to urinate, the black side to defecate. Do you understand?"

"You said that there's a brown card green on one side and black on the other. I don't understand."

"No, no, no, a round card, a round card! Do you understand?" she squealed.

"Oh, a round card."

"Yes, green on one side, black on the other. Green to piss, black to shit."

Two officials dressed in blue led me into a circular room similar to the one at the Wagon Wheel. In the wall of the circle, there were five large double doors, each leading into a row of cells called a cellblock. I astutely made the observation that the double doors were bolted and padlocked and that access to any cellblock had to be through the circular hub. Too, a guard armed with a burp gun stood directly in front of each double door. They unlocked one of the double doors and led me through it and took me down the corridor to Cell Number 10. I was searched again before they removed the leg irons and handcuffs. Next they took away my filthy Red Chinese padded pants and jacket, my G. I. sweatshirt, my shoes and socks, and even my cruddy underwear. I was glad for that, because the underwear was literally rotting on my body. In return they gave me a pair of dark blue pants, a dark blue shirt, and a pair of black cloth shoes.

When they left me alone, I immediately began to examine my new cell. It was about 10 feet square and had the typical heavy wooden door in the wall facing the hallway. The door was a faded maroon color on the inside. I later learned it was painted black on the outside and was barred with a huge steel bar. To the right of the door and situated about four feet off the floor was a barred window. A paper screen covered the bottom half of the window, and there was a small flap in the screen through which the guards kept a watchful eye on inmates. On the outside wall, there was also a barred window, the lower half of which was covered with chicken wire and a wooden picket fence. The window panes were covered with heavy brown paper, and the upper portion of both windows was covered with a fine mesh cloth. However, the cloth was riddled with small holes. An extremely low-wattage light bulb was perched close to the ceiling and sandwiched between two plates of glass reinforced with chicken wire. There was also a wire grate nailed up outside the plate glass. The lone dim bulb provided light for two cells: mine and an adjacent one. The outer layer of the walls, which were one-and-a-half feet thick, was made of a white, plaster-like material. The interior was made of cement and stone. From the concrete floor and extending up for about two feet, there was a light gray wainscoting that jutted out a half- inch or so. My bed, another "Red Chinese board," was about six feet by two-and-a-half feet and appeared to be about a half-inch thick. It rested on two sawhorses eight inches above the cold concrete floor. I later learned that the cellblock I was in contained fourteen cells and a primitive toilet.

The next morning, April 6, 1953, the sun crept into the cell, and I woke up. I lay on the board and watched the sun until seven o'clock. That's when the guard pounded on the bars and motioned for me to get up.

I arose, folded my blanket and pad, sat down on them, and waited. Shortly, a tall fellow opened the door and gave me a pan with a quarter inch of warm water, a bar of soap, a pack of toothpowder, and a small, green tin cup. The soap was yellow. It looked, smelled, and acted like Grandma's lye soap and produced no lather. The toothpowder came in a green and brown package with a large red rooster on it.

After I washed my hands and face and brushed my teeth, I started to strip down to give myself a sponge bath. The houseboy (caretaker) happened to lift the observation flap to my cell and saw what I intended to do. He quickly dropped the flap, opened my cell door, and rushed inside. His anger was revealed in the way he scolded me and removed the washbasin.

At eight o'clock the houseboy brought my breakfast: a small portion of wormy rice gruel and a small bun. I ate the stuff, and a few minutes later he gave me another bowl of gruel. This really caused me to wonder what was going on, because they had never been liberal with their food before.

A couple of hours later a guard came and escorted me to the toilet. It was none too soon, for I was in a great deal of pain from containing myself even though I had a very strong urge. Actually, I couldn't have held it back much longer. In spite of my pain and my need for time, the guard kept his eyes glued to the slit in the door and continually prompted me to hurry. I pretended not to hear or see him, so I took my time.

"What a life," I thought, as I squatted over the filthy, smelly slit trench. "A man can't even go to the toilet when he has to. And finally, when he does get to go, he can't even take a crap without being hounded."

At noon the houseboy brought my meal in a small, green mess kit. It consisted of a small bowl of very thin soup, an extremely small portion of some type of grass or seaweed, and a small portion of steamed rice with worms and tiny white rocks in it.

I sat on my hard board most of the afternoon. Occasionally the guard asked me to walk around the cell. Mostly I reconsidered my opportunities for escape. Being in a new location somehow revived a small hope that it might now be possible. In my mind I devised a plan of action, such as it was, to study my new surroundings and be particularly alert for any weakness in the security that might be in my favor. I stopped short of becoming optimistically hopeful, lest I be severely disappointed later on. However, I nourished a glimmer of hope that the change might introduce some weakness in the enemy's overall practices that could be used to my advantage.

My reflections on escape and the means to accomplish it were interrupted by supper. It consisted of about the same slop as lunch, except that I received small buns instead of steamed rice.

From my first day there, I formed a habit of either sitting down after supper and thinking about things or walking around and thinking about things. On rare occasions, I would be given a cup of boiled water at seven o'clock, and boardtime (bedtime) was always at nine o'clock.

In general, the above paragraphs describe my daily routine in my new prison, the Spider Web. I will spare you the weighty boredom we prisoners were forced to endure and relate to you only the more interesting and unusual incidents dealing with cell life.

The guards at the Spider Web worked two hour shifts, and I noticed that I had four different guards. I also noticed that about every half hour an ammo guard (guard equipped with an ammunition pouch) passed through the cellblock to check on the regular guards.

In my cellblock there was this really gung-ho Redchink guard who tried to make me walk during his whole shift. My feet and legs were really bothering me. At times the pain was almost unbearable.

Even though it was painful to walk, I really didn't mind doing it because it helped me to pass the long, empty hours a little faster. I immensely resented this guard's obnoxious attitude and his attempting to force me to walk for two hours. Whenever I became tired or when I was in excessive pain and didn't feel like walking any more, I would jump up and look outside over the screen in the window. Sometimes I would push out the guard's observation flap in the window and look through the opening into the hallway. That kind of behavior aggravated the guard, and he would order me to sit down. At other times, when I wanted to alleviate the boredom, I would count cadence or sing Air Force songs as I marched around the cell. Alternately, I would goose-step and shout "Seig Heil!" The more the guard sputtered, the more I goofed off.

But the aggravation worked both ways. That particular guard thought I was a smoker, so he would smoke outside my window and blow smoke into my cell in an effort to upset me. I never told him I was a non-smoker because it didn't bother me that much. Also, I didn't want to deprive him of his innocuous way of striking back, lest he find some other more brutal and painful way to get his revenge.

Several days after arriving at the Spider Web, several guards and houseboys tried to make me sit at attention on the edge of the hard board. While sitting in such a cramped position, I had to look straight forward at an imaginary spot on the wall. A guard or houseboy would come into my cell and physically position me on the edge of the board, use a finger to trace an invisible letter X on the wall, and insist that I stare at it. I would smile at him and flash an "okay" sign. I also gave the "okay" sign to the guard or houseboy who spied on me through the window flap. However, as soon as the guard or houseboy left my cell and closed the door behind him, I would resume a more comfortable sitting position on the pad—even before they slid the locking bolt into place on the outside of my door.

My insubordination induced a loud scream from whoever raised the window flap to look at me. Immediately the door would fly open again, and one of the Redchink pricks would storm back into my cell. I would be admonished in a loud stream of Mandarin words, words which I couldn't understand but which gave me some secret satisfaction through their definite tones of anger and frustration. At

69

the end of the unintelligible diatribe, I would be re-positioned the way they wanted me and again be instructed to stare at the wall. But no sooner than they left my cell, I'd do the same thing over again, and we continued to repeat this incredibly stupid game for three days.

On the afternoon of the third day, after being physically and forcefully seated at attention on the board by an exceedingly obnoxious Redchink houseboy for the umpteenth time and ordered to stare at an imaginary "X" on the wall, I gave him a big smile and agreed to comply. I was amazed at their persistence in the matter and amused at their gullible acceptance of my intention to obey each time they demanded it. From past experience, they had no basis to believe that this time I would behave differently, and I remained true to the pattern I had set: as soon as they left the cell, I relaxed again. When the houseboy raised the flap in the window and saw me, he shouted some obscenities, slammed the flap closed, and trotted down the hall muttering aloud, presumably expressing his dissatisfaction of my behavior to the guards on duty along the hall.

A few minutes later, I saw the corner of the flap being slowly lifted. Finally it was raised high enough that I could see the assistant warden glaring at me. He uttered something in Mandarin. I didn't understand what he was saying, so I just sat and glared back at him. He slammed the flap shut, opened the door, and rushed into my cell. I could tell by his flashing eyes that he was as angry as hell.

He spouted out something, which I took to be an order to sit at attention, but I shrugged my shoulders and just stared at him. I guess he realized there was a language problem, so he demonstrated just how he wanted me to sit. I meekly assumed that position. He grinned triumphantly and left the cell, and I immediately resumed a more comfortable position.

A houseboy peered at me through the flap and saw me in an almost prone position. He began shouting, and immediately the door opened again, and the assistant warden and a houseboy returned to my cell. They again ordered me to sit up on the edge of the board, and this time their words contained a menacing quality. I complied with their command, not because I was afraid, but I just wanted to see how far they'd take this game.

I soon found out. When they left and I again relaxed in defiance of their order, they rushed back into my cell and peppered my ears with abusive language and obscene gestures. Then they grabbed my blanket and pad and carried them out. A few minutes later, the houseboy returned and removed my board and the sawhorses that supported it. He closed the door with a loud bang when he left.

I walked around for awhile mumbling and singing. About an hour later, the houseboy returned, and he talked with the guard on the outside of my cell for a few minutes. Suddenly, the door flew open, and the houseboy rushed in. He closed the windows, gave me a dirty look, and left like a man with diarrhea heading for the toilet. I sat down on the cold concrete floor because I was tired of walking and my feet and legs were really aching.

I spent the rest of the day alternately sitting on the cold floor and goose-stepping around the cell. I aggravated the guards and houseboys even more by singing, counting cadence, giving the Nazi salute, and laughing at them.

At boardtime the houseboy returned my board and bedding, so I lay down and tried to sleep. Almost every night the obnoxious guards would shine a flashlight in my eyes or toss small pebbles at my head. I would cover my head and try to sleep. The guards tried to make me uncover my head by pounding on the bars. I never yielded to that pressure. However, I had to contend with the games the guards played and with the crabs racing around my flesh as if it were the Indianapolis Speedway, so I seldom got much sleep.

On rare occasions when I did fall into a deep sleep, it would be interrupted by those chilling, blood-curdling, agonizing screams, which I remembered all too well from my stay at the Hotel and which were no less disturbing at this new location. That obstacle was enough to contend with, but not the only one: sometimes I was still shaken awake and hauled off to the dreaded interrogation area.

About five days after my arrival at the Spider Web, the houseboy brought a wooden honey bucket into my cell. The bucket soon started to leak. I sat for hours watching the liquid contents seep slowly from the bucket and spread out on the floor. I pretended the puddle was a huge cloud. It gradually grew larger and frequently changed shapes. I observed the different shapes and identified them with different

71

objects, or even scenes. At one point, the puddle formed the definite shape of a head with ears on both sides and a ragged top, like a silhouette of hair. Later those features were transformed by the dripping addition of more liquid, and the result was an unidentifiable glob—like a huge inkblot design in a Rorschach test. As I watched the puddle grow, I thought of how communism was slowly spreading across the Free World.

Idleness is extremely difficult to endure. If you let it, idleness can conquer you. I knew my fellow crew members were probably suffering the same cruelties and deprivations as I, as well as having to deal with idleness, a sinkhole into which all productiveness and hope can fall. I tried various ways to occupy myself and to make the time pass somewhat faster. While sitting on my board one day, I noticed a spider moving across the ceiling. Moments later I spied another spider approaching the first one, and shortly the two were facing each other. One spider fled across the ceiling, and the second one pursued it. When the aggressive one caught up to the escaping one, a battle began. The first one would fight awhile, and then try to escape, but the aggressor always chased it. I watched this overhead combat for several hours, and I never knew which spider was the winner because, in spite of my idleness, I eventually lost interest.

I learned that such mundane and uninteresting things as spider-watching provided a welcome break in the monotony of idleness. I developed a habit of counting the daddy-long-leg spiders that occupied my cell every morning, and each day there were more of them. I never knew the exact reason for the increase in number. I discounted rapid breeding as the reason because they were mostly beyond the baby stage. I finally decided it was shyness on their part, a reluctance to initially show themselves to a grungy, obviously alien, individual who had been suddenly thrust into the midst of their habitat. They further revealed themselves as they grew accustomed to me and realized that I was not a threat.

One day while I was watching my fuzzy cellmates, I happened to glance at the window flap. A nosy guard was peeking in trying to figure out why I was so quiet. The next time I heard a guard approaching the flap, I looked up at the ceiling and moved my head back and forth as if I were trying to follow the movement of something. The guard strained and craned his neck in an effort to get his eyes in a position to see what I was looking at. I motioned to him with my hands that there was a large creature on the ceiling. The guard rushed down the hall and returned with a houseboy. When they came into my cell, they looked around and saw nothing. They discussed the matter for a few minutes, looked at me strangely while they were talking, and finally left.

At other times I sat and watched the bugs crawl around on the floor and up the sides of the walls. Sometimes I caught an ant or some other insect and let it run back and forth on my hand. Those insects, and other pests, contributed enough mental diversion for me to keep my mind off my troubles for awhile, and in so doing, they were helpful to me in passing the long, weary hours of my imprisonment.

Since I had become discouraged with any idea of an escape, I was able to devote my time to inventing other ways of breaking the monotony rather than by expending many futile hours planning something I had concluded was certainly improbable, if not impossible. One of the things I came up with was to play silly little games with the guards. They stared at me frequently at all hours of the day and night, even when I was eating. I got aggravated with this continuous harassment, so I came up with a plan. When my meals came and I started eating, as soon as a guard started staring at me through the flap in the window, I would stop eating and stare back at him until he dropped the flap; only then would I resume eating. Every time he raised the flap to stare, I would stop eating and stare back. When he wouldn't let the flap down and he continued to stare too long, I would shout at him and return some of the abuse I was receiving. I usually said, "Get the hell out of here, you yellow-bellied son-of-a-bitch! Get lost!" The response I usually got was a similar yell from him. In retrospect, it was foolish of me to taunt the guards. I was taking a chance on losing the meager rations they so begrudgingly gave me.

Another thing I did was to wait until a guard came near the flap in the window. When I was sure he was close by, I would blow on my arm and simulate a loud, ripping fart. The guard would usually lift the flap immediately, give me a disgusted look, hold his nose, and slam the flap with a loud bang. These little diversions helped my morale by showing my enemies that they were not in as total control of me as they thought. And the reactions I got from the dumb, uneducated guards were sometimes very amusing.

A week after I arrived at the Spider Web, my interrogations were resumed. One big difference was that they would send two type-written questions and about 20 sheets of blank paper, a staff pen, and a bottle of ink to my cell. Of course I understood that they expected me to fill up the blank sheets with a lot of information which they could analyze to determine its validity and value.

Another difference was that I was taken to an office near the big, round room and questioned by one English-speaking officer. Those one-on-one sessions were generally of a political nature during which time I received an angry reprimand for failing to cooperate. The root of the reprimand was my lack of cooperation in filling out the blank sheets; they wanted more "writing" than I was willing to give. It was totally illogical that a couple of questions would require 20 pages to answer, and I told them so. Of course they were not satisfied with that, so they usually extended the scope of the reprimand to include my behavior in the cell. The sessions were unnecessarily long and tedious, and night sessions were not a rarity.

In other ways, my treatment at the Spider Web was similar to my treatment at the Hotel. The guards wanted me to keep my head down on my chest as they escorted me to the interrogation room, and that was enforced rigidly and painfully at the Hotel. But at the Spider Web, when I walked with my head high and looked all around, the guard would force it down. I would jerk it back up, and he would shove it back down. This battle of wits took place on my walk to and from the interrogation room. The result of my stubbornness was a very sore and stiff neck, but it paid off: after about a week of trying to force me to keep my head down, they gave up. My interrogation sessions took place almost every morning in a small room near the large circle, or hub, of the web. To me, they were nothing more than "bull sessions," and they were repeated again and again and again.

One day toward mid-April, I was walking around my cell when suddenly I saw this huge object whiz past my barred, outside window. Initially I thought it was some type of aircraft, but then I heard a squawking sound. I kept my eyes glued on the window, and shortly several others whizzed past the window. They were large, black birds with a white breast and one white feather among the black feathers on their wings.

I could look out my window and over the roof of another cellblock and see a tall, dead locust tree with a large nest perched in the top.

The noisy birds would light in the locust tree and on top of the roofs of the other cellblocks. Because they made a sound resembling the "dits" (dots) of Morse code, I called them "Ditty Birds." These fine-feathered friends provided me many, many hours of distraction from the rigors of captivity.

On April 16, 1953, I received my first haircut since I had been in Red China. A houseboy came to my cell in the company of another joker who wore a filthy, white robe and carried hair clippers. The houseboy carried a stool and a huge pair of scissors. He placed the stool in the center of the cell and motioned for me to sit down. I complied, and the "one-armed-barber" began removing my months-long growth of shaggy, dirty hair. I called him the "one-armed-barber" because he placed one hand in his hip pocket and sheared me using only his other hand. He started the clippers from the back and went straight forward toward my brow. Within a few minutes he had "scalped" me to the point that I looked like an onion-head. As a final act, he brushed off what loose fuzz I still had on my head and dabbed some powder on it.

When the barber finished his scalping job, the houseboy started cutting my exceedingly long fingernails. The huge scissors, which looked more like sheep-shears, were duller than the Redchink communists whom I'd been exposed to so far. He mangled the nails and tore them down to the flesh with the crude tool he was using. In view of the poor sanitation they provided, I thought it was contradictory, maybe even hypocritical, that they even bothered to pick up all the jagged pieces of fingernails and sweep up the bushel basket of shorn hair that lay on the floor. But they did.

As soon as they left, I had a sudden, unpleasant thought: they were not only trying to make me into a communist, they were also trying to make me feel and look like a Chinaman. Nevertheless, I was glad for the haircut and manicure. It made me feel better physically, and there were certain hygienic advantages I could not ignore. I dared the damned crabs to wander across my head where I could now smash the little critters flat by one good smack with the flat of my hand.

One bright, sunny day toward the end of April, I was sitting on the board picking crabs from various places on my body and squashing them between my thumbnails. I realized that what I was doing was not only personally distasteful, but it was also an utterly disgusting spectacle for someone to watch. I had noticed that the guards, the houseboys, and the prison officials were thoroughly disgusted when they witnessed my premeditated and carefully executed extermination of the little varmints. In fact, they were so upset about the practice that they ordered me to stop it. My sentiments were that if they didn't like it they could give me something to get rid of them. Since they chose not to, I continued to disobey their order, openly and defiantly.

The guard on duty that day was watching me with a disgusted look. He poked his ugly face into the window slot and ordered me to stop. I continued my practice of non-cooperation and ignored his order. Usually, other guards and officials would not persist after ordering me to stop. They would walk away, probably thinking I was an incurable degenerate of some sort, and I was left alone to pursue the loathsome task of picking off the bothersome parasites. But there was one gung-ho guard who would glare at me, curse at me, and continue noisily to taunt me in an effort to make me stop.

I decided to respond to his harassment. I picked off a couple of extra large crabs, jumped off my board, and bolted toward the window where he stood watching me. As I did so, I held them between my thumb and finger and poked them toward him threateningly. He jumped back immediately. He must've been furious as he ran down the hall to report me to the houseboy.

Moments later I heard footsteps approach my window and stop. I glanced up and saw someone peeking in, so I continued to pick off the crabs and mash them flat. The houseboy watched me for several minutes before he went to the door and jerked it open. When he entered my cell, he motioned for me to stop. I just glared at him and continued what I was doing. My disobedience caused him to storm out of the cell and to slam the door so violently that it seemed to shake, which was no small matter for such a heavy door.

The next morning the same houseboy brought in a small bottle of clear liquid and indicated that I should apply it on the area around my genitals. I took the bottle and doused the infested area. Apparently, they had finally gotten tired of watching me squash crabs between my thumbnails and of my upsetting the guards by throwing crabs at them. For the next four mornings, the houseboy brought me a bottle of liquid medication, which I immediately applied. This treatment successfully eliminated the crabs, and I finally was able to have more rest.

Toward the end of April, the houseboy took away my blue clothes and gave me a set of blacks with no pockets. Cloth knots served as buttons, and the new clothes had a strange effect on my outlook. After I put them on, I became extremely morose and felt as if I were doomed. Since the blues were still in excellent condition, I figured that they had given me the blacks for some special, sinister reason. Many terrifying thoughts kept running through my mind: Perhaps they were going to execute me on May Day; maybe they were going to parade our crew through Peking to show off the big bad Capitalist aggressors to the poor ignorant masses; they might have plans to get rid of us by shipping us off to Siberia, and no one would ever know what really became of us. That thought reminded me that no one in the Free World knew where we were or whether we were alive or dead. The mangy Redchink bastards openly boasted about that. They said that they hadn't notified our government that they were holding us. I felt so insignificant and helpless. I wanted to do something, but couldn't.

"Hell, it's hopeless," I thought. "The only things I can do are to sit and wait and pray. Oh Lord, I'm scared!"

For the next few days, and especially on May Day, I was exceptionally jumpy. Every time I heard strange footsteps in the corridor, my imagination would run away with itself. I had to struggle to conceal my anxiety and fear. In order to take my mind off the horrible thoughts which were flitting through it, I would pester the guards.

On May Day I noticed that all of the guards had received a new O. D. summer uniform, and every prison official had received a new blue summer uniform. I also made the observation that the only difference between a Red Chinese holiday and any other day was that the prisoners had even less to eat on holidays. Not only that, but on May Day morning, the prisoners began getting a quarter inch of cold water in their washbasins.

I was pretty sure that there was at least one other American in the cellblock with me. From the time I had arrived in the hellhole I had dubbed "Spider Wed," I sat and listened any time anyone was taken out of his cell. I would listen to the footsteps, and soon I was able to distinguish one set from another. I could differentiate the prisoners' footfalls from the steps of the guards and the houseboys. With daily practice, I learned to recognize the footfalls of each guard and houseboy in the cellblock.

Throughout the month of April and much of May, I kept hearing a set of footsteps which was completely different from all the others. In fact, the footsteps sounded familiar, so they awakened my curiosity. Every time I heard that particular set coming down the hall on its way to the toilet, I got off my board and started walking. When the prisoner passed my door, I rushed to the window, looked into the hall, and tried to see who it was.

"Smoker," an extremely obnoxious guard, used to tear holes in the paper screen on the window in an effort to cause trouble for me with the prison officials. I made use of the holes in an attempt to see the owner of the familiar footsteps. On some days, I became bold and pushed out the flap on the window for a peek into the hall, but the mangy guard usually stood right in front of it and completely blocked my view. I thought I knew whom the footsteps belonged to, but I wanted to confirm my belief.

One day when Smoker was standing at the flap staring at me, I gave him the finger and said, "Up your ying-yang (rectum)!"

This irritated him, and he slammed the flap shut. Almost immediately, he jerked open the flap again and glared at me.

I glared back and said, "Up your ying-yang! Sobee! (The Mandarin translation for our over-used "F-word" followed by "you") Hey tongwa (Chinese), go tell migwa (American), 'Up yo ying-yang, sobee'." I pointed down the hallway toward the cell where I thought my fellow crew member might be. Smoker closed the flap and hurried down the hallway toward the other fellow's cell.

Momentarily, I heard him say to someone, "Yo ying-yang. Sobee migwa!"

Then I heard someone in the cell yell, "Sobee, you no good son-of-a-bitch! Don't give me the finger, you yellow-bellied Redchink (Red Chinese) bastard!"

It was Daniel Schmidt, the Central Fire Control gunner on my crew.

Smoker was highly annoyed with me for the way I had used him. He was also annoyed with Schmidt, probably because of Schmidt's bombastic and graphic response to his taunting statement. Smoker got his revenge by making me wait when I needed to go to the toilet. He made it a practice to ask everyone in the cellblock if they had to go before he asked me. As a result, most of the time he went off duty before "my time" came, so I was usually forced to wait until his replacement took over.

None of the guards were dependable or consistent in their actions and their treatment of me. All of them at times would refuse to let me go to the toilet when I asked. If there was urgency in my need, I would pull down my pants and squat over the honey bucket, an action the guard saw as a serious threat for a violation of the rules. When confronted with such an explicit "request" for toilet facilities, the guard would usually relent and escort me to the latrine. However, I made a tactical error by using the method even when there was no urgency, so they got wise to me and reverted to making me wait again. I found it necessary to invent a new way to address the problem.

One day I was struggling to contain myself, and I told Smoker I definitely had to go. He grossly and uncaringly ignored my request. I told him that I was about to shit right in the middle of the floor, but he shrugged his shoulders, as if to say he didn't give a damn. He obviously thought I wasn't serious about it, because I would be the one to have to smell it all day and all night.

Not willing to give up, I approached the window flap and told him I was going to do it on the window ledge in front of the flap. He didn't believe that, either, and just laughed at me. His resistance, his disregard for my need, and his scornful laugh were too much. I pulled down my pants, grabbed hold of the bars, pulled myself up so that my bare bottom was square in the disbeliever's face, and started grunting. Flabbergasted by my action, he jumped back and yelled for me to wait. He ran to the door and opened it; then he escorted me to the latrine.

Of course, Smoker wasted no time in reporting me to the houseboy. Soon, the houseboy came into my cell, as I expected he would, and lectured me on the prison rules and the adverse effect shitting on the floor and on the window ledge would have on the prison's sanitation. He was very forceful in telling me that I should use the toilet instead.

While he lectured me on sanitation, he hacked and spit a huge glob of phlegm on the floor and rubbed it in with his foot. His hypocrisy angered me, and I told him spitting on the floor was almost as bad as shitting on it. However, he waved off my complaint and explained that spitting was "okay" as long as you "rubbed it in." All of the Red Chinese with whom I'd had contact indulged in the filthy habit of spitting on the floor, and I couldn't help but be annoyed and disgusted by the practice.

Smoker and the other guards also irritated me with their habit of sneaking up to the flap, peeking in, and watching me. They did this regularly and too often for it to be a simple matter of satisfying a depraved curiosity. I was sure they had orders to regularly observe me, and they probably recorded their observations and made sure they got to the interrogators. It was all part of their "plan" to know all about me and to "break" me and covert me to communism. Nevertheless, I grew tired of that kind of invasion of my privacy. I decided to fight back; so, when I sensed that there was a guard outside the flap, I squatted down and edged my way right under the window. When I heard him lift the flap, I jumped up, let out a loud yell, and poked my finger toward his eye. Sometimes I grazed his cheek before he could jump back. I couldn't understand all the things he yelled at me, but some of them were obscene and abusive. After he finished yelling, he ordered me to sit down. I deliberately disobeyed and began walking around my cell.

The things I conceived to retaliate, to show them I still had spirit, were not without consequence. The result was always hot scoldings delivered at any time of day or night, a calling in of reinforcements—a houseboy, an official, or another guard—and threats of severe punishment if I did not renounce my rebellious behavior and obey the prison rules. I reveled in the fact that I was able to exasperate them. I gloried in the frustrated looks on their faces, their disorganized and helter-skelter reactions, and sometimes I secretly gloated about the fact that I still possessed some powers that I could exert, even though they were minor ones compared to what I'd lost by my imprisonment.

Late one afternoon the houseboy opened my cell door and put my green mess kit on the floor just inside the door. I picked it up and returned to my board. When I started to open the kit, I noticed that the outside of the container was covered with snot. I became nauseated and thought I was going to vomit. However, since I was starving and the morning meal was 12 hours away, I opened the kit. Much to my disgust, I found snot inside the kit. I turned my head away, closed my eyes, and forced myself to eat the scanty contents. I was THAT hungry!!!!!

I had finally gotten used to the maggots in the rice. I even considered them a treat compared to some of the garbage they fed me, but giving a human being a mess kit covered with snot was despicable, totally depraved, and barbaric. But they found other ways to harass me that could be similarly classified. Many of the guards stood near the window at mealtime, hacked up phlegm, and spat it out. A few of the Redchink pricks lifted the flap and spat toward me. The meals themselves were unappetizing enough, but the coarse actions of the guards made mealtime even more revolting. Their crude, inhumane behavior and their barbaric treatment of their captives made me even more determined not to cooperate with them; I remained firm in my commitment to do all in my feeble power to annoy them and defy them as much as I possibly could. Nevertheless, I nearly always paid a price. Whenever I "misbehaved" in my cell or in the interrogation room, they usually punished me by cutting down even further on my meager food ration. In addition, they withheld my cup of boiled water, which in my circumstances was a treat.

I don't know whether it was an accident or was done on purpose, but the rice almost always contained tiny white rocks. It was very difficult to distinguish the stones from the rice. When I put rice in my mouth and began chewing it, I would often bite down on a rock and almost break a tooth. Of course repetition is a good reminder; I soon learned to approach the act of chewing with the most delicate care.

In early May I was given a new set of blacks with a white patch containing a black character. With it came a set of white underwear which had a similar patch. The shorts were crudely constructed, and the excessively rough seams cut into my scrotum. I soon contracted a genital rash that was red and smooth. It was an extremely painful rash that drove me crazy with its itching and burning. If I scratched, the itching grew more intense; if I didn't scratch, both the burning and itching intensified to such an extent I felt like climbing the walls. Whenever I walked, the rubbing of my flesh against my shorts and trousers irritated the infected areas. Eventually, the whole area (scrotum, crotch, and penis) became raw, and the pain grew almost unbearable. Many times the thought that "I couldn't take it anymore" oppressed me to the point that it was all I could do to keep myself from screaming out my anger and pain.

I asked for medication, but it never materialized. I fervently begged the guards, the houseboys, and the prison officials for proper medication for the malady, but I was continually refused. They continuously pointed out to me that my attitude was "incorrect" and that I would have to start cooperating if I wanted my conditions to improve.

One morning near the end of the month, the houseboy entered the cell and motioned for me to follow him. He made a circular motion with his hand. I didn't understand the gesture, but I got up from the board and followed him out of the cell and down the hallway. He led me through a side door into a small courtyard between the cellblocks. I still didn't understand what was up, but I followed him to the center of the open area. He motioned for me to walk around the courtyard in a small circle.

The open area, or courtyard, was enclosed by three cellblocks. The only way to exit the courtyard was through a side door into one of the cellblocks. Flowers were planted along each cellblock and throughout the courtyard area. I noticed a lonely grapevine and several small trees, one of which was a mulberry. The cellblocks fanned out in wings from a common circular building, like spokes on a huge wheel. A round structure connected the extreme ends of my cellblock and an adjacent cellblock. The houseboy kept telling me not to look around, but I had seen enough to know that I was completely enclosed; there was no chance for me to make a desperate escape attempt by running away.

The houseboy had a clock with him that he kept looking at. After approximately 15 minutes of walking exercise, he took me back to my stuffy, oppressive cell.

For the next three weeks I was taken out about three times a week for a 15 minute walk in the courtyard. Then, without any explanation, they discontinued the short exercise sessions. I made an assumption that I was being deprived of the walks because of my conduct, my continued failure to "cooperate" with them either in my cell or in the interrogation room.

About two o'clock in the morning of June 1, 1953, I was awakened by a commotion down the hall. Someone was being moved into a cell. I rolled over and went back to sleep.

Several hours later, the guard pounded on the bars in my window to wake me up. By the noises and the footsteps I heard, I suddenly realized that the cellblock was teeming with a bevy of new guards, and I wondered what was going on in the minds of my captors to instigate such a drastic change and what it would mean for me and my fellow crewmen.

Later on, I noticed a new set of footsteps being led to the latrine. I was excited, because there was the distinctive sound of a crippled person using crutches. When the cripple finished his business at the latrine and headed back to his cell, I jumped up and rushed to my window in an attempt to see him. I was disappointed because I failed to get even a glimpse of him.

Late that afternoon I heard the new prisoner coming down the hall again. I got up and tried again to see him. From that first day of June until July 18th, I heard and watched the newcomer make his way to and from the latrine twice daily. I surmised that he was really special, a V.I.P. (Very Important Prisoner), because he was allowed to use the latrine twice a day. Many times, by jumping up and looking over the window screen or by looking through the holes around the flap made by Smoker, I was able to get short glimpses of him. By incrementing those fleeting visions, I managed to create a fairly good picture of the man. He was a male Caucasian, about five feet nine in height, with a medium build, and he had a shaved head. As time went by and his hair started growing back, it looked black or dark brown. His complexion was fair, and he wore clothes like mine—black with a white patch. I didn't recognize him, so I wondered who he was and whether he was military or civilian.

I made attempts to communicate with him at times when he passed my cell. I tapped out Morse code on the wooden door in an effort to attract his attention and let him know who I was, but I got no recognizable response. When that failed, I tried coughing out Morse code, but that also failed.

I refused to give up, however, and got pretty bold in my efforts. I started jumping up to look over my window screen and at the same time calling out my name. I also asked the newcomer his name. Hoping to get lucky and hit on the right name, I mentioned others also. I thought he might be the instructor pilot who accompanied our crew on the ill-fated mission; he had been wounded in the leg and probably needed crutches. Whoever he was, he either ignored my attempts to communicate, or he was afraid to try to respond.

About that same time, I ceased to hear Schmidt's footfalls going to and from the latrine. I suspected that he had been moved out of the cellblock because we stubbornly continued to have minimal communications between us. Any time he passed my door, I pounded out Morse code, and quite often he would acknowledge my signal by coughing. But we were both being watched too closely to be able to complete any lengthy communications or exchange any kind of information other than the fact that we were who we were and that we still existed.

During the period I was observing the newcomer, I noticed that another prisoner was experiencing much difficulty moving down the hall on his way to and from the latrine. It was obvious from the sounds I heard and the time it took him to make the trip that he moved very slowly. I tried to get a look at him, but the guard or the houseboy would make me sit down before he came near enough to my cell for me to steal a peek. They would also stand in front of both my window flap and my door while he was passing my cell.

In early June 1953, I was escorted to a room in the vicinity of the interrogation area where they X-rayed my chest. This really caused me to wonder what the wily communist were up to. I thought that perhaps the war was over and that they were going to send me home.

Beginning in June, all prisoners, at the sound of a bell, had to take a two hour siesta from twelve o'clock noon until two P.M. Usually I was just finishing my lunch when the siesta bell rang. At that very instant, the guard would aggressively urge me to finish my meal. He raised the window flap and heckled me until he became agitated and I became upset. Finally, I learned to fight off this unwelcome intrusion into what I considered my own private time; I began to stop eating completely and then just sit and stare at the guard until he gave up and closed the flap, after which I resumed eating at my own pace. I regarded this as my personal "sit down strike" for a good cause, and it worked quite well.

My "siesta time" aggravation did not end when I finished eating. There was still the chore of rinsing out my mess kit with a cup of cold water the guard gave me. I made it a point to work slowly in completing the task, during which time the guard fussed and fumed at me because I was such a slowpoke. I merely laughed at him and then crawled upon my board to take my nap.

But, as in all the other aspects of my captivity, the various guards who were victims of my willful aggravation had to have the last say in the matter in order to show me who was "boss" and to pay me back for my lack of cooperation. Therefore, they disturbed my siesta by talking and laughing just outside my cell, and I rarely got the full benefit of the rest period. The siesta breaks lasted through the summer months.

During the months of May and June, the political commissar apparently became concerned over my "incorrect" attitude and "improper" behavior. As a result, the political indoctrination and "re-education" sessions became longer and more frequent. I was subjected to endless hours of lectures dealing with the birth and history—the entire spectrum—of communism: communist ideology,

85

goals, aspirations, guerilla techniques, and finally the plan for world domination. They made a fervent endeavor to convert me to communism through continued indoctrination sessions, despite my fervent objections. The strong convictions and the visible dedication of the lecturers to the ultimate party goals really impressed and frightened me. They made no bones about it: their main goal was the eventual destruction of our free democratic society. All lecturers stressed the view that time was of no essence. It really didn't matter whether it took five years or 100 years, they would persist until they achieved their goal.

Many references were made to my family origin. Repeatedly, they belabored the theme that I wasn't really an American and that I should seriously consider to whom my allegiance should be directed. After all, I was still young, and there was still time to make amends. Their intensified harassment and indoctrination efforts extended through July and into August.

During that time I found myself reflecting on World War II, which was an impressionable event in my boyhood. I remembered myself as a youthful civilian who, through news clips and movies, learned about the terrible tragedies our fighting men and women suffered. Sometimes, through imagination, I vicariously participated in those tragedies and performed heroic deeds of great magnitude. Those years, though not so long ago, crowded in upon me, and I realized that those past idealistic fancies I indulged in did nothing to prepare me for my life of captivity.

Presently, I was still a young man, only 21, and some days I felt like an old curmudgeon. That mind set was a product of facing moment-by-moment ugliness and brutality, a heavy load that robbed my youth and created an unnatural precociousness I struggled to accept and live with. Knowledge of that change and its effect did little to comfort me or to assuage the anger and bitterness I felt. Yet, a small peephole of hope emerged in the darkness of my thoughts, and it inspired me to hang on, to confound my enemies in spite of their treatment of me.

By the middle of July, my cloth shoes were starting to smell terribly putrid. I took them off, carried them to the flap, and shoved them under the guard's nose. He jumped away and slammed the flap shut. From his action, another weapon was born that I could use to fight back. Whenever I got fed up with the almost constant surveillance of the guard, I yanked off my smelly shoes and headed toward the flap. He never failed to close the flap and move away.

On July 18, 1953, the day started off as usual. Somewhere around ten o'clock I heard a commotion in the hallway. I listened and tried to determine what was happening, but I was uncertain about what the noise meant. Shortly two houseboys came to my cell and made me help them move my belongings. One carried the bed board and sawhorses, and the other one carried the honey bucket. The only thing I had to carry was my blanket and pad.

They escorted me down the corridor until we reached the large circular area that served as the hub for a number of cellblocks. I followed them through some double doors to another cellblock, and they led me the entire length of the hall to the last cell on the left. I had learned enough Chinese to determine that the character above the door was the number 15. They opened the door, deposited the bed board, sawhorses, and honey bucket; then they went back down the hallway toward the hub. I was left alone without any explanation as to why I had been moved to Cell 15.

This cellblock was longer than the one I had just left. As I made the long walk from the hub to the cell, I counted eight cells on each side of the hallway. There was also a dirty, rat-infested toilet on each side; they were actually no more than small cubbyholes in the walls. On each end of this cellblock, there was a circular room with double doors. Except for those differences, the new cellblock was much like the old one.

In Cell 15 the position of the door and the inside window were the reverse of what they were in Cell 10 in the cellblock from which I had just been moved. In Cell 15 the door was on the right, and in Cell 10 it was on the left. Also, the door in my new cell had a 4 inch by 4 inch hole cut out at eye level, and this hole was covered with a cloth flap. The inside (hall) window was on the left, and its screen was made of cloth, not paper. It, too, had an observation flap, thus giving the Redchinks two peepholes to spy on me.

Cell 15 had no mosquito netting on the windows. I regarded this as a plus because I used them as a diet supplement. One of my more zestful pastimes was chasing and killing mosquitoes. With a little imagination, I made the chore a source of entertainment by pretending the mosquitoes were MIG 15 jet fighters. Whenever I "downed" (killed) one, I would yell, "Ole, ole! Another MIG bites the dust!" Sometimes my exuberance would bring the guards running to find out what the commotion was all about. I explained to them that the mosquitoes were Tongwa figi (Red Chinese aircraft) and that I was shooting them down. When they understood how happy this made me, they admonished me not to entertain such thoughts. Naturally, I ignored their advice.

It was an unfortunate experience to have to use the toilet in my new location. I couldn't help but be diverted by the rats that scurried around the hole below where I had to squat. To me rats were repugnant even in the best of environments, and to see them in and around a hole filled with excrement was absolutely sickening. Nevertheless, some vulgar impulse caused me to move my bottom around in an attempt to bombard the filthy pests. When I figured I had accurately zeroed in on one, I shouted "Bombs away" at the same time I let go with a full load. Occasionally I managed to spatter one of the sorry little disease carriers.

One day, during one such strategic maneuver, I was overcome with a great loathing. "My God!" I thought, "Is this the level to which I have sunk?"

About 10 A. M. on July 20, 1953, I was escorted to a cell in another cellblock off the big round room. There was a desk in the cell with medical paraphernalia scattered all over the top. Two Red Chinese were in the cell: one wearing a dingy white smock and the other wearing summer blues.

"Can you see?" asked the interpreter as the "doctor" held a card in front of my eyes. "Can you see it?" I told him that I could see it, and he said, "Eyes okay," and put a check by "eyes" on the medical form in front of him.

The quack then picked up a tuning fork off the top of the desk and hit it against his left hand, causing the fork to vibrate; then he held it to my left ear. "Can you hear it?" asked the interpreter. I told him that I could hear it, and he marked "ears okay" on the medical form.

"Open your mouth," said the tongue (interpreter). I did and the quack shoved a flat stick into my mouth. "Now say ah," the tongue told me. I said, "Ah." The tongue told me to open my mouth wider. I did and the quack peered into my mouth and down my throat. The tongue asked me to say "ah" again. I uttered a long "aaahhh" sound, and the quack said, "How." The tongue reported, "Tonsils okay," and put a check by "tonsils" on the form.

"Step up on the scales," ordered the tongue. I did and the quack checked my weight, and the tongue recorded it. Neither said, "Weight okay."

The quack then placed his stethoscope against my chest and listened to my heart. Moving it back and forth, he listened some more and mumbled a few words in Mandarin, and the tongue recorded it on the form.

"Pull down your pants," said the tongue. I did and the quack checked my rectum and mumbled something, and the tongue marked it down on the form. Then he told me that I had hemorrhoids.

While my pants were down, the quack examined my genitals and the surrounding area. The whole area around my genitals was still raw and red with cracks in the skin. The quack asked "Tong? Tong?" (Does it hurt?) I assured him that it did and told him that it burned, itched, and hurt intensely. I again asked for medication to treat the area. The quack listened and grunted something, and the tongue wrote it down on the form.

The tongue told me that the doctor wanted to know if my legs and feet were still giving me much pain. I told him that they were still aching something awful and that they felt as if someone were sticking long, sharp needles into them.

"The doctor wants to know if your stomach bothers you much," said the tongue.

"Very much," I said. "Being on a starvation diet coupled with the rotten crap you so begrudgingly dole out to us, one can not expect not to have stomach trouble."

"Show the doctor where it hurts."

I showed him and he put his hand there and pressed down and asked, "Tong, tong?" I emitted a long, loud "ooowww" sound and told him that it damn well did hurt and hurt bad.

With that the half-assed physical was completed, and the guard hurriedly took me back to my cell. Needless to say, I wasn't going to hold my breath waiting for medication to treat my painful and annoying rash. But I wondered, "Why the physical?" I thought that perhaps the war was over and that they were going to send me home.

My bed board was arranged in Cell 15 so that it was against the wall that faced the outdoor exercise area. After I had been there a few days, I was sitting on my board trying to figure why I had been moved. I thought the reason might have been because of my attempts to communicate with the newcomer. On the other hand, they really didn't need a reason; but, if they were looking for one, my continued defiance and sassiness were probably numbers one and two on their list.

Anyway, it was hot and muggy in the cell, and the window above my bed board was propped open. I happened to look up at the open window, and I saw the reflection of someone walking in the courtyard. The window was papered except for two panes. Evidently they had been broken and replace, and the Red Chinese forgot to paper the new glass.

I continued to watch, and I saw that there were two men walking around outside on the far side of the patio. From what I could see, they appeared to be Caucasians. One was built like our Aircraft Commander Gene Vaadi; he was even baldheaded. The other one looked enough like our Pilot Wally Brown to be his brother. I was pretty sure both men were white, but I couldn't be positive. I really needed a better look.

In about 15 minutes they were apparently taken back to their cells, and two other men were brought out. The two new ones were also kept on the other side of the courtyard. Their movements and their exercise actions (swinging arms, side-straddle hops) were not oriental in nature, so I assumed they were from a Western nation, probably Caucasians. I watched them until they, too, were taken away. Then two more were brought out, and one had a crippled, or injured, leg because he had a crutch and a cane. The longer I watched them, the more convinced I became that they, too, were white. I was careful to do my watching in a nonchalant manner to avoid the displeasure of the guards; if they even suspected me of "breaking the rules" by trying to see outside, they would have punished me or moved me to another cell.

That same afternoon during the siesta period, I noticed another man walking on the patio. He walked around the circle, and as he approached my side of the courtyard, I saw that it was John Thompson, our Right Scanner. I watched him until he was led back through the door that was located between my cell and the hub. Of course I was unable to determine which cellblock he entered from the hub. But I was elated by the discovery. I felt pretty sure that all surviving members of our crew were somewhere nearby, and I vowed to be alert and try to confirm it.

After Thompson was taken back to his cellblock, about 12 Chinese prisoners entered the patio and walked around for awhile. I noted that, during the course of the afternoon, several different groups of Chinese prisoners were allowed in the patio where they puttered around the flower garden and took advantage of the exercise and fresh air. I was not interested in the Chinese, so I finally ceased my observations and chased a few mosquitoes.

The next morning I was sitting on my "bed" thinking. I interspersed that boring activity by occasionally glancing up at the window. I happened to see a man walking around in the patio, and he passed within six feet of my window. I saw that he was definitely white, of medium build, had light hair and complexion, and stood about five eleven. He wore black pants and shirt, and both the shirt and pants had a white patch with a black character inside. The man was quite active and walked at a lively pace. He looked very familiar, and I had a feeling that I knew him.

I was interrupted by the houseboy. He came into my cell and took me for a walk in a different courtyard from the one just outside my window. When I came back from my walk, the light-haired man I'd seen earlier was just then being returned to his cellblock; he was taken into the same cellblock where I was sure Thompson had gone the day before.

In the afternoon, after siesta, I saw the baldheaded one and the slim one walking in the patio again. I watched. When the guard went to the other end of the cellblock, I stood up on my board and tried to get a better look. I saw that they were white, but they were just too far away for me to identify. I was careful because the ammo carrier could enter the cellblock at my end, so it was possible for him to surprise me.

I watched those men for more than two weeks, and I could never quite see enough or hear enough to make a positive identification. However, I was able to get a better look at the light-haired man that was so familiar-looking; I finally recognized him as the extra Radar Operator who had accompanied us on our ill-fated mission. When he passed nearby, I pounded code on the wall with my cloth shoe to let him know who I was. I also called out both my name and his whenever he was in the vicinity of my window. But he was watched very closely, and the only response he could give me was a smile and a nod of his head.

PART V

CONFESS OR DIE

Steve E. Kiba

One of the things I did to pass the time and keep from going berserk was to create names for guards and other Red Chinese officials. I had no specific criteria for doing this. It was an exercise that just came naturally as I was exposed to various unique individuals. When I moved to Cell 15, I encountered a new guard. He was an overgrown Mongolian ape-like creature. He was well over six feet tall and weighed between 250 and 300 pounds. I recognized right away that he was kind of dumb and definitely a slow learner. I named him "Big Stupe."

On July 27, 1953, Big Stupe escorted me to the interrogation room. All the way there, he kept forcing my head down against my chest so I couldn't look around. I kept jerking my head up, and he kept pushing it down. This defiant refusal of mine to cooperate was accepted by most other guards, and they had quit trying to force my head down when they were with me. But not Big Stupe. He persisted all the way to the interrogation room, where he took me to the center of the room and made me face three Red Chinese officers seated behind a large desk. I was stopped 15 feet from the desk, next to a stool. The dreaded Napoleon, with whom I'd had many difficult sessions, was seated in the middle.

"Sit down," Napoleon said.

I sat down and placed my right hand inside my shirt in the manner I always used to imitate him.

He noticed and said, "I see you have not changed your 'wrong' attitude yet." Then he got down to business. "Where did you land after we shot you down?"

"On the ground."

"You wise son-of-a-bitch! I mean what country?"

"North Korea, of course."

"Are you sure?"

"Positive."

"Why are you positive?"

"Because we have the best crew in the Air Force, and there's no possibility of our being mistaken in our position."

"Now, where did you land?"

"On the ground."

"What country?"

"North Korea."

"You landed in the People's Republic of China."

"Like hell we did."

"You landed in the People's Republic of China. We had you on radar, and we saw our fighters attack you. One came in from this angle." He swooped his flat hand through the air to simulate the angle of the fighter. "And another one came in from here, and here, and here, while others followed."

His gestures reminded me all too well of the sudden attack by MIG 15s and the tragic results for me and my crew. But he was a liar. We knew exactly where we were when we were shot down, and it was south of the Yalu River in North Korea.

I said, "Hell, I didn't even know you barbarians had radar. Besides, what does that prove? You could just as well have tracked us in North Korea."

"What did you see when you landed?"

"I couldn't see. It was dark."

"Do not be a wise guy. What did you see?"

The room was extremely hot. Napoleon and the other two at the desk had sweat rolling down their faces, and all three were vigorously fanning themselves with round, paper fans.

"After I hit the ground, I saw a train. Further down the tracks, I saw what I believed was a train station. The men running the station kept turning their lights on and off. Red China is not officially at war, so why should a railroad station in Red China have a blackout? Undoubtedly, the station was in North Korea, and they were using blackout procedures due to an air alert that we caused."

"Kiba, they do not have trains in Korea. What kind of lights were they?"

"Electric lights."

"They do not have electric lights in Korea. You Americans have bombed out all of the railroads and power stations in North Korea, so how could you expect them to have trains and electric lights? What color clothes were the people wearing?"

"Some were wearing black, some white, and some dark blue."

"You see, I told you that you were not in Korea. Everyone in Korea wears white. Now, why do you not confess that you were in the People's Republic of China as everyone else has done?"

"I told you already that I was in North Korea. N-O-R-T-H K-O-R-E-A!"

"You will confess sooner or later. Take your hand from your shirt. Are you trying to make fun of me?"

"I'd never think of it."

"You would not have to think of it. Kiba, you are too damned arrogant. You could make things so much easier on yourself if you would only cooperate and conduct yourself properly—like a prisoner should."

"I've never been a prisoner before, so how should I know how to conduct myself?"

"You can start by telling us what we want to hear from you and by signing a confession. Then you must obey our rules. Of course, if you do not sign, you will not have to worry about the rules, or anything else, anymore."

Napoleon had a nasty grin on his face, and I wanted to smack him. I was finding it harder and harder to contain my thoughts and emotions and not strike back.

"Are you threatening me again?" I asked.

The nasty grin never left his face, as he said smoothly, "This time we are not threatening you. It matters very little to us whether or not you sign it. It is your life which is at stake. Are you going to confess?"

"Confess?"

"Yes. Are you going to confess?"

I screwed up my face to affect a puzzled look. "Confess what?" I asked.

"Your crime against the peace-loving Chinese people." He lost his control and practically screamed out the words.

"What crime?"

"Do not try to act dumb. Confess!"

"I haven't done anything."

"Your aircraft violated our air space," he said.

I couldn't contain myself, so I screamed back, "Like hell we did."

97

He ignored my outburst. "We have proof," he said. "Now confess."

I called his bluff and said, "Show me the proof."

He ignored my demand and continued to hammer me with accusations and questions.

"You landed in the People's Republic of China."

"North Korea," I said.

"You had better confess that you landed in the People's Republic of China." He made this sound like an "or else" demand.

"Is North Korea a part of Red China?" I asked.

"No, of course not."

"Then we did not land in Red China."

"You violated the territorial air space of the People's Republic of China. Our brave People's Air Force shot you down, and you landed and were captured in the People's Republic. Now you had better confess. Your Wing Commander Colonel Arnold has already confessed. Your Aircraft Commander Captain Veedee has already confessed. The entire crew of Stardust Four Zero has already confessed. Why do you not confess? Who are you trying to fool? You are no hero. Do not be melodramatic! This is not the movies. As you have undoubtedly observed, it would be most difficult—if not impossible—for any of you to escape. There is only one way for you, and that is for you to confess. Now, either you will sign this confession or it will be your end."

"Which end?"

"I see that you insist on being a wise guy. We are tired of you and your horsing around. Let us inform you that there are very few people who know that you are alive. So, if we so desire, we can eliminate you or send you to the Far North, and no one will ever know what happened to you."

Actually, I believed Napoleon really enjoyed his job. His gestures and his expressions were transparent, and his evil smile during that threat certainly showed his level of depravity. However, I was spurred to respond.

"What? Why you mangy sons-of-bitches. You mean to say you haven't notified our government yet that we have been captured and are prisoners?"

"That is correct." The three at the desk laughed. I even heard Big Stupe let out a subdued giggle, although I doubt he really understood the gravity of the situation.

I said, "According to the rules of the Geneva Convention, you were supposed to notify our government as soon as you captured us."

"The People's Republic of China is not a signatory nation of the Geneva Convention."

"That doesn't surprise me," I said. "Your inhumane treatment of prisoners and your perverted actions prove that."

I heard a commotion coming from the door behind the interrogation desk.

"Are you going to sign this confession?" Napoleon said.

"I still maintain that our plane was shot down in North Korea."

"Nevertheless, you must sign this document which states that your B-29 type aircraft intruded into the People's Republic of China."

"Even thought we bailed out in North Korea?"

"Yes."

"You said all other crew members had signed. I'd like to see their confessions."

"Okay. Come up to the desk."

I got to my feet and started walking toward the desk. The officer seated on Napoleon's right picked up the two top folders from a stack and brought them to me. One was signed by Colonel Arnold and the other by Captain Vaadi.

"Do you recognize the signatures?" Napoleon asked with a smug look on his ugly face.

"No, I can't say that I do."

"You have seen their signatures before?"

"Yes, a few times."

"Are these their signatures?"

"I don't know. I don't recognize them. They could be forgeries, so I need more proof that they actually signed these papers. This isn't enough."

"There is a fingerprint on each statement."

"The hell there is! Colonel Arnold's doesn't have one. And the print on Captain Vaadi's statement could be yours for all I know. I can't tell one fingerprint from another."

"Blast you Kiba! Will you sign or not? And take you hand from your shirt!" Napoleon was either very angry or putting on a good show.

"Why should I sign your friggin' false paper when you starve me and keep me in solitary confinement? Besides, you have kept our imprisonment a secret from our government, and according to you, they don't even know we're alive. What good would the 'confession' be if it comes from a 'dead' man?"

"Hah! So you think you have been starved and ill-treated. Well, it is just now starting."

I heard more noise coming from the door behind the desk, and it confused me. The interrogation and the unidentified noise had almost unnerved me.

"Let me see more signatures," I said. "You said everybody had signed. I want to see the signatures of Van Voorhis, Weese, and Hart."

"No!" he said very adamantly. "You must confess or die!" His eyes bulged, and the veins on his neck stood out.

For some reason, I sensed that they were not bluffing. The strange noises coming from behind the door had increased in both volume and frequency, my mind was numbed by exhaustion, and I was physically, mentally, and emotionally beaten down to the point that I could no longer function normally. Worst of all, I was scared—damn scared. I truly believed they were about to execute me, or even worse, to send me to Siberia. I had a sick feeling deep down in my stomach and had to fight back the urge to vomit.

Finally, I said, "Okay. I'll sign your scrap of paper, but I still say we bailed out over North Korea."

"Bring your stool up here," he said.

I carried the stool up to the desk and sat down.

Napoleon handed me a staff pen, a sheet of blank paper, and a typewritten statement.

"Now write on the blank sheet in your own words what it says in the typewritten statement," he said.

I wrote: "I was told that we violated the territorial air space of the People's Republic of China in a B-29 bearing arms, ammunition, and radio sets and are hereby subject to the laws of the People's Republic of China."

I signed the statement and handed it to Napoleon. He read it and became very angry because I had written "I was told" in my confession.

He handed me another blank piece of paper and said, "Write it over and omit the first three words." If looks could kill, his mean stare would have destroyed me immediately.

"In my own words?" I asked.

"Yes, in your own words."

I began writing again, using "my own" words.

"No, no, no! Stop! I told you to omit those first three words."

I just grinned at him and reminded him that he told me to use my own words.

"Yes, but leave out 'I was told'."

I started writing again on a clean sheet of paper. Again I aroused his wrath.

"No, no, no! Stop! You wiseass! Here, I will help you write it. Copy what I tell you: 'We violated the territorial air space of the People's Republic of China in a B-29 type bomber bearing arms, ammunition, and radio sets; we are hereby subject to the laws of the People's Republic of China.' Now sign it!"

"These are not my own words," I said.

"If you do not sign, we will kill you NOW! You have exhausted our patience and wasted much of our valuable time. Now, for the last time, you sign or you die!"

I was absolutely terrified. I took the staff pen and signed the false statement, which was in Napoleon's words, not mine. He pulled it from my hands and looked at it.

The door behind the desk flew open, and five or six Red Chinese officials dressed in dark slacks and light blue long-sleeved shirts rushed out. One was a very distinguished-looking man; he was evidently a high ranking official in the Central Committee.

The distinguished looking man seized the false confession, beamed, and said something in Mandarin to Napoleon, and Napoleon translated it for me.

"You were smart to sign. Otherwise, you would be dead. Do you believe that you landed in the People's Republic?"

"No. Since when has North Korea been a part of Red China?"

The distinguished looking official, who was still holding the false statement, seemed irritated. He said something to Napoleon.

Napoleon turned to me and said, "You MUST believe it! And stop saying Red China. My superiors do not like it."

"I still say I landed in North Korea."

"Then why did you sign?"

"Because I figured you'd kill me if I didn't, and I'm too young to die."

"Now you are smart, but my superior says that you MUST believe it. Now, go back to your cell."

"How are the others? How are Van Voorhis, Weese, and Hart?"

"We don't know."

"You mangy liars!" I yelled.

"Never you mind about the others. You just worry about yourself. Do not forget that you are a prisoner, and you must conduct yourself accordingly. Now go!"

Big Stupe escorted me back to my cell. I sat down on the hard board and waited for supper and my usual cup of boiled water. I soon realized that supper and water had been doled out while I was being interrogated, and I wouldn't get any. Hell, I didn't feel like eating, anyway.

While I was waiting for boardtime, horrible thoughts and images kept creeping into my numb mind. I felt as if I were in an unreal and grotesque alien world. I tried to sort out the twists and turns in my thinking that led to my perfidy. Yet, even though I was possessed by some unidentifiable compulsion at the time, I was disappointed that I yielded to that compulsion after having resisted them for so long. Why was I so terrified? Why hadn't God answered my fervent prayer for merciful deliverance from the hands of these barbarians? What was wrong with me? Where had I failed?

I remembered our briefing at Yokota Air Force Base in Japan just before we left on our leaflet dropping mission. We were warned that if we were captured the communists might attempt to coerce us into signing false confessions or making propaganda broadcasts. The briefing officers told us to try to avoid signing anything. However, they said that if it were a matter of life and death, to go ahead and sign, but be sure to include falsehoods or something unusual. In spite of that qualified permission and in spite of not understanding the value of the false confessions to the Red Chinese, I was still troubled. My numb mind was still active enough to think "What if?" What if our briefing team in Japan denied their advice to us? Since the communists had what they wanted from us, what if they slowly tortured us to death? What if they shipped us to an isolated hellhole somewhere for the remainder of our lives, without ever telling anyone?

I was alone, abandoned, and harboring a fear so deep it threatened my sanity. Still, questions kept popping up in my mind. What were our fellow Americans doing to hasten our release? What *could* they do? If our torturers had been truthful, our government, our families, and our friends had no idea where we were or that we were even alive.

Would my death be slow and painful, as they had promised me? Or would they tie my hands behind my back and blow a bloody, gaping hole in my head as they had done to so many of our men in North Korea? When would they do it?

Finally the boardtime (bedtime) bell rang. I lay down on the hard, hard board and tried to get some sleep, but it was no use; I couldn't turn off my mind. I spent a long, sleepless night plagued by feelings of guilt, and I kept chiding myself for being so weak.

Next morning I was still devastated by my forced treachery. I endeavored to lift my crushed spirits by killing as many mosquitoes as I could, while pretending that they were enemy fighter planes. At the usual time, I had my customary bowl of watery rice gruel and a small bun. I noticed that there weren't as many worms in my gruel as usual, and I thought sardonically that things must be getting really bad for me.

I hastily gobbled down my scanty breakfast and paced the floor for an hour or more. Then I sat down and stared at one blank wall and then another. This dull routine was broken occasionally by an upward glance at the outside window. I saw large groups of Chinese prisoners, undoubtedly Kuomintang, working in the courtyard. Later

I got a glimpse of the two Caucasians I'd seen before, and I named the bald-headed one "Baldy" and the slender one "Slim." Just before noon I was taken to the patio for a 15 minute walk. In the afternoon, after I took my siesta, I again saw Van Voorhis, one of our Radar Operators, as he walked in the patio.

At four o'clock, Bluebeard—one of my political instructors, came into my cell with a Chinese copy of my false confession. I couldn't read Chinese, so I didn't understand a word of what was written on the paper. Bluebeard assured me it was an official copy of what I had already signed in English. Therefore, when he asked me to sign it, I believed I couldn't do any more damage than I'd already done, so I signed it without argument. Bluebeard took the signed copy, gave me a pamphlet, and told me to read it carefully. He grinned and said, "It is very good. I have read it five times myself."

When Bluebeard left, I sat down and thumbed through the 81 page pamphlet. It was entitled TRUTH ABOUT THE AMERICAN DIPLOMATS. It condemned our foreign policy and our way of life in general, and it claimed that all United States Embassy workers were professional spies. It criticized democracy and praised communism.

The more I read, the more disgusted I grew. Occasionally I had to vocally vent my anger and distress. "Bull! What a bunch of malicious lies," I cried more than once. Of course I had no audience, but nevertheless it felt good to purge myself and, at the same time, to excoriate the principles set forth in the propaganda I was forced to read. It seemed to me that the basic prerequisite for being a good communist was to be a professional liar.

By the time I finished reading the propaganda pamphlet, I was boiling mad. I tried to return it to the guards and the houseboys, but all of them refused to take it.

The next day, since I had nothing else to do and since I was sick of staring at blank walls and the ugly guards, I picked up the obnoxious pamphlet and read it again. My Red Chinese instructors knew I would do just that.

Through the long, tortuous days, I continued to see and watch Van Voorhis, Thompson, and the other Caucasians, as well as the groups of Chinese prisoners in the courtyard. From time to time I would stand on my bed board and pull myself up onto the window ledge in an attempt to get a better look at the Caucasian prisoners. This act was forbidden, and it was extremely dangerous because the guards, both those assigned to watch the prisoners in the courtyard and those assigned to watch me, supervised us very closely. Whether or not they suspected me of taking unauthorized peeks outside was irrelevant; they suspected *everything,* and that is why they continuously and unexpectedly threw up the flap and looked in on me, day and night. But somehow—most probably through miraculous Divine Intervention—I managed to avoid being caught.

I saw the poor, unfortunate Van Voorhis walk in the courtyard for the last time on the morning of August 3, 1953. This was about a week after I signed the false confession. That same afternoon I was escorted to the warden's office and accused of talking to the prisoners in the patio. I feigned ignorance and told them that their accusation really hurt and that their distrust in me deeply pained me. The warden and his cohort glared at me, uttered some obscenities, and then forced me to endure three hours of boring re-education.

On August 4, 1953, the houseboys moved me to another cellblock and put me into the first cell on the right, next to the toilet. This move definitely confirmed my belief that they knew I had been watching Van Voorhis and the other inmates. It was no accident that in my new cell I no longer had a view of the patio.

Periodically, the Chinese inmates were made to empty the toilet with large buckets. With an incredible perversity, they always chose the time immediately before we were fed. The putrid garbage they fed us was incredibly unappetizing, and we had to force it down our own gullets to have any nourishment at all. So it was truly a cruel and unusual form of torture to be forced to eat at the same time they dipped out the foul-smelling excrement and waste right next to us.

Yet, there was an advantage to living in my new cell: I was allowed to exercise more freely. Most of the guards even encouraged me to exercise, and they usually stood at the flap and watched me when I did calisthenics.

At ten o'clock on the morning of the 9th, I asked permission to go to the latrine. The houseboy opened the door and let me out. As I stepped into the "one-hole" john, my eyes almost popped out of their sockets. There, on a sawhorse over the slit trench, sat a white man. Both of us were so shocked that neither of us could speak. I stood and he sat with our mouths wide open gaping at each other in disbelief. Before we could compose ourselves sufficiently to speak, the houseboy realized his mistake and rushed me back to my cell. When I sat down, I was trembling all over; the man was the first person, other than Red Chinese guards and officials, whom I'd been in close contact with in about eight months.

That evening I sat on my board and periodically dozed off. Every time I did, the guard pounded on the bars to rouse me. I sat with my head bobbing and slowly sinking into slumber, but I was never allowed to reach that point, until *they* were ready for it. Finally, the bell rang, and I lay down on my hard, hard board and went to sleep.

It was an incomparably miserable experience to be exhausted and not be permitted to sleep. I learned this to be a fact because the Red Chinese had used sleep deprivation to break my resistance ever since I'd been captured. They also used it to demoralize me and force compliance to their will so they could extract information from me. It was just another facet of their overall scheme of torture.

On August 12, my 212th day in hell, the houseboy led me down the hall and into another cell. There was an oval-shaped wooden tub in the middle of the floor. It was about 10 inches deep by 18 inches wide by 30 inches long, and it was half full of lukewarm, dirty water. I was allowed to undress and crawl into the tub. It was too good to be true! It was the first bath I'd had since being captured, and I celebrated by splashing water all over myself. I thought I might be dreaming, but that thought passed as quickly as it came. I marveled that dirty water could make me feel so good, but there was disappointment in the event: I was not allowed to use soap because others had to use the same water after me. Of course I realized that others had used it before me, too, but I tried not to think about that. Instead, I thought about the early days of my confinement and how self-conscious I was about my body odor. But, after awhile, I got used to it and pushed it to a lower level of priority in my thinking. What else could I have done?

Actually, dirty water or not, there are hardly any words to adequately express my feelings while taking that bath, which at the time was apparently a privilege reserved for a cadre of higher echelon people in the communist hierarchy. It lifted my morale 100 percent, and I felt sure that I would be homeward bound by Saturday, at least. Alas, the pleasant experience was limited to five minutes, and I was made to get out and dry off with a small hand towel provided to me by the houseboy. After he took me back to my cell, I sat on my board and thought about the exciting things I would do when I got home.

About the middle of August, my "re-education" lectures were temporarily discontinued. I thought that perhaps they had given up on remolding my mind because I had proved to them how incorrigible I was. Perhaps they had come to the conclusion that I would make a poor communist. I would learn later that the hiatus was definitely only temporary, and that much more effort than I had imagined would be expended by the political commissars to convince me of the virtues of the communist system versus the evils of the so-call "Democratic" system of the Capitalistic-Imperialistic Warmongers of the United States.

Eight days after my first bath, I was moved again. This time they kept me in the same cellblock, only moving me to the fifth cell on the left side of the corridor. I was certainly glad to get away from the smelly latrine.

Shortly after I had settled in, Big Stupe came and motioned for me to follow him. He escorted me to the interrogation area. This time he didn't even attempt to force me to keep my head down. As we entered the interrogation room, I saw Ratface (the warden) and Bluebeard seated behind the desk. Bluebeard told me to sit down, and I did.

After a few moments of silence, Ratface said in Mandarin, and Bluebeard translated, "We are going to make things more comfortable for you. We are going to put you with one of the other crew members, and we will give you more books to read. We ask that you take good care of them and that you study them very carefully. We will be asking you questions about them. They will show you the truth about your corrupt government and point out how communism is much better. Another thing, we ask you to obey prison rules: you must not fight with your cellmate, whistle, sing, make loud noises, write on the walls, talk to the guards, talk to other inmates, or look out the window. Do you have any questions?"

"Do I have a choice of who my cellmate will be?"

"What person do you want to be with?"

"Hart or Weese or Van Voorhis," I said.

He frowned, and said, "No. We will decide who will be with you."

"Why not put us all together?"

He ignored my question and said, "The guard will take you back to your cell now. Remember what we told you; and, if you do not behave, we will split you up."

I said, "Wait, I have another question. Is everyone okay? How are Hart, Weese, and Van Voorhis?"

"I do not know about them. I only know of you. Do not worry about anyone but yourself. It will be much healthier for you if you take this advice."

Within an hour after I returned to my cell, I heard a commotion in the corridor. My cell door opened, and a houseboy carried in a bed board. Another houseboy came in carrying bedding. Finally, my fellow crewman Daniel Schmidt hobbled in. He was extremely thin and had such a pitiful, weary expression. He wore black summer clothing and sported a cleanly shaven head.

When the houseboys left us alone, we apologized to each other for not having exchanged a few words on our chance encounter on the ninth, but the encounter was so unexpected and brief—and such a shock—that we were both rendered speechless.

We discussed our unfortunate predicament for a short time. Then, as we continued to chat, I learned that he had not been moved from the cellblock in early June as I had suspected. Rather, he had contracted some sort of disease that caused his right knee and leg to swell over twice their normal size, and he had much difficulty in moving around. He said that, on his way to and from the latrine, he had heard me and wanted to reply; but, he was in excruciating pain, and the guards stayed with him like flies on cow dung. A cute little Red Chinese nurse came to his cell daily and gave him shots. The injections didn't help much, so they kept experimenting with different types of drugs.

Early in the afternoon of that first day we were together, the same cute nurse he mentioned came into our cell and gave Schmidt his shot. Later, a female doctor came in and examined him. Due to our prolonged period of sexual deprivation, the mere sight of these members of the opposite sex was enough to trigger our carnal appetite. When we were left alone, our conversation was dominated by our intense craving for sexual gratification. We discussed in great detail the attributes of the nurse and the female doctor.

That evening we heard more commotion in the hall, and we assumed that others of our crew were being moved into the cellblock. Our assumption was correct. We discovered that John Buck and Wally Brown were in the first cell on our side of the block. Eugene Vaadi and Elmer Llewellyn were in the third cell; and Howard Brown, Harry Benjamin, and John Thompson were in the sixth one.

There were also inmates in the fourth cell on the other side of the cellblock, across the hall from Schmidt and me. But who were they? Where were John Arnold and Bill Baumer? Where were Henry Weese, Paul Van Voorhis, and Alvin Hart?"

After they rang the boardtime bell, Schmidt, who had been lying on his board in pain, got up and hobbled to the honey bucket. While he was there, the guard rolled up our window flap, and also the flaps on the windows of other cells.

On his way back to his board Schmidt said, "Hey, Kiba! There are two Americans in the cell across the way."

I jumped up from my board and rushed to the window. I looked out and saw two Caucasians. One was short, about five eight, and the other one was about five ten. Both were dressed like us. Their hair was cut short just like that of the other Americans. One was brushing his teeth.

Schmidt and I started talking loudly. We called each other by name with raised voices in hopes we could be heard by those in the other cell. The guard, upon hearing our uncommonly loud discourse, rushed down the hall and ordered us to shut up and go to sleep. He rolled down our flap and stood by our window until we obeyed him. Yet, both of us were so excited we could hardly sleep. Intermittently, throughout that first night together, we kept waking up and talking to each other in a low voice. This aggravated the insensitive guard, and he kept shouting at us to keep quiet and sleep.

The next morning, Friday, August 21, 1953, we awoke early but didn't get up. It was a luxury to just lie on our boards and talk. Our premature awakening and subsequent visitation were not in accordance with prison rules, so we were continually admonished by the guard to shut up, but we ignored him.

At seven o'clock the wake-up bell rang. I hopped off my board and started exercising. A few minutes later the houseboy came and let us out, one cell at a time, to get our own wash water. While I was at the water barrel, I heard John Buck and Wallace Brown talking in one of the cells. As I was returning to our cell, I heard Gene Vaadi and Elmer Llewellyn. I also heard some other voices that resounded down the hall; but, even though they were speaking in English, I couldn't identify them.

Since we were both starved for news and company, we spent the rest of the day talking. We discussed our situation and compared the interrogations we had been subjected to. We discovered that the Red Chinese interrogators had used different tactics on us. We also compared the different places where we had been—the food, the treatment, and various other details—and we learned that although we had been at the same prisons, we had been treated differently in almost all respects.

Schmidt described in detail bailing out and being captured. He described the terrain where he landed and remembered a certain patch of evergreens; I had passed the same spot that night. He said that he heard footsteps and thought they belonged to an enemy search party, so he didn't call out. We decided that we were near each other, at least for awhile, and that our precautions to remain undetected by the enemy quite possibly kept us from finding each other.

The remembrances of our ordeal were often broken by nostalgic thoughts of home and of our longing to be there. Yet, our thoughts could not completely escape the undesirable situation we were in, and sometimes the past and present became intertwined. In one such instance, Schmidt commented on how beautiful and nice his little Red Chinese nurse was, but in the next breath he described how beautiful and sexy his wife was and how much he missed her.

The next day, Saturday, August 22, 1953, we spent a lot of time raising our voices in an effort to get other crew members to reciprocate, but we were not successful. But on that same day there was a welcome change in our treatment: they began serving our food in bowls. From that day on, we got watery soup in one bowl, and some unrecognizable, unappetizing food we called "grass" in another. A third bowl contained steamed rice or a bun. Our drinking water now always came in a green crock, and we were rationed to about a cup and a half per day.

After our morning meal, a houseboy brought us three books. The titles were as follows: THE MOVING FORCE, THREE MONTHS IN NEW CHINA AND THE SOVIET UNION, and WOMEN OF CHINA BUILD FOR PEACE. Of course we had been ordered to read what they brought us. It was part of their attempts to "re-educate" us. Therefore, we began reading the books.

THE MOVING FORCE, by Tsao Ming, was a story about how old Sun organized the people and how he engineered the repairing of a power station in Manchuria, which the Japanese had destroyed in World War II. Old Sun was a staunch communist. The story stressed that only a communist could accomplish such feats. It was a trashy story, poorly written and very dull. If it hadn't been for the concrete walls and steel bars, we definitely would never have read past the first page. The same was true for most of the reading material they forced upon us.

THREE MONTHS IN NEW CHINA AND THE SOVIET UNION was written by a Ceylonese named K. Vaikunthavasan, who had attended a trade conference in Peking with his wife. They toured Red China and the Soviet Union. The naive author described the things which he and his spouse had seen during their brief sojourn. The book also contained many photographs taken by the author. Anyone with an ounce of knowledge would readily perceive that the author and his wife had been used by the communists in the Soviet Union and Red China: they only showed them what they wanted them to see. It was even trashier than THE MOVING FORCE. It was strictly propaganda.

WOMEN OF CHINA BUILD FOR PEACE was a pamphlet loaded with pictures showing and telling how the heroic Red Chinese women were—in addition to raising a large family—working in the factories and on the collective farms to build a more prosperous Red China and to take a *piece* of the world. It pointed out that the communist government was encouraging ultra large families and that any woman who had ten or more children was awarded the Mother's Heroine Medal.

So, because we had to, we read their trash and looked at the pictures. I must admit that we examined the pictures of the opposite sex with much more interest than we did the printed propaganda. Just seeing pictures of young women intensified our desire for female companionship, and we spent many, many hours fantasizing. We would undress them with our eyes and verbally discuss the various parts of their anatomies. Without fail, these erotic discussions would lead Schmidt to recount in minute detail his courtship and lovemaking with his wife. Sadly though, most of the propaganda material contained very few pictures, especially those of women. We figured the omission was purposeful. What better way to add to our torture than to give us limited exposure to pictures that would tantalize our natural physical needs?

We knew that others in our crew were also receiving the reading material because we heard a voice across the hall from us reading aloud in English. Sometime later we received another pamphlet entitled CHILDREN OF NEW CHINA. When we examined it, we discovered that it was the same article we'd heard from the mystery voice across from us. We attempted several times to contact those across from us by shouting our names and asking them who they were, but those efforts failed.

On the evening of the 23rd, we began chatting with the enlisted men in the sixth cell. We accomplished this by facing the inside window and talking so that our voices would carry out into the hallway. Although this method had its limitations, it worked, and we were able to reach our fellow inmates. They learned to use a similar technique, and the end result was some minimum communication between us. Our talking upset the guard, and he continually told us not to talk so loud. When I explained to him that I was hard of hearing, he refused to believe me. Whenever he thought that we were talking to the other crewmen, he kept harassing us, essentially interfering with our attempts to communicate. We learned to wait until he was at the other end of the cellblock making his rounds; then we had a short interval to talk to the men in the sixth cell before he returned to our end.

At eleven o'clock the next day, the guard we called "Fugstick" told us that our inside window was dirty. He gave me a damp rag and ordered me to clean the window. I climbed up onto the window ledge and started wiping the glass. I noticed the door of the "mystery" cell across the hall was open. This was the cell housing the two Caucasians with whom we'd been trying to communicate, but unsuccessfully. We had heard the noise of the cell door earlier when it had been opened, and we assumed that the inmates had been taken out to walk. When they didn't return within 30 minutes, we thought our first assumption was wrong and that instead of walking they were being interrogated. So, as I strained hard to see everything I could while I cleaned my window, I noticed the cell door was standing open and the cell was empty. The two "mystery" Caucasians were gone. So were their bed boards and honey bucket. It was obvious that they had been moved.

One morning in early September, Schmidt and I were having a conversation when we heard someone pounding on the bars. It was the houseboy we called "Sam, the three-thumbed Chinaman." He motioned for me to come to the flap. I assumed we were going to be reprimanded again for talking too loud; but, to my surprise, instead of rebuking us, he handed me two small, red objects and grinned like an opossum eating shit. I took them and tossed one to Schmidt. We examined them and found, much to our surprise, that they were little apples about the size of a walnut. We hastily gobbled them down—core, stem, and all—before Sam had a chance to change his mind.

We continued trying to establish contact with the four officers up the hall from us, and about the middle of September contact was made and certain signals were agreed upon. Schmidt and I provided the others with a brief refresher course on Morse code. We designated the cells as Able, Baker, Charlie, and Dog. Short unique signals were established for certain things, and finally a workable communications system was set up. John Buck and Wallace Brown occupied Able Cell; Eugene Vaadi and Elmer Llewellyn were in Baker Cell; Daniel

Schmidt and I were in Charlie Cell; Howard Brown, Harry Benjamin, and John Thompson were together in Dog Cell.

The officers found it harder to talk, so they had to be more careful. The guards and the houseboys didn't seem to mind too much if we talked back and forth with Dog, but they were highly irate when we talked to the officers and when the officers attempted to communicate with us enlisted men. The Redchink perverts even became vexed when Able and Baker Cells tried to talk to each other.

About mid-September Dunghead gave the five airmen on our crew (Kiba, Schmidt, Howard Brown, Benjamin, and Thompson) a bar of soap and escorted us to the shower building. The soap was like laundry soap; it was yellow in color and very strong. The water was alternately scalding hot and ice cold, but we became accustomed to it and really enjoyed it. We stayed under the shower for about five minutes, and then they turned off the water. We dried off, put on our smelly, dirty clothes and were marched back to our respective cells. After we were returned to our cells, they took the officers out two at a time for their showers. After that, during our bathing periods, one houseboy led us to and from the shower building, while another houseboy and a Redchink we called "Babyface" stayed in the shower building and kept us from communicating with each other. Babyface appeared to be the immediate superior of houseboys and in charge of taking care of American prisoners. Of course, the new privilege of being permitted to bathe boosted our morale considerably.

Later in the month, the two younger airmen in Dog Cell were given chores. They had to sweep the hall with a straw broom that had no handle and wash off the little tables on which the chow (food) bowls were kept. For some reason, the houseboys wouldn't let Howard Brown out into the hall to help them.

From late September through early December, we heard Red Chinese news broadcasts almost daily over the public address system. Schmidt and I could understand enough to know that they were talking about American and Red Chinese troops. We were fairly certain that the war was over and that they were exchanging prisoners. We were bubbling over with enthusiasm, and we relayed our opinions to the others.

About that same time, Sam and Dunghead showed a strong desire to learn English. They frequently visited Dog Cell where Brown, Benjamin, and Thompson were kept. Benjamin and Thompson tried to teach them a few words in English in exchange for Chinese words, but Brown ignored the houseboys, whom we all considered "mangy."

Everyone was getting restless and anxious to go home. Schmidt and I pestered the guards to make things more bearable. In addition, probably out of a pure desire for some kind of revenge, we harassed them. We made a practice of either laughing at or cursing the guards whenever they peeped in on us.

We continued getting trashy books and pamphlets. Our current reading material was a three part novel, FAR FROM MOSCOW. It was about construction workers who were building an oil pipeline across a bay in Siberia. The author over-emphasized the importance of the communist party in achieving the goals of the workers. The way the commies pledged to achieve 400 percent to 500 percent—and even 1,000 percent—over their quota amused us to no end. There was always a villain in their novels. The villain was always a non-party man paid by the Imperialistic-Capitalistic Warmongers to slow down, wreck, or disrupt the project.

Schmidt was still being treated for his ailment. One day the little nurse came in to administer his shot, and Dunghead—a particularly obnoxious man with obviously poor hygiene habits—came with her. I was sitting on my board and looking through a slanderous pamphlet called THE PAPER TIGER, which contained political cartoons denouncing and ridiculing the United States and its leading personalities. Dunghead walked over to me and asked to see the magazine. I handed it to him. He leafed through it, giggled, and pointed to the nurse who was squatting to give Schmidt his shot. I pointed at her and motioned that I was patting her fanny. Dunghead burst out laughing and imitated my gestures. Then he pointed to a cartoon and said Americans were no good. The cartoon pictured an American briefing room with a Colonel on crutches briefing a pilot. The Colonel was pointing to Red Chinese hospitals and schools as if to indicate that these were targets. I pointed to the cartoon and told Dunghead that the characters in it were Red Chinese. Then I found another cartoon where General MacArthur was running down a map of Korea with chickens in his hands. A Korean soldier with a pitchfork was chasing him and yelling, "Stop thief!" I showed it to the houseboy, pointed to the fleeing figure, and said, "Look! Mao Tse-tung."

"No, no. MacArthur," Dunghead said.

"Mao Tse-tung!" I repeated. "MacArthur dinghow." (MacArthur is good.)

This agitated Dunghead. He said, "MacArthur pu-how!" (MacArthur is bad, no damn good!)

I shot back, "Mao pu- how. Tongwa (Chinese) pu-how!" (Mao is bad, no damn good. Red Chinese are no damn good!)

Dunghead was frowning angrily when he left with the nurse.

A few days later the public address system was blaring all over the prison again. (As they were at the "Hotel," loud speakers were placed strategically throughout the prison for the benefit of both prison personnel and prison inmates.) The day's hot topic was about Eisenhower, Panmunjon, and Red Chinese and American military personnel. We knew that Panmunjon was where the so-called peace talks were being conducted. From all the bits and pieces of information we had accumulated, Schmidt and I were almost certain that some kind of an agreement had been reached and that the war was over. We also thought that a prisoner exchange had already taken place, or maybe was in progress. These beliefs gave us a strong hope of being released soon. We looked to the treatment we received and the attitudes of our houseboys and guards as a sort of indicator of where we stood. This was an inexact science, because they would be cooler toward us for a time, then suddenly warmer. Their attitude changed periodically between hot and cold, and we assumed that their attitudes depended on how the Monkey (Mao Tse-tung) turned them with his edicts and propaganda.

One night in mid-October 1953, after the sijo bell (bell to announce it was bedtime) rang, Schmidt and I prepared to lie down. Fugstick motioned for us to close the outside window and to hand him the stick which was used to prop open the window. We ignored him and lay down on our hard bed boards. Our disobedience caused him to become irate, and he jerked open our door and rushed toward the outside window to close it and remove the stick from our cell.

Schmidt and I jumped off our boards and grabbed Fugstick, the raunchy son-of-a-bitch, by his arms, carried him to the door, shoved him out into the hall, and returned to our boards.

Fugstick screamed abuses at us as loudly as he could. Shortly, the houseboy rushed out of his office and down the corridor to investigate. He listened to Fugstick's complaint and then came into our cell and tried to get us to close our window. After discussing the issue with us, he gave in and permitted us to keep the window open.

Schmidt and I lay back down; and, whenever Fugstick looked in on us, we gave him a big horselaugh.

One day in late October, I was opening the window in the outside wall to get some fresh air. When I raised the window and tried to insert the stick to hold it up, it slipped and shattered a pane. The guard immediately sounded a warning, and in less than a minute the cellblock was swarming with armed guards and houseboys. Sam and Fugstick came into the cell, picked up every sliver of glass, took them to the houseboy's office, and pieced them back together. A small sliver was missing, so they returned to our cell and searched until they found it.

Several days after the broken window incident, the houseboys gave us the same blue padded jacket and pants which they had taken away from us in April. They also gave us a black skull cap.

Steve E. Kiba

PART VI

HELL ISN'T ALWAYS HOT

Steve E. Kiba

By early November 1953, the never-ending boredom was showing its effects. Everyone was getting touchy and grouchy. Even little things would upset us. We fought boredom by exercising, by reading and re-reading the trash they put before us, and by telling and re-telling each other our experiences. Idleness and uncertainty held absolute control over our every thought, our feelings, our attitudes, and our actions.

We always hungered to know more about our situation, so we questioned the guards the best we could using sign language, limited broken Mandarin, and English. One day I used this technique on a guard we had named Junior. I asked about Colonel Arnold and wanted to know his whereabouts. I also asked him how many Americans were in the prison. Junior told me there were 14 Americans that he knew about personally. Then I asked him about the news broadcasts on the public address system, and Junior said they were talking about American and Red Chinese troops in Korea. He said that soon many of his comrades would be set free and return from Koje Island. When I asked how soon we would be going home, he shrugged his shoulders to indicate his complete ignorance and then clammed up.

Then, on November 15, 1953, we noticed that we had a whole set of new guards. They appeared more seasoned and professional than the pigs they replaced, and they were all wearing medals. Immediately following their arrival, we tried to find out where they came from. We conversed with the more friendly ones and made fun of the others. The more infuriated a guard became, the more we teased him and laughed at him.

"Hey, Schmidt, we have a new guard."

"So I see," muttered Schmidt.

"Look, the little monkey has medals."

"He must be a model guard."

"Yeah, a real hero."

"He's going to get pooped toting around all that junk all day."

"You shouldn't say junk," I said jokingly. "The poor fella probably had to work really hard to get all those medals."

"You think maybe he helped Ole Sun break the ice?"

"Or perhaps get them rationed rice."

"I bet he found them in a Cracker Jack box," laughed Schmidt.

Another new guard appeared at our flap and stood there just staring at us.

"Look at the little ape," said Schmidt. "I bet he even has a tail."

"Just look at those medals," I exclaimed. "He must really be a **big** hero!"

"Look, Kiba, he has a PEACE DOVE Medal."

"I've noticed that most of these new guards are wearing it."

"Look at his filthy uniform; it looks like it's never been washed. They all wear the same set of clothes year round, or at least all winter."

"They have two sets: one for winter and one for summer. They probably even sleep in them."

"Their clothes sure smell like it. I'd wager they don't bathe more than once a year."

"Whether they need it or not."

"Most of these jokers smell like billy goats."

"You can see the garlic fumes pouring from their nostrils when they exhale."

"From those who don't wear those silly looking masks, that is."

"Say, Schmidt, I just figured out why these mangy apes wear those stupid-looking masks."

"Why's that, Kiba?"

"They're all so friggin' ugly, and they're too damned ashamed to show their faces."

"Ain't that for the birds!" exclaimed Schmidt.

"What's that?" I asked.

"Our being cooped up like wild animals while these repulsive apes are free."

"Just uncaged, Schmidt, just uncaged," I said. "They're not really free; they're nothing but slaves, slaves of the MONKEY and his tyrannical regime."

"By golly, they're freer than we are!" exclaimed Schmidt.

"True, but I bet you wouldn't trade places with them for all the wormy steamed rice and all the rotten potato peelings in Red China. Now would you?"

"You got that right! There's nothing like being an American!" exclaimed Schmidt.

From some of the friendly guards, we learned that they were from the Korean Front and that the fighting was over. We became extremely optimistic and worked even harder at digging up information. It was our fervent hope to learn when we would be going home, but the job of getting any kind of information from them was very difficult. The guards were forbidden to talk to American prisoners; and, if they got caught doing it, they would be transferred from the cellblock and presumably punished. Even so, a few took the chance; the boredom of pacing up and down the hall making their rounds and visually watching us overcame them.

On Friday, November 20, 1953, a stranger paid a visit to our cellblock. We heard him enter and leave Able Cell; then he entered and left Baker Cell. From the loud noise we were hearing, we knew that we were in for a bombastic reprimand.

Sure enough, several minutes later our cell door was violently jerked open, and a rather tall, ugly, bug-eyed stranger dressed in all black and his interpreter stormed into our cell. Bugeyes started screaming loudly something in Mandarin, and the tongue translated: "You have been talking too loud and talking to the other criminals. You have also been calling us bad names, and you have not been obeying the prison rules. I warn you that if you do not change your reactionary behavior and attitude, I will have to punish you severely."

Bugeyes continued his harsh tongue lashing, all the while, pointing and threateningly shaking his finger at us.

Schmidt and I looked at the screaming, bug-eyed maniac and then at the tongue and then at one another and then shrugged our shoulders.

Bugeyes and the tongue stomped out of our cell, slamming the door behind them with such force that it almost pulled away from its hinges.

"Don't slam that friggin' door, you idiot!" I shouted as loudly as I could.

The visitors went into Dog Cell and repeated the same tirade that they had just performed in the other cells.

Thanksgiving Day on November 26, 1953, was bitterly cold. Schmidt and I sat on our cold, hard bed boards in our frigid cell and shivered the whole day long. Our optimism, which bubbled up from the well-spring of knowledge we had gathered, fizzled out in the presence of unrelenting truth. In its place, profound feelings of despair began to grow, and we found it difficult, actually impossible, to be thankful for our scanty ration of wormy rice.

As the day progressed, our depression intensified. We exchanged views about our wretchedness and wondered whether or not anyone really cared about us. In our despair, we concluded that few, if any, did. We decided that most people were just too greedy and selfish and inconsiderate and that most people didn't have the time, or didn't want to take the time, to worry about a handful of fellow countrymen who were unfortunate enough to be "left behind." Of course, we realized that there was an element of self pity in our assessment of things, but what the hell—if anyone had a right to feel that way for awhile, we damn sure did.

I suppose we could have predicted it if we'd thought about it, but Thanksgiving Day didn't get easier as it progressed. Our thoughts of home and the sumptuous dinners we would be enjoying with our families made it extremely hard to swallow the wormy rice and seaweed they served us. Our first-hand experience made us acutely aware of how lonely and difficult holidays were for any American captive in some far-off communist hellhole, because the reality of their predicament cannot help but be amplified to an almost unbearable pitch by the good memories of times past. Nevertheless, we got through the day, and I can truthfully say it was a Thanksgiving Day I'll never forget; bad memories are just as effective as good ones in marking the mind.

A few days later we were eating one of our usual unappetizing Red Chinese meals that consisted of clear plastic-like noodles mixed with a kind of greens. I took several bites and suddenly hollered out with pain.

"What's the matter?" Schmidt asked.

"Felt like something cut me," I said.

I put my fingers into my mouth and pulled out a huge, dirty, filthy, yellowish toenail. I showed it to Schmidt, and he almost lost the little he had already eaten.

The cruddy toenail had cut the inside of my mouth, and blood was trickling down my chin. I walked over and dropped the toenail into the honey bucket and spit out the blood. Then I went back to finish eating the sorry food, and the cut kept oozing blood while I was eating. The blood-greens combination certainly wasn't tasteful, but I was very hungry. While I was finishing the meal, I kept thinking of what humans will stoop to eat when they're starving.

November turned into December, and we were still feeling low because it was quite apparent that we would be spending Christmas in a frozen hell. It was so cold in the corridor of the cellblock that the water barrel had an inch of ice on it. Our cells were even colder. We endeavored to ward off the biting cold in various ways: covering ourselves with a thin blanket, sitting huddled up on our boards, walking around the cell. Ice crystals formed on the front of our padded jackets; this was caused when the warmth of our exhaled breath came in contact with the bone-chilling air. My extremities were numb, and it felt as if I had stubs at the ends of my arms and legs. My hands turned beet-red, and the pain in all my extremities was unbearable. Neither Schmidt nor I was able to control our shivering. I even shook severely as I circled the icy cell.

"I never knew Hell was so friggin' cold," I told Schmidt.

Several days later we were having a light conversation to pass the idle hours and take our minds away from the frigid conditions of our cell. The dialogue went like this:

Schmidt: Kiba, we have 13 shopping days until Christmas.

Me: Maybe our benevolent captors will turn us loose in Peking to do our shopping.

Schmidt: We'll be out of here soon.

Me: This stupid black beanie cap I have to wear makes me feel like a monk.

Schmidt: You're too corrupted to be a monk.

Me: You're puncturing my dreams!

Schmidt: How's that?

Me: I was planning on becoming a preacher.

Schmidt: You, a *preacher? You!* He laughed until his sides hurt and tears came to his eyes.

Me: You don't think I'd make a good preacher?

Schmidt: You wouldn't even make a good church-goer.

Me: Well, I was joshing you. But speaking of preaching, did I ever tell you how services are conducted in a Holy Roller Church?

Schmidt: No, but it sounds like it might be interesting. Go ahead.

Me: When I was ten years old, we lived in West Virginia.

Schmidt: So?

Me: We lived in one of those small coal camps along Buffalo Creek. Usually, there weren't more than 30 houses in a camp. Our camp had a general store and a post office combined in one building. The next town down the creek had a movie house, a gas station, a store, a drug store, and a grade school.

Schmidt: What's all that got to do with church?

"Well, they had a church too, right next to the grade school. Now, getting back to my story, there was an old brick building in our camp. The locals converted it into a church. Every Sunday, and almost every night during the summer, church services were held there. I used to go to some of the services with my brother and his friends. We always sat on the back row and just listened.

"Normally, they had a different preacher every night, and everyone went around calling each other "brother" and "sister." The preacher screamed at the top of his voice and clapped his hands vigorously and told everyone what big sinners they were. One particular preacher would jump up on the railing that ran along the side of the pulpit. As he was preaching, he walked back and forth on it. Although he shouted the whole time he was walking on the railing, he never lost his balance.

"At some particular time during the service, numerous people from the congregation walked up in front of the pulpit and started talking in an unintelligible jargon. Oftentimes they screamed out their gibberish. Some pulled on their hair, and some rolled around on the concrete floor. At the same time, they shouted that the "Holy Ghost" was in them and that they had been saved. My brother was saved once, too, and he was baptized in the polluted water of Buffalo Creek."

"Which brother?" Schmidt asked.

"The one just older than me. But two days later he became a backslider. I noticed that there was a congregational pattern where people would get saved, and shortly thereafter they would backslide; then they got saved again, after which they would backslide again. I think I witnessed some that were saved and baptized at least 30 times.

"One elderly woman was saved and boasted that she could walk on water and move mountains. Some of the more intelligent members of the camp didn't believe her and called her bluff. She agreed to prove her new-found abilities.

"One bright Sunday afternoon, she and an enormous group of curious people ambled up to Cold Creek where she was "led" to perform her miracle. She took off her shoes, walked over to the edge of the water, and gingerly put her right foot on the surface of the water. She withdrew it instantly and explained that she was unable to perform the miracle that day because the wind was blowing a little too much. Of course, most people laughed about her excuse because there wasn't even a faint breeze at the time. She also failed to move the mountain. That whole congregation was a real weird group of people."

"Weird ain't the word for it," said Schmidt. "They were downright looney."

"Wait till you hear this," I said. "I had a pet groundhog named Elmer. I used to go home after watching the Rollers and preach to Elmer. He would sit up on his hind legs and listen to me for an hour or more at a time."

Schmidt laughed. "You were just a little weird yourself, weren't you?" he said. He turned over on his side, propped his face in his right hand and said, "Say, Kiba, did these commie jokers try to convince you that there is no God?"

I said, "Yes, quite often. They've repeatedly told me that I was too intelligent to believe such nonsense. Their continual argument is that religion is nothing but a tool by which the rich capitalists keep poor people subjugated. Naturally, they wouldn't let me express my opinion. According to them I am too young and naive to know the real, genuine truth. My mind, they say, has been saturated with the "incorrect" religious and political propaganda of the church and the Wall Street Warmongers."

Schmidt said, "According to their god, Karl Marx, religion is an opiate of the poor, downtrodden people. It is merely a tool the rich use to keep poor people happy and ignorant."

I could see in his shivering that our conversation had not made us warmer. I, too, was very uncomfortable from the frigidness of our prison cell, and no matter how hard I tried to keep from it, I couldn't control my shaking.

I said, "You know, Schmidt, before we were shot down and captured, I sure didn't give the appearance of being a good Christian. I was raised better, too. I'm really ashamed of those lapses in my behavior that I know were wrong."

"Me, too," he said. "I'm just glad my Mom and my wife don't know about the raunchy things I've done. But I still believe in God, and I'm gonna try hard to do better from now on."

"Good, and I'm making that same commitment. I know that God exists; the atheistic commies can talk until doomsday, but they'll never convince me otherwise."

"Me neither," Schmidt said. "The Bible says that we're to love our enemies and to pray for those who persecute us. I'm sure having trouble with that."

"I understand, because I've had the same hang up."

"How can we NOT hate our captors? They are mangy, inhumane pigs!" Schmidt said.

I said, "I agree. Before we were shot down, I had no ill feelings toward the Chinese people. But the way they've treated—and are still treating us—has caused me to immensely dislike the damned heathens. I've seriously tried not to hate them, but I do. The longer we're here, the more I hate them."

"So do I," Schmidt said.

Despite the intense cold, our conversation held our attention for awhile and made our discomfort more bearable. It also made me think about some things I'd not thought of before.

I said, "Schmidt, do you think we can ever overcome our anger and hatred?"

"I don't know," he said. "One thing's for sure, though. I don't think I can do it on my own. I'm gonna need help."

"Yeah," I said. "I don't think any of us will be able to do it alone."

About the middle of the month, we were given another haircut, or—as we called it—a scalping. Dunghead took us one-by-one to a Red Chinese "tonsorial parlor" (an empty cell) where the one-armed barber performed his specialized task.

Afterwards, when Schmidt saw me, he laughed and said, "Kiba, now you really do look like a monk."

"Yeah, smooth head, monk cap, black outfit and all," I said.

"Can't gripe too much," he said. "As cold as it is, these silly-looking beanies at least help keep our bald heads warm."

"I agree. Don't know why these dumb Redchinks even bother to build buildings if they're not going to heat them. I'll bet it's at least as cold in here as it is outside: below zero."

Schmidt asked the houseboy for some nail clippers; and Sam, the three-thumbed Chinaman, handed him a pair engraved with the brand name of *TRIM.* He laughed and read the brand to me.

I said, "It's really funny that these pigs claim to hate the United States, yet they use all kinds of products manufactured by us."

"Yeah, they probably shot us down with U. S. shells," Schmidt said ruefully.

I said, "Not only that, but they also guard us with American weapons, transport us in American cars and military vehicles, interrogate us with officers educated in the United States, and shackle us with American made handcuffs and leg irons. It's enough to make you really think about what's going on in the world." My bitter complaining didn't make me feel one bit better.

"What puzzles me is the fact that they knew so much about us, things I would've thought that no one but my family would know," Schmidt said.

"Yeah, and so quickly, too," I said. "They undoubtedly have agents in the United States, the Philippines, and Japan because they knew all about us from the moment we were shot down. Aren't you through with those clippers yet?"

"Almost," he said.

"Well, hurry up," I said. "Did the Redchink bastards tell you that they were waiting for us that night."

"Yeah, something to that effect."

I said, "They told me they knew we were coming out that night and that they knew our aircraft was not fully armed. They also admitted that they knew the Bird (Colonel Arnold) was on board."

"Thirty MIGs against one measly B-29 armed only with a tail gun! Catch," Schmidt said. He tossed the nail clippers to me.

I grabbed them in mid-air and said, "Thanks. It's about time."

"Kiba, what's the hurry? You goin' somewhere?"

Our first Christmas Eve as captives was a cold, somber, dreary evening. We wrapped ourselves in our blankets, sat on our boards, and waited for the "sleep time" bell. We passed the time griping about the miserable cold temperature in the cell, reminiscing about Christmases past, and regretting the fact that our socks were too rotten to hang up, even if we could. We also faced the probability that we would not go home any time soon, maybe not even until after Easter.

The thoughts of holidays and our remembrances of home and family did not assuage the unpleasantness of our situation, and our lack of freedom intensified the repulsiveness of our ordeal. Thanksgiving Day was bad, but not nearly as bad as Christmas. There is nothing more cheerless, doleful, lonely, or pitiful than to be locked up in a distant foreign prison during the Christmas Season, a time that is traditionally full of joy, goodness, comfort, and peace. As prisoners of the communist, we were denied all of those things, not only during holidays but constantly through the day-by-day perverse treatment and rules from our sadistic captors.

During my short life I had never thought about what being a prisoner would be like, nor had I dwelt on the idea during my service in the Air Force. Of course that possibility was a small part of our training and mission briefing. But none of that prepared me for actually being a prisoner. Since I was captured and tortured, I had feelings and thoughts I would never have dreamed of having before. There was an acute awareness that everyone in the Free World was happy and cheerful as they made preparations to celebrate holidays or to live their daily lives according to their own ideas and beliefs. Therefore, the dingy gloominess of my cell depressed me; there was a certain amount of disillusionment in its reality, and I was constantly disheartened. I even wondered if my government, my family, and my friends would even take a few moments of their hectic schedules to think about me. My mind and thoughts became so morbidly gloomy that I often wondered if God had forgotten me. Of course, I realized that I was not alone; my crew members undoubtedly suffered the same agonies.

In spite of its loneliness and depression for us prisoners, Christmas 1953, came and went uneventfully. In the long, cold days that followed, things returned to "normal."

Our "re-education" sessions resumed, and the political instructors harassed me unceasingly with their foul propaganda, threats of violence, and other horrible consequences if I persisted in harboring my "reactionary" attitude. They repeatedly screamed at me that I would never leave the People's Republic of China, that no one knew I was alive, and that if they so desired they could kill me. They could also continue to torture me, or they could keep me chained and caged forever.

Most of them delighted in telling me their torture techniques. It was especially delightful to them when they taunted me with the threat that I would never go home. They constantly reminded me, while wearing a wicked grin, that my government and the people I knew—including family—really didn't give a damn about me or they would do something to secure my release.

When we returned to our cell after the intense interrogation sessions, we prayed for relief from the miserable existence created by our illegal and unjust detention. We kept hoping to hear the droning of American bombers overhead and the cheerful shouts of friendly Marines rushing down the corridors of our cellblocks. Our fantasizing was so desperate and real that I could "hear" the steel bolts of our cell doors slid back by our liberators. Then the ugly truth would set in, and we were again faced with the utter hopelessness of our captivity: the American bombers did not come; no bombs fell on Peking; the U. S. Marines did not charge down the corridors; and, the steel bolts were never drawn back.

Yet, we were not beaten. At some point in our captivity, we all adopted some kind of "instinctual survival." I'm sure there was some overlapping of ideas and actions in this respect, but also some unique ones, too. Every night Schmidt and I lay on our hard boards and dreamed of a good life back in the States. It was an "escape mechanism" that temporarily gave us renewed courage and hope, but it was a "come-and-go" escape from our tedious and painful reality; our fantasies were almost always shattered by nightmares; and, when morning came, we found ourselves still chained and caged.

The growing hunger pains, the incessant thirst, the various and numerous body aches and rashes, the fears, the frustrations, and the terrible disillusionment all worked in unison to debilitate our bodies and minds. The thought that no one knew we were alive, that they even cared, kept invading our minds and slowly eroded our morale. As our morale deteriorated, our hopes of ever being released were also diminished. The vicious promises of the interrogators to never let us go home, to let us rot in our filthy cells, were fast becoming a reality.

We had reached the point where we would try anything. We believed "anything" would be better than just wasting away physically and mentally. We discussed plans to "move on," but we kept them short and held them at irregular intervals to keep from arousing suspicion. We recognized that the odds of our escaping were very slim, but we made ourselves hope that it would happen. We were sure we could devise a workable plan—we just *had* to. We were so serious about it that we began exercising more in order to build ourselves up for the long hike across the Red Chinese countryside.

For some reason, which we didn't quite understand yet, the Red Chinese considered us, the Stardust Four Zero crew, their "golden goose," and they kept an extremely close watch over us. A guard would lift the flap to our cells about every 30 seconds. There were also several "ammo guards" who roamed in and out of the cellblock. Before they moved most of our crew into one cellblock, the ammo guards were used primarily to check up on the regular cellblock guards. Now they were being used to help the regular guards keep an even closer watch over us.

Beyond the double doors in the circle, there were at least six guards armed with burp guns. Our portions of food were meager and lacking in vitamins and minerals. Consequently, we were kept in a very feeble physical state; we received barely enough food to stay alive. Therefore, because of the meager rations and constantly alert guards, it was absolutely impossible to store any food to take along should we manage to escape.

In short, everything was against us: too many armed guards; physical weakness; inability to build a food reserve; towering outside wall around the prison lined with electrified and barbed wire; lack of shoes, proper clothing, and other necessary supplies; and our very color. Nevertheless, we maintained a mental attitude that escape might be possible, and we stayed alert for an opportunity that would make it feasible.

In the afternoon of New Year's Day 1954, Schmidt was reading aloud from a book entitled THEY ARE BETRAYING PEACE, by Jean Catala. Suddenly our cell door flew open and an important bug-eyed communist official rushed in. He was accompanied by an interpreter—whom we usually called "Tongue" —and a houseboy. We recognized the man as one of the so-called "judges" who had harangued us mercilessly in various sessions when they both interrogated us and tried to indoctrinate us with Red Chinese Party dogma during the early months of our captivity.

The bug-eyed "judge" pointed his finger at us menacingly and loudly spouted out something in Mandarin. Tongue translated his message: "You have your nerve talking so loud while I am in the cellblock. I have warned you many times about your 'incorrect' attitudes. The warden has also warned you that you must not talk to the other cells and that you must not talk to the guards. This is a prison, so why do you not conduct yourselves like prisoners? Our Chinese inmates do not give us trouble. You are making it very difficult for us to follow our lenient policy. I warn you for the last time, either you start obeying prison rules or else you will bear the consequences. Do you understand?"

We were surprised by the vehemence of his charge, and it showed on our faces when we stared back at him.

I said, "You must be mistaken. Why, we'd never think of talking to the others, or to the guards, either. We are model prisoners, real

Stakhanovites." (A term used in Soviet propaganda books that refers to a "very efficient person.")

"Do not look so surprised," he said, and Tongue translated. "We know that you talk with the others; we are not fools. As for being model prisoners, that is ridiculous. Kiba, all you are is a model goof-off. Since Schmidt has been with you, that is all he is. Keep in mind what I have told you."

The trio left, and Bug-eyes slammed the door behind him.

I shouted at him, "Don't slam the friggin' door, you pig!"

Then Schmidt yelled, "What's the big idea? You tryin' to shatter our nerves?"

Bug-eyes didn't respond, and we heard the inspection team go into Dog Cell and chew them out, too.

Schmidt started to read the book again, but I interrupted him and told him to give the books we had to the guard. He thought that was a bad idea and suggested that we "play it cool" for awhile. I disagreed and insisted that we quit reading and return the filthy, lopsided propaganda books they'd so eagerly given us; none of them had any redeeming value of any kind, and they served only to intimidate us.

Schmidt finally agreed and gave me his books. I took all of them to the flap, shoved them into the guard's face, and ordered him to take them. He backed away from the flap and refused to take them. I told him that if he didn't take them I would throw them on the corridor floor. My determination distressed the guard, and he walked off toward the houseboy's office down the hall.

The guard returned a few minutes later accompanied by the houseboy Sam, who asked us why we were so upset. I explained the situation to him and shoved the sorry books into his hands. He tried to calm me and make me take the books back, but I refused them and walked away from the flap. He took the books away hurriedly— probably took them to his office and hid them—because he was surely afraid Bug-eyes would see them and accuse him of losing control of the inmates in his cellblock.

Several minutes later the inspection team left Dog Cell. As they passed our cell again, Bug-eyes lifted the flap, gave us a dirty look, and then slammed the flap. We heard them march down the hall and leave the cellblock.

Apparently Sam was watching, because he came back as soon as Bug-eyes left. He tried to return the books, and we refused to take them. He wanted to know why, so I explained to him that the bug-eyed son-of-a-bitch just chewed us out and told us not to read.

Sam tried his best, through gestures and broken English, to make us understand that Bug-eyes only meant for us not to read too loud and that it was a rule for us not to talk to other inmates in the cellblock. He lingered in our cell for five minutes or more trying to get us to take the books, but both Schmidt and I continued to refuse. Finally, he made us understand that there would be some bad repercussions from his superiors, both for him and us, if we didn't read the books.

So we agreed to take a copy of CHINESE LITERATURE, but we made it clear to Sam that he had to tell that bug-eyed, Redchink bastard not to shout at us or threaten us anymore. He smiled and nodded his head in understanding, and we took the book. We never believed for a minute that he had the power or the courage to make demands on Bug-eyes. Nevertheless, it felt good to "fight back," even in such a small way.

As it turned out, Sam did us a favor, although I'm sure he didn't know it. When we read the copy of CHINESE LITERATURE he brought us, we learned for sure that the Korean War was over. However, there was no specific date given as to when the end occurred.

Twelve days after Bug-eyes made his surprise visit, the houseboy named Dunghead entered Baker Cell and for no reason started giving them a bad time. Llewellyn lashed back at him, and this angered Dunghead; he immediately moved Llewellyn out of the cellblock.

After Dunghead left, we tried to find out from Vaadi, his cellmate, what happened. Eventually we all decided that the Red Chinese officials had found out about "Hank Snow," our code name for escape plans, and they probably moved Llewellyn because he was more or less the ringleader.

There was definitely a downturn in their attitude toward us from that point on. They kept an even closer watch and clamped down on the intra-cellblock and inter-cellblock communications. They were extremely peeved and on edge about something, and even the propaganda material slowed down to a trickle.

In the evening of January 14, 1954, Schmidt and I were teasing the guards as they peered into our cell. There were now at least six or seven guards zipping up and down the hall at regular intervals. Each time one appeared at the flap, we heckled him with derogatory remarks and obscene gestures. Sometimes we'd even ridicule him by laughing at him in an insulting way. Naturally, this treatment did what we expected it to do: it upset them, but they had never retaliated. I was about to lose interest, but I wanted to try one more thing to make them lose their composure: I started singing THE YELLOW ROSE OF TEXAS. They really reacted to this, even became jumpy. Schmidt advised me to "cool it" for awhile, but I ignored him and continued to sing.

Shortly, Dunghead appeared at the flap and screamed at me to stop; it thrilled me to know my caterwauling was irritating them.

He glared at me through the flap. I smiled at him, and said, "Why, no shit, if it isn't old Dunghead." Then I began singing again.

Dunghead was angry. He shouted "Bushing!" (Don't.)

I ignored him.

I could see the wild look in his eyes, and he ground his teeth so furiously I could see his jaw muscles quiver. He was infuriated, a madman.

Again he shouted, "Bushing! Bushing! Ah la la bushing!" (Don't! Don't! Don't ah la la!)

I reveled in the fact that I was inflicting something—hopefully discomfort—on my enemy. I ignored his panicky voice and kept on singing, or rather caterwauling.

He slammed the flap shut. I stopped singing and yelled, "Don't slam the flap, you stupid queer!"

Dunghead opened the flap again and tried to appear calm. He said, "Bushing, ah ah ah bushing." He made sign language for me not to shout.

My nerves were totally frayed. Everything upset me. Sitting and waiting and not knowing what was going on nibbled on my sanity like a mouse chewing on a big hunk of cheese. One thing I did know now was that the war was over. So why were the Redchinks still holding us? Why hadn't they notified our government that we were alive? Would they ever?

Being caged and treated like an animal was turning me into one, and I couldn't control it. The constant, endless surveillance bugged me, and I felt like screaming.

"Oh God," I thought. "How much longer will this go on?"

A little later I started tapping code on the edge of my board. In the meantime, Dunghead had returned to the vicinity of our cell. When he heard my tapping, he rushed to the flap, jerked it open, and said, "Bushing! Bushing!" (Don't! Don't!)

I just smiled at him and kept right on tapping.

He came into the cell and demanded that I stop tapping. I told him I would if he would give me a pencil and paper, or find something else for me to do.

Dunghead lost his patience with me and moved me into a cell across the hall. He ordered me to remain silent. Before he locked me in, he closed the inside window so it would be more difficult for me to communicate with Schmidt and the others.

I walked around the new cell trying to keep warm. I sang at the top of my voice, and I tried to make as much noise as I could. While I was thus engaged, I also did a cursory examination of the cell. I found a calendar scratched on the wall with the dates of 20, 21, 22, 23, and 24 August 1953. These were the exact dates when Schmidt and I had seen the two Caucasians in this cell. I also found two marks over the door. I stood against them and compared them to my own height. One was about 5' 9" high, and the other one was about 5' 10".

After the sijo (sleep) bell rang, Dunghead moved me back to Charlie Cell. Schmidt was already asleep when I got back.

The next morning, wrapped in our pads and still shivering from the intense cold, Schmidt and I discussed our plight. In several of our bull sessions with the political instructors, we were told that they were discussing the possibility of exchanging an unspecified number of Americans for Formosa and a seat in the United Nations. We both agreed that we would rather rot in their filthy hell than see the mangy communists be rewarded for illegally detaining American servicemen.

137

During our conversation, we discussed many topics, ideas, and theories. Among them were the possibility that the war had broken out anew in Korea, plans for escaping, our "missing" status, and how much concern they had for us back home. There were moments when we doubted that anybody cared about us and our miserable predicament.

On January 20, 1954, there was another complete change of guards. The new guards turned out to be real pricks, but there were a couple who, though not friendly, were less obnoxious than the others. Yet, they all had one thing in common: each one sported many medals on their plain uniforms.

On January 27, Benjamin and Thompson had a disagreement. This caused the houseboys to transfer Benjamin into the cell across from Schmidt and me.

Later that same day Dunghead escorted us to the shower building. As we were undressing, Babyface made us stop and step into some stalls while another man was brought in. Howard Brown and I were in one of the bath stalls, and we were able to see the stranger undress. He was about five-nine, or ten, and weighed about 140 pounds. He was white, had brown hair and whiskers, and appeared to be around 50 years old. His sides were caved in, and he was pitifully emaciated.

When the old man finished undressing, Babyface put him into the bath stall next to the one where Howard Brown and I were waiting. We wanted to communicate with him somehow, but we couldn't: the Redchink goons were watching us too closely. Once the old man was in the tub, Babyface allowed us to finish undressing. We entered the shower stalls and adjusted the water the best we could, but it still came out alternately cold and almost scalding hot. Nevertheless, we were thankful for it and for the infrequent opportunity to indulge in a simple pleasurable activity that most people in the civilized world take for granted. So we savored every moment, every drop.

After only five short minutes of enjoyment, the attendants shut off the water. We dried ourselves with scratchy, soiled towels and dressed quickly so Dunghead could escort us back to our cold, cold cells.

Ever since Llewellyn had been moved from our cellblock, which we called "Carnegie Hall," the rest of us had been trying to contact him. We tried hardest at night, after the sijo bell rang. Eugene Vaadi was elected to cough the messages, and occasionally Able Cell (John Buck and Wallace Brown) would also give it a try. Occasionally someone in the next cellblock coughed back. We wondered if it might be Llewellyn.

About the middle of February 1954, we learned that the Chinese prisoner in cell nine understood English. Much to our consternation, we also learned that he told the houseboys what we talked about, and the houseboys in turn reported it to higher authorities. On several occasions, they took Number Nine himself to the office to give a full report. We had to consider two scenarios: One, that he was "planted" for that very purpose; or two, he was indeed a prisoner trying to ingratiate himself with the prison officials by ratting on us. Of course we were disgusted and did not conceal our contempt for him, the mangy Redchink stool pigeon.

From the moment we learned about him, all of us joined in frequent verbal assaults launched over the "open air" of the cellblock with full knowledge that he would hear some of them. We'd say:

"What would Chang Kai-shek think of you now?"

"If I could only get my hands on you, you'd never rat on us again. I'd wrap my hands around your dirty neck and squeeze until your eyeballs popped out of their sockets."

"Hey, Number Nine, when are we going home?"

"Come on, answer us, you rat. We know you savvy English."

"Tell us what's going on, and we'll make it easier for you when we get our hands on you."

"We know the war is over. We know we'll be out of here soon, so you'd better cooperate with us. We can do something for you. The communists have nothing to offer you but a ten-by-ten cell, so why play watchdog for them? Tell them to shove it. Are you a man or a mouse?"

"He's a no-good, rotten, mealy-mouthed commie."

"Yeah, there's nothing lower than a commie."

Sometime later, after we discovered the rat in cell nine, Schmidt was up walking around and noticed something outside our window. He stopped and said, "Hey, Kiba! What's this?"

I jumped off my board and walked over to look.

"Looks like a mike," I said.

Schmidt asked me to watch for the pussyfoot guard. When it was all clear, he climbed up into the window for a better look.

He whispered, "I see a wire and something that could be a mike."

He jumped down, said he'd watch for the guard, and told me to take a closer look.

I climbed up, took a quick look, and climbed down.

There was no doubt now. They knew everything we'd talked about and probably everything we'd communicated to each other through Morse code and even our "Hank Snow" escape plan. We figured that all the cells were bugged somehow. The discovery corroborated our belief that Llewellyn had been moved into isolation because of his leadership in the plan. It also explained why the food had gotten worse and why the houseboys and guards were so super-cautious and ill-tempered.

Schmidt and I decided to fill their sneaky ears to the fullest. Using the crudest language we were capable of, we berated them and criticized their communist system, their military prowess, and their leaders. We said Mao Tse-tung was nothing more than a stupid puppet and Red China was a mere satellite of the Soviet Union. We told them that their communist literature reeked and that they could shove their Marxism-Leninism up their bungs. Simultaneously, we whistled and screamed into the mike.

Immediately after our harassing tirade, we were literally swamped with Marxist-Leninist reading material. We read it, but we added a word here, left out a word there, and changed words around until no one, especially Marx and Lenin, would have recognized it.

Near the beginning of March 1954, the stoolie in cell number nine was transferred to another cellblock. We also noticed that the bug outside our window had been removed.

Even though our jailers tried to keep us from working out in our cells, we were able to sneak in some conditioning exercises. We still had hopes of escaping, so we did every type of exercise that could be done in such closed in quarters. Some of the crew were able to do up to 1,500 sit-ups and 1,000 side straddle hops in one exercise session. Most of us averaged 500 push-ups daily, and we usually exercised about three hours per day.

The meager quantity and quality of food we received scarcely supplied the calories we needed to exist, much less support the long and strenuous exercises we were doing. So I often wondered what kept us going. Was it the will to live? Perhaps, but we did not consider being caged up like rats as "living." Then what could the reason be? Without proper diet, where did we get the physical strength to carry on the way we did? Was it love of country? Was it maybe faith in a Superior Being? Or was it our unflagging hope that we would return home and live in freedom again?

I concluded that it was all of those things combined; they were qualities and ideals so ingrained in our beings that they helped us sustain a fighting, driving spirit in our hearts and souls. Some of us were religious. Others were not, or at least they were less religious than some. There was no doubt that all of us loved our country dearly; we harbored deep hopes to return to it as soon as possible, and we were willing to risk our lives to get there. Every one of us hated communism and our Redchink jailers. It is very probable that our hatred also helped us in our struggles. We didn't view ourselves as heroes; we believed that live heroes were few and war heroes were usually dead ones.

Simply put, we were men who met misfortune while doing a job; our imprisonment was a continuation of that job, and from our own experience we knew absolutely that there was nothing heroic in the life of a prisoner of war. Sometimes I got a depressing feeling that, because I was taken prisoner, I had failed in the performance of my job. Yet, the fact that I was captured did not terminate my job. On the contrary, the most difficult part of my job began with my capture. So the question: "Had I really failed?" became polar in my thinking.

The answer, I believed, depended entirely on my personal conduct and my unique view of things. A job was a job: whether I was a crewman on a B-29 or sitting in a political prison endeavoring to resist interrogations and survive torture, the result was the same. I could do a good job or a poor job, but who would judge the quality of my work? How could I be judged?

With most kinds of employment, a qualified superior or supervisor can critique and evaluate an employee's performance, skills, and conduct. But who was qualified to evaluate me and my

141

crew, political prisoners whose performance, skills, and conduct were bred and grown in indescribable agony? Surely not anyone who hasn't endured the same torture, the same humiliation and deprivation, the same far-off hell-hole prison where we were isolated and starved beyond belief and where we suffered daily from unbearable cold or heat and feelings of abandonment.

Thus were my thoughts sometimes in moments of frustration and indignity.

On or about March 10, 1954, we were allowed to take another short shower. We saw the same emaciated old man again, and we speculated on who he was. A former pilot, maybe? Or perhaps a newsman held by the communists who didn't like his reporting.

When we got back to our cell, Schmidt said, "Do you ever have nightmares, Kiba?"

I said, "Yeah, quite often. How about you?"

"Sometimes I dream that I'm back home in Coeur d'Alene, Idaho, and all my old friends are around. I can't enjoy myself like I should because I know I'm not home to stay. It's like I'm on furlough; and when it's over, I have to come back to this prison."

"And when your leave is up, you refuse to come. Right?" I said.

"That's right. The weird part is that my wife, my friends, and the government all force me to come back."

"Back at the 'Hotel' I was tormented by exactly the same dream almost every night that I wasn't being interrogated. I still have it occasionally. Really strange, isn't it?"

"Sure is," Schmidt said. "What do you think it means?"

"I don't know," I said. "My nightmares center around one theme: this damn prison. Although they usually vary slightly, different people or different town, for example, they all end up the same—right back here."

"Mine, too," Schmidt said.

"What a riot! We can take a furlough from prison any time we want to—in a dream."

"Yeah, and it gives me a creepy feeling when my friends force me to come back. Who the hell needs friends like that?"

I said, "Yeah. Good thing it's only a dream. Say, speaking of strange things, while I was back at the 'Hotel,' I took off my sweatshirt one day and noticed a big spot of dried blood on the front of my T-shirt. The spot was in the shape of Africa."

"What happened? Were you wounded somewhere?"

"No," I said. "All I had were a few scratches on my hands and a bruised tailbone."

"Are you sure your nose didn't bleed, maybe while you were asleep?"

"I'm sure. I still can't figure out where the blood came from. I had no cuts on my body, and both my T-shirt and sweatshirt were tight-fitting."

"Sure is puzzling," Schmidt said.

"When we got shot down, Llewellyn and Baumer were both wounded, but my back was toward them. I got some of their blood on the back of my head and my jacket, but there was no way that their blood could've gotten on the front of my T-shirt without getting all over my sweatshirt."

Schmidt laughed and said, "Maybe you were sweating blood."

"Another funny thing is that when we were still at Clark Field in the Philippines—you know, before we went to Japan and then got shot down—I had another weird nightmare."

"Say, this 'dream' business is getting more interesting by the minute. Tell me about it," Schmidt said.

"I dreamed we were shot down in Korea. It happened in my dream exactly like it happened that night, January 12, 1953. I woke up in a cold sweat and sat up in bed. For a long time, I just sat there staring off into space. I think I was half-asleep and half in shock because of the dream. It was around two in the afternoon, and Castor, our Filipino houseboy, was squatting near my bunk and shining my shoes. He stood up and asked me what was wrong, and the sound of his voice snapped me out of my daze. I told him everything was okay, and he went back to shining my shoes. I sat shaking on my bunk for awhile and thanked God that it was only a nightmare."

"When did you have the dream?"

"In October 1952," I said. "At that time, we didn't even know that we would be sent anywhere else, much less Japan and Korea. I should have taken it seriously and left the crew, but I was too hard-headed."

Schmidt frowned and said, "Why didn't you tell me this back then?"

"You, and everyone else, would've laughed at me. Besides, it wouldn't have made any difference with you. You're just as hard-headed as me."

On March 23, 1954, the houseboy took us five airmen to the patio for a short walk. While we were out there, I noticed something new.

"Hey, Schmidt! Do you see what I see?"

"What's that?" he said.

I pointed and said, "That filthy red rag flapping on top of that building."

"Sure, and it's polluting the air," he said.

"This is the first time I've ever seen their rag flying," I said.

"I've been looking out toward that building since I started walking in this courtyard, and today is the first time it's been there."

I said, "I've seen it next to the Monkey's (Mao's) picture in the interrogation and indoctrination rooms."

"So have I," he said.

The Red Chinese (communist) flag was red—blood red—and in the upper left hand corner it had one large yellow star and four smaller yellow stars. According to our political indoctrinators, the four smaller stars represented the four steps to achieve socialism, that is, their four revolutionary-civil wars. The large star represented their ultimate goal, communism.

On March 27, 1954, Dunghead took us five airmen for another short walk. As we circled the patio, we heard a voice call out from behind the third window in what we called the "Skid Row" cellblock.

"Damned if it ain't…," the voice said.

We stopped in our tracks and stared at the third window. We saw an indistinct face and a hairy arm, but we couldn't tell who it was. Evidently the houseboy in Skid Row reacted quickly because the mystery man was taken away from the window and the window was quickly closed. The "mystery man" event prompted Dunghead to cut our walk short and immediately return us to our cells. On the way back, we speculated as to who it might've been, but no one really knew. However, it was obvious that he had recognized us.

The weather was beginning to warm up. When the houseboys left our cellblock, they left open the double doors leading into the small hub (circle) which connected Carnegie Hall (our cellblock), Skid Row, and Shower Corridor. We took advantage of that and tried to make contact with Llewellyn who, we believed, was in Skid Row.. Our coughing efforts to that end made our cellblock sound as though it were housing tuberculosis patients. It was fruitless, however, because we never received a "valid" message from him.

After we saw the "mystery man," they changed the location where we walked. Thus we were excluded from going anywhere near his cell, and it made us suspect that the "mystery man" was either Llewellyn or one of our other missing crew members.

Steve E. Kiba

PART VII

BRUISED, NOT BROKEN

Steve E. Kiba

Maybe it was a touch of spring fever or just pure cussedness; but, whatever the cause, Schmidt and I were exceedingly restless. Not only that, we were highly discontented, bored, and frustrated. We were literally sick of being confined to a stuffy cell where our liberties and freedoms, even the most basic ones, were denied to us. We were fighting mad at the automaton guards who monitored our every action and spied on us relentlessly with a depraved sense of satisfaction in the "job" they did. They and their immediate superiors were extremely inhumane flunkies of the communist "system," and our very existence—through them—hinged on the whims of some irrational, atheistic crackpot leader who used them to maintain his power and achieve his goals.

We endeavored to cope with all of our situational problems and to retain the little sanity we had left by ridding ourselves of some of our pent up frustrations. Our primary method of release was to direct our rage toward the lower echelon people: the guards and the houseboys. Fortunately, Schmidt's knee and leg were much improved, and that fact contributed much to our ability to pester the guards.

One day Schmidt looked at me with a glimmer of evil in his eyes.

"Watch this," he said and squatted down beside our cell window. The next time the guard approached it and started to encroach upon our privacy by lifting the flap and peeking in, Schmidt straightened up and shouted "Boo!" right in the guard's face.

The guard was so startled that he jumped backwards away from the window.

Schmidt and I burst out laughing; and, when the guard came back and cautiously lifted the flap again, he gave us a long, dirty look, uttered some unsavory remarks, and then slammed the flap closed.

"Sobee!" I hollered back at him. (Mandarin for our over-used - F- word.)

The guard raised the flap again and glared at us.

"Sobee!" I said again.

"Sobee bushing!" yelled the guard. (Don't say sobee!)

Schmidt yelled back, "Sobee! You ugly, Redchink son-of-a-bitch!"

"Bushing!" Screamed the guard. (Don't!)

"Go bug yourself and leave us alone," I said.

He closed the flap and left our cell to continue his round. Every time he reappeared at our window, either Schmidt or I would yell "Screw you!" in Mandarin.

Being constantly confined and having nothing to do really got on our nerves. We sought ways to intimidate the guards and houseboys to grant us privileges that would occupy our minds, things that could be done in the cell, or even outside—anything to alleviate the boredom. Even though Schmidt was convinced that I'd never get them, I became obsessed with obtaining a pencil and some paper to draw on.

"Why try?" he told me. "You'll never get them."

I was never one to give up easily, so I ignored his advice. The next time the guard lifted the window flap and looked in on us, I pointed toward the office and asked him to get the houseboy. He refused and kept repeating, "Miyo!" (No!)

I got angry, raised my voice, and belittled his ancestors. He kept telling me to shut up. Our houseboy—Sam, the three-thumbed Chinaman—rushed out to investigate. He lifted our flap and said, "Sheema, sheema?" (What? What?)

I told him I wanted a pencil and some paper. He glared at me, said "miyo" (no), and slammed the flap closed.

"Don't slam the friggin' flap!" I hollered at him.

Sam opened the flap again and asked, "Sheema?" (What?)

I went through the act of slamming the flap and said, "Wham, wham Puho! (no damn good) Wham, wham! Bushing, bushing!" (Don't slam the flap!))

Sam had difficulty disguising his anger. He slammed the flap as hard as he could and started to walk away.

I was angry too, so I yelled out, "Don't slam the friggin' flap you stupid Redchink pimp!"

Sam came back, jerked the door open, and rushed into our cell.

"Sheema?" he said. "Sheema pimp?" (What? What's a pimp?)

"You stupid pimp," I said.

"Bushing! Miyo walla walla!" (Don't! No speak).

"Give us a pencil and a pad, and we won't yell. Okay?"

150

"Miyo, miyo," he said. Then he went on to explain that the last time he gave us paper we wrote nasty notes on it about our treatment and the Red Chinese.

I got disgusted with him. "Okay," I said. "Shove it up your dirty bung!"

He left in a huff and slammed the door behind him.

"Don't slam the blasted door, you no-good bastard!" I yelled.

Sam went to the flap, lifted it, and gave me a dirty look. He motioned that he would put handcuffs on me if I didn't keep quiet.

Our not-so-nice battle of wits continued for quite some time. Sam finally got fed up and called in Assistant Warden Babyface for reinforcement. I didn't understand why he thought the two of them could deal with my stubbornness better than one; but, apparently they thought that, by sheer numbers, they could "tame" my overzealousness and disobedience.

When Babyface lifted the flap, I repeated my request for paper and pencil. He became angry right off and denied my request. He also repeated the threatening gesture of handcuffs for me if I didn't settle down.

I didn't let his threat deter me. I said, "Ah, screw you! Sobee! Your threats don't scare me." I held up my wrists and said, "Go ahead! I just don't give a damn!"

Both Sam and Babyface were now totally exasperated. They left and came back in about five minutes. When I asked them again for a pencil and some paper, Sam whipped out a shiny pair of manacles from his back pocket and quickly placed them around my wrists. I just grinned at them and asked for a pencil and paper again.

I knew that through the entire scene Schmidt thought I was crazy. There might've been some truth in the assumption, but in order to emphasize our solidarity, Schmidt—and the other airmen who'd listened to it all—asked them for handcuffs, too. Sam and Babyface just shook their heads and left our cell, slamming the door behind them.

"Don't slam that friggin' door!" I hollered.

Babyface jerked open the window flap and stared into our cell. I stared right back at him and repeated, "Don't slam that friggin' door!"

He continued to glare at me, and I at him. He mumbled something under his breath, slammed the flap, and stormed out of the cellblock.

My defiant behavior created a collateral problem I did not anticipate. Although it was the middle of April and the weather had warmed to a tolerable level, we still wore our padded winter clothing. When Sam placed the handcuffs on me, he did so in such haste and spite that I was not allowed to take off my padded jacket. This sent me off on another series of confrontations with the witless Redchink jailers, who refused to acknowledge the discomfort I was in.

At nine o'clock when the sijo bell rang, the guard peeked in to make sure we'd gone to bed. I was still up, and when he ordered me to lie down, I asked him to bring me the houseboy. He refused and repeated his command for me to lie down. I told him I wasn't going to lie down until I could get my padded jacket removed. His reaction was the same as any guard who faced disobedience or who was irate because of his loss of control: he screamed out for the houseboy.

Sam came running down the hall and came into our cell. He immediately ordered me to lie down and go to sleep. I told him I would if he would unlock my manacles and let me take off my padded jacket. He refused. I asked Schmidt to rip it off, and he jumped off his board and began pulling on the jacket.

Sam didn't like that tactic either, and he spouted out his loud, Chinese sing-song objection: "Miyo, Miyo! Dalee, Dalee!" (No, no! Wait, wait!) He then turned and left the cell.

A few minutes later Sam returned with Babyface, and they came in with angry looks on their faces. Babyface ordered me to lie down. I tried hard to make them understand that it was hot and I needed to take my jacket off. In order to do that, they had to temporarily remove my manacles. It was no use, however. Neither comprehended the word temporary nor my gestures to that effect. The language barrier was too great, and they were too thick-skulled to understand common sense. Babyface was very adamant when he reminded me that I had been bad, that I had asked for the bracelets, and that I could damn well sleep in them.

In frustration, I asked Schmidt once more to rip off the jacket. He got back up, came over, and started ripping and grunting. This infuriated both Sam and Babyface, and Sam cried out, "Hundota! Maubee! Miyo!" (Two swear words; No!)

The jacket tore a little, but Schmidt didn't have enough strength to do greater damage.

Babyface pointed his finger at me like a kindergarten teacher about to reprimand an upstart and said, "Sijo, sijo." (Go to sleep; go to sleep.)

"Go screw yourself," I said.

They were obviously disgusted with me and at the end of their patience in trying to deal with a problem which they did not fully understand. They left the cell and conversed excitedly as they stomped down the hall toward the houseboy's office.

I knew Schmidt was tired and needed rest, so I quieted down long enough for him to go to sleep. Nevertheless, I remained very uncomfortable and recalcitrant. I walked around the cell quietly; and, every time the guard peeped in, I glared at him, made faces at him, or did both simultaneously. Finally, Shorty came on duty. He was a guard who treated us with some decency, so we reciprocated by being more cooperative when he was on duty. He would let us talk from cell to cell and warn us when the houseboy or a hostile guard was approaching. In deference to his better treatment, I finally went to bed.

The next morning I hopped off my board and started clanging my handcuffs together. I knew such early noise would anger the guard, and sure enough it did. He uttered profanities and chided me vehemently, but only for a short time; he had grown used to my stubbornness. When I continued my clanging, he called a houseboy.

Sam came down the corridor, jerked open our flap, and glared at me. I stopped clanging my new toy and told him I had to go to the latrine. I explained and illustrated that it was impossible for me to squat over the slit trench and empty my bowels wearing both jacket and handcuffs. I pointed out that the jacket would have to be removed or I would mess all over it. He finally understood and said, "Dalee, dalee!" (Wait, wait!) Then he hurriedly left the cellblock.

Within minutes Sam returned with Babyface and a key to the manacles. Babyface berated me again for my "incorrect" behavior during the night and told me I was nothing but a no-good troublemaker.

Sam unlocked the manacles and removed them, and I took off my jacket. Then Sam replaced the manacles and escorted me to the toilet. Once there, I fumbled around trying to pull down my padded pants in order to squat over the slit. Sam watched me for five minutes before he lost patience; finally, he came over and helped me get my pants down.

A few days after my altercations with Sam and Babyface, our padded winter pants and jackets were replaced with summer blacks. The blacks were the same as we had previously worn: both the pants and the shirt had the white patch with a black Chinese character on it. Since the last time we wore them, we had learned that the patch symbolized "a man in irons."

While they had me handcuffed, I found a way to mystify the guards. While sitting on my bed board, I slipped my feet through my cuffed hands, thus moving my hands from my front to my back. When the guard peeped in, he was totally puzzled as to why my cuffed hands were no longer in front. When he dropped the flap, I quickly slipped them back the other way. The next time he looked, my hands would be back in front. We played this game for hours, with the guard peeking in trying to surprise me making the switch, but he never caught me. Schmidt had fun watching the silly little game, and he said, "Even a ten-year-old American could figure that out. That shows the intelligence level of the Red Chinese prison guards."

On April 20, 1954, Ratface, Bluebeard, Babyface, and a houseboy we called "Smokey" made an unexpected inspection of our cellblock. Every cell was inspected and thoroughly searched. We wondered what was going on, if anything, but we never had a clue as to why they had made such a detailed inspection.

Exactly a week later, they took us one-by-one to the front office for a reprimand and a bull session. I was seated on a stool in front of a desk. Ratface and Bluebeard were seated behind the desk. Both were very amicable throughout the session. They scolded me for my misbehavior in the cell and promised to remove the manacles if I would start behaving. Their version of "behaving" was for me to be totally subservient and kowtow to their every wish and demand.

Schmidt and I had read in the 1953, Fall Edition of the CHINESE LITERATURE that the war was over, so I asked them why we were still being held. They both denied that the war was over. Then I complained that our treatment was inhumane and cruel. They suggested that if I were to change my "hostile attitude" and commence behaving myself, the treatment and conditions would improve, and I would receive more literature. In other words, if I yielded to their indoctrination and accepted communism and behaved accordingly, I would be treated better. I went back to my cell with the realization that the communist bastards were either going to have to kill me or just let me die in misery, because I would never accept their doctrine and their way of life.

The next day, April 28, 1954, Llewellyn was moved back into Baker Cell with Eugene Vaadi, and Benjamin was returned to Dog Cell. We chatted for quite a while asking each other questions and bringing Llewellyn up to date on what had transpired during his absence from our cellblock, Carnegie Hall. He told us that it was not he who yelled at us on March 27th and that he had been in Rheumatism Row, not Skid Row as we had suspected. He also had a session the day before, but the Red Chinese would not tell him why he had been removed from Baker Cell and put in solitary confinement.

A couple of days later, Schmidt and I were sitting on our bed boards when suddenly he yelled, "Hey, Kiba, look at the rat!"

I immediately looked at the flap-covered opening where the guards spied on us; I expected to see the face of an ugly guard, but no one was there.

"I don't see anything," I said.

"It's gone now," he said.

"Are you sure it was a rat?"

"Yes. I saw it run across the ledge. Watch and it might come back."

We both stared at the ledge, and the guard saw us concentrating on the ledge when he looked in. He had to crane his neck to see what we were looking at, but of course he couldn't see anything because the rat was gone.

"Sheema?" The pussyfoot guard asked. (What?)

I walked to the flap and told the guard that Schmidt had seen a big rat race across the ledge. He grunted something unintelligible and went to get the houseboy.

A houseboy we called "Buttercup" was on duty, and he came to our cell. He looked over at Schmidt and said something in Mandarin; then he looked at me and grinned. I interpreted his actions and his silly grin as meaning that Schmidt was "touched in the head" and was probably hallucinating.

Schmidt explained to Buttercup what he'd seen, but Buttercup just looked at him sorrowfully and shook his head. Then he looked at me, put his index finger to his head, and made a circular motion with it to imply that perhaps Schmidt was demented.

"Looks like Buttercup didn't believe you," I said to Schmidt.

Although it was not intentional, my statement irritated Schmidt. He sat up stiffly on his board and said, "I tell you it's true. I *did* see a rat."

"I believe you," I said.

"It was there on the ledge, just plain as day," he insisted.

"They sure have plenty of them around," I said. "I'm probably responsible for their skepticism."

Schmidt gave me a funny look and said, "What do you mean?"

"Before you came, I used to play games with the guards just to annoy them. One thing I did was to wait until the guard lifted the flap and then pretend that I was hiding something. When he looked in, I'd jump up and act guilty. The stupid agot (West Virginia slang for a slow-witted person) would run for the houseboy, and he would sneak up to the flap and peek in. Of course, I sat quietly and acted like a model prisoner while the houseboy was looking; so, he never was able to visually confirm what the guard was telling him. I repeated this silliness until the houseboy would finally search my cell. After finding nothing, he would leave and chew out the guard for his false alarms' before he went back to his office. So you see, Buttercup probably didn't believe you because he thought you were playing the same game."

"Well, I'll be damned," Schmidt said with a grin on his face. "Maybe next time I can conjure up a pink elephant."

Every morning from mid-April to almost mid-May, as soon as I got off my bed board, I greeted my fellow inmates and my dimwitted jailers by clanging my manacles together. This "special greeting" drew angry protests from both the guards and the houseboys. The louder they protested, the more vigorously I brought my hands and wrists together, thus increasing the intensity of the noise as metal struck metal.

On the morning of May 14, 1954, Sam came into our cell (Charlie Cell) and removed my handcuffs. I really didn't know why they decided to free me, because I was continually giving them a hard time, but we all concurred that it was probably due to a change in their thinking about the way they treated us. I was certainly ready to be rid of the uncomfortable and inhibiting pieces of iron, but some of the other crew members teased that I should have put up more of a fight to keep them.

The next day the houseboy Smokey took us out for a short walk. I was wearing a pair of black summer pants that were completely split at the seat. My previous efforts to get a new pair of pants, or at least get the torn ones mended, were unsuccessful. I had no underclothes on, so my bare fanny was visible. We were walking around in a small circle, and Howard Brown fell in behind me and started horsing around. He moved in close behind me and played like he had an overwhelming urge to caress my naked behind, so I started running and pretended that I was deathly afraid of his advances. Our innocent horseplay was misinterpreted by the houseboy; he got panicky and immediately rushed me back into the cellblock and gave me another pair of trousers that were intact.

On May 19, 1954, the Red Chinese moved us from Carnegie Hall into Skid Row, the cellblock which fanned out from the opposite side of the small circle or hub. We kept the same cell designations we used in Carnegie Hall: Able Cell, occupied by officers John Buck and Wallace Brown; Baker Cell, occupied by officers Gene Vaadi and Elmer Llewellyn; Charlie Cell, occupied by Airmen Steve Kiba and Daniel Schmidt; and Dog Cell, occupied by T/Sgt. Howard Brown and Airmen Harry Benjamin and John Thompson. As we entered Skid Row from the small hub, Able was the first cell on the right,

Baker the third, Charlie the fifth, and Dog the last. Skid Row was similar in design to Carnegie Hall.

We examined our new cells thoroughly and found nothing of any value. I could look out of Charlie Cell and see a small building just a few feet from the cellblock, and the outside wall was just on the other side of that structure.

All of us wondered why we had been moved, but we could not find a logical answer. Some of us thought that it was because we'd be leaving soon, and others thought it was because we'd continue to be imprisoned for a long time to come. However, we all agreed that we could not out-guess the Red Chinese; they did things without reason; logic and common sense were not functional qualities of their modus operandi.

On May 28, 1954, they moved us back to Carnegie Hall and into the same cells we had vacated just ten days before. On my first trip to the toilet, I learned that our short stay in Skid Row was to give Red Chinese workmen time and opportunity to make repairs to the "one-hole" ("one-slit trench") latrine. I also learned that three Chinese prisoners had joined us in Carnegie Hall: one in the cell across from Able Cell and two across from Baker.

A week or so later I was circling the cell, and suddenly I got a bad attack of stomach cramps that made it absolutely necessary for me to use the latrine. I asked the houseboy for permission to go. He refused my request and gave me a look that showed his "superiority." I asked him again and accompanied the request with gestures to indicate the urgency of my need. This time he just grinned and told me to "wait." I told him to go screw himself and then used all my willpower to avoid soiling myself with my own excrement. I wasn't sure if I could hold back or not, or for how long if I continued to try. I managed to restrain myself for a miserable half-hour; then at last that no-account son-of-a-bitch Smokey finally opened the door to let us out of our cell to use the latrine. I made a mad dash for the "one-hole" and barely made it. Squatting over the smelly slit, I was humiliated and angry for the many ways the Red Chinese used our human needs to treat us with cruelty and perversity. If I'd had the means and the opportunity at that moment, I could have killed without impunity every friggin' Redchink bastard in the whole damned prison.

On my way back to my cell, Smokey ordered me to help Thompson and Benjamin sweep the filthy hall. I told him to go screw himself. He shoved a broom without a handle toward me and said, "Sama sambee." (Sweep.) He insisted that I sweep his cruddy, phlegm-spattered floor. I shoved the broom back at him and told him to jam it up his nasty bung. He threatened to slap me in irons. I told him to go ahead because I wasn't about to sweep the friggin' snot-covered floor. He was baffled by my staunch resistance and acted as if he didn't know what to do. Finally, he reluctantly accepted my refusal to kowtow to his demand and returned Schmidt and me to our cell.

"That bastard really had his nerve," I said when the cell door slammed behind us.

"Well, you really pushed him," Schmidt said. "I thought he might bang you on the head or put you back in solitary."

"He made me wait," I said. "Even though the toilet was unoccupied, *he made me wait.* He almost caused me to dirty my pants. The son-of-a-bitch can sweep his cruddy floor himself."

About ten minutes later, Smokey returned and made me follow him. He led me to the water barrel and pointed to the gourd in the barrel. Then he pointed to the smelly john. I got the message: he was telling me to clean out the filthy, stinkin' slit trench in the toilet.

I pretended not to understand, and he went through the same motions again. We played that game for a few minutes, until he got so angry he grew pop-eyed. The veins in his neck and forehead became protruded. He trembled with rage as he repeatedly screamed his order for me to clean the john. I continued to scream my refusal right back at him.

I knew I was pressing my luck, as Schmidt reminded me, but I didn't care what they did to me. My pent up hate and frustration would not allow me to be pushed around by this obnoxious Redchink brute with a Neanderthal mentality.

Smokey lost his patience, grabbed me by the arm, and tried forcing me toward the toilet. I knocked his hand away, assumed a fighter's stance, and shouted, "Keep your filthy hands off me, or I'll clobber you!"

Sam, the houseboy, heard the commotion and came into the hall. He took Smokey aside, and they had a short conference, which I was barely able to hear. That didn't matter because I couldn't understand much of their gibberish anyway.

The conference was short. Apparently Sam convinced Smokey it was better not to force the issue, so he escorted me back to my cell. His frustration with me was evident during the trip back; he looked at me as if he could kill me, and he made strange muttering sounds all the way to the door. Then, when I stepped back into my cell, he forcefully slammed the door shut, and the sound of the locking bolt sliding back into its slot rang out like the strike of a huge bell clapper.

June 17, 1954, was a busy day for all of us; they escorted us, by cell, to the front office for more indoctrination. Our instructor, whom we referred to as "Bluebeard," told us that they called us in to learn if there were anything they could do to make our stay more bearable and comfortable. I told him they could send us home, especially since the Korean War was over and there had already been a prisoner exchange.

He denied that the war was over, and he refused to even talk about our being brought by force into Red China when we brought it up. He made it clear that we were war criminals, not prisoners-of-war. He insisted that we had violated Red Chinese air space and suggested that, unless we changed our "incorrect" attitudes and allowed ourselves to be re-educated, we would be in the People's Republic of China for one helluva long time—whether or not the war was over. He scolded us for our unruly behavior, disobedience, disrespect, and our failure to show appreciation for "all" that they were doing for us.

I again asked about our other crew members, the ones none of us had seen yet; but, as usual, I was advised to forget them and worry only about myself. Then I asked for us to be put with the officers. They flatly denied the request because, they said, the officers were bad and might corrupt our minds even more.

All of us still wondered about our three missing crew members: Hart, Van Voorhis, and Weese, so I decided to be more specific. I accused them of brutally murdering them by tying their hands behind their backs and blowing their brains out. I substantiated my accusation by pointing out that many American soldiers were found in North Korea with their hands tied behind their backs and with gaping, bloody holes in their heads. The accusation really unnerved Bluebeard, and he was at a loss about how to answer; he remained silent for a long time. Finally, he said that the People's Republic of China followed a lenient policy toward the "many" American prisoners she **was holding.**

Schmidt and I elaborated on what was wrong with the way they were treating us, and we suggested many changes and methods that would improve our deplorable plight. Yet, it was quite apparent that any changes or improvements that would make our lives better relied on our willingness to surrender our will and allow our minds to be cleansed of all the corrupt ideas which permeated them. Without that cleansing, we remained vicious enemies of the People's Republic of China and the peace-loving Chinese people. According to Bluebeard, our "only hope" of staying alive and of ever getting out of prison was to cooperate fully and unconditionally. Of course we were vehemently opposed to their "cleansing" proposal and to the "mind control" methods they used, but we had to face the reality that they were the captors and we were the captives. We went back to our gloomy cells feeling as disheartened as we'd ever felt.

Several days after our session with Bluebeard, the airmen in Dog Cell succeeded in getting a pencil and a pad from the houseboy. Otherwise there was no improvement in our treatment: no salt, no additional drinking water, no nutritional meals—just the same poor treatment and conditions.

Then, on Tuesday, June 22, 1954, the houseboy gave us each four small pieces of hard candy. Once again our hopes of going home soon skyrocketed.

On Tuesday, June 29, 1954, T/Sgt. Howard Brown and Airman Second Class John Thompson had a disagreement, and Brown was moved into the cell across the hall from Schmidt and me. This left Benjamin and Thompson still together in Dog Cell, which we thought was better for all concerned. Three people in one small cell were just too many. Even with just two in a cell, stress was a factor. I know that I got on Schmidt's nerves, especially with continuous shenanigans with the guards and houseboys. But mostly he was a good sport, patient, and even-tempered. I was glad to have him for a cellmate.

Several hours after T/Sgt. Brown was put back in solitary, Smokey gave everyone but him a level teaspoonful of salt. It seemed to us that the Red Chinese were giving in little by little to some of our demands. From that time on, our "benevolent" jailers gave us four small pieces of hard candy every ten days or so and very rarely several pinches of salt. That first day Smokey took it upon himself not to give Howard Brown any salt as a punishment for fighting with Thompson.

A week later, July 6, 1954, the houseboys (Sam and Smokey) took the five airmen on our crew to Skid Row and made us clean it up. We swept out every cell, swept down the walls, cleaned the latrine, and swept the cruddy hall floor. After that, we carried bed boards, saw horses, honey buckets, spittoons, and other junk from a cell in Skid Row and put them into cell number one in Carnegie Hall.

The following day they moved the nine of us (the four officers and the five airmen) from Carnegie Hall to Skid Row. Benjamin and Thompson (Dog Cell) were assigned to the first cell on the right nearest the hub, Schmidt and me (Charlie Cell) the second cell, Howard Brown the third cell, Vaadi and Llewellyn (Baker Cell) the fourth cell, Wallace Brown and Buck (Able Cell) the sixth cell. The houseboys also moved the three Chinese inmates who were with us in Carnegie Hall into cells on the opposite (left) side of Skid Row. The chow buckets were kept in the cell directly across from Schmidt and me. Thus, for whatever reason, we were forced to "adjust" to a new environment which, although much like our old quarters, had differences that required a certain amount of acclimation on our part.

A few days after being moved into Skid Row, Schmidt and I were reading a Russian physics book: ENERGETICS. I took the book to the window flap and started teasing the guard we called Shortcrotch. I showed him a picture of a monkey and told him that it was a picture of a "Tongwa (Chinaman), Tongwa Mao Tse-tung," and both Schmidt and I roared with laughter.

Shortcrotch screamed, "Bushing, bushing!" and angrily slammed the flap.

"We hurt his feelings, shame on us," laughed Schmidt.

"Yeah, just because we showed him a picture of his brother and berated his glorious leader, Chairman Mao."

On Monday, August 2, 1954, Schmidt began to complain about a sharp pain in his right side. I advised him to lie down and take it easy. I approached the flap and asked the guard to summon the houseboy. The guard ordered me to shut up. I continued to try to make him understand that Schmidt was hurting really bad, but the baboon was just too dense to comprehend. Vaadi and Llewellyn let us know that the houseboy was out of the cellblock, but should be back shortly.

Schmidt remained in a semi-prone position on his board and continued to moan and groan. Finally, a half hour later, the houseboy came. I called out loudly to get his attention as he walked down the hall, but he ignored me. He entered the cell just across from us where the chow buckets were kept. He picked them up and started to leave the cellblock to go after chow. While he was still nearby, I shouted, "Hey, Sam!"

Sam walked over to our flap and asked, "Sheema?" (What?)

I told him that Schmidt was very sick; but, instead of coming in to see about him, he told me to wait and walked away.

About 15 minutes later Sam returned with chow. When he opened our door to bring us our meager rations, I cornered him and made him listen. I asked him to get a doctor for Schmidt. He promised he would and left the cell hurriedly.

While we waited for the doctor, I urged Schmidt to eat his watery soup; I thought he was mainly suffering from hunger pains. However, when he ate it, the pain did not go away, and it was clear that the hunger pangs that gnawed on his stomach were negligible compared to the pain caused by whatever else was wrong with him.

About six o'clock Sam returned to pick up our chow bowls. He asked about Schmidt's condition, if he were any better. Schmidt told him the pain was getting progressively worse and asked why the doctor wasn't here yet. Sam told him to be patient and that the doctor would soon be here. After Sam left, I did my best to comfort and to console Schmidt, but I could see that wasn't enough.

Steve E. Kiba

At seven o'clock Sam returned with drinking water for everyone. When he stopped at our cell, I begged him to hurry up and bring the doctor. He asked again how Schmidt was feeling, but Schmidt didn't answer; all he could do was hold his right side and groan. Sam left again, but he promised that the doctor was on the way. Just as he was leaving, Babyface opened our flap and looked in on us. Sam went out and had a brief conversation with Babyface. The warden showed up, too, and he had to peek in on us.

Shortly, Sam and Babyface returned with a female doctor, an interpreter, and several other people whom we'd never seen before. Sam took me to an empty cell down the hall, which happened to be between the officers' cells. I immediately tapped out messages on both walls to let the officers on our crew know what was going on. About fifteen minutes later, Sam came and took me back to my cell. Babyface was still there, and he was in the process of taking Schmidt's toothbrush and tin cup and removing Schmidt from the cell. Sam said they were taking him to the hospital.

While Schmidt was in the hospital, I was occasionally assigned to help the airmen in Dog Cell with clean-up duty. We swept the hall floor, cleaned the latrine, and worked slowly, which extended our visiting time with each other. When we were in the vicinity of occupied cells, we lingered long enough to exchange greetings with our fellow inmates, including the Chinese prisoners.

Of course I missed Schmidt's company, but it was with mixed feelings; I learned that I also liked my privacy, so in that sense Schmidt's absence was not a great burden. Being alone again gave me the opportunity to reflect on my situation, and through introspection discover new things about myself.

My uppermost thought was of the time I was losing. I was only twenty when I was captured and imprisoned, a stubborn youth with a hopeful determination to build a good life for myself. Since then I had experienced indescribable hardships and stress that had never entered my mind before as being humanly possible. I had passed my twenty-first birthday in captivity wondering if I were going to live or die. The happiness and promise of that right of passage was nullified and sullied by the brutality of my Red Chinese captors, and the hope

164

of future existence was offset by almost constant feelings of futility; when would it end? *How* would it end?

Yet, I was a changed person; I felt as if I had made a giant leap from frivolous youth to old age. Coincidentally, there emerged in my mind more mature thoughts, and I knew—*I felt*—the gist of my higher maturity was in new values that had grown up in the fallow fields of my youth. Those values, though good and appropriate, were flavored with the bitterness of captivity and cruel treatment. On one hand, I imagined myself back home living a happy life with my new-found values to guide me. On the other hand, I was forced to constantly face the ugly realities of my existence and deal with them from moment-to-moment. The vision I had from this introspection was crystal clear: my mature, idealistic values and behavior were no match for the brutal realities I had to face.

My realization that there is no correlation between maturity and survival allowed me to behave freely in whatever manner I deemed necessary to harass my enemies and escape death as long as possible. My captors did not understand freedom, human dignity, or compassion. Their minds were occupied with power through suppression, and human needs and qualities were only important to the extent that they promoted their goals. Therefore, my new-found maturity was vindicated by the facts, and I continued to harass the guards and houseboys with the infantile games and language that they reacted to the best. In other words, I found the right buttons to push, and I pushed them. It didn't matter to me that they were sometimes stupid and sometimes dirty; what mattered were results.

One thing I did was to write with chalk on the walls and door of our cell. I'd found the chalk when I helped sweep the hall and clean the latrine. I was severely reprimanded for "stealing" the chalk, and they pointed out that defacing property was strictly forbidden. They threatened me with severe punishment if I continued to do it.

The writing on the walls precipitated a reprisal by Sam, the houseboy. He came into the cell one day and verbally chastised me for writing on the cell door and walls, talking to other inmates, sassing the guards, swearing at the guards, writing on the walls of the latrine, and a whole series of other trivial matters, all of which were true. He reminded me that I had been warned repeatedly not to break prison rules and that I still insisted on misbehaving and not even trying to cooperate. At that particular moment, my nerves were particularly irritated and my patience was as thin and fragile as tissue paper. I felt myself losing control; I had an overwhelming urge to seize him by the throat and squeeze until his eyeballs popped out. However, I was able to keep my homicidal desires in check until he finished his verbal attack. Nevertheless, as he was leaving my cell, I picked up my blue tin cup and threw it toward the door. The cup missed Sam's head by about a foot and hit the cement wall to the right of the door facing. He rushed back in and started yelling like a crazy man; during his tirade, he slowed down enough to accuse me of trying to hit him. I told him that his accusation was ridiculous, that if I had been aiming at him I would certainly have hit him. My answer didn't produce a smooth disposition to his outburst. Instead, he continued to rave and spout profane and abusive language for several minutes, after which he picked up my crumpled tin cup and, still raging, left the cell.

We had another confrontation later that day when he brought water for my washbasin. I asked for my cup, and he exploded in anger again. He told me that I would not get another cup and that I was lucky to be getting the drinking water.

After he left, I put the washbasin on my bed board and waited for the boiled water to cool off. When it was cool enough to drink, I knelt down on the board and began lapping up the water like a dog. The guard peeked in at me, so I barked at him and growled like an angry dog. He dropped the flap and ran down the hall to fetch the houseboy. When Sam's face appeared at the flap, I lapped some more water, barked, and growled at him. This time I bared my teeth. He slammed the flap down and left.

As I hoped, it wasn't long before Babyface, the assistant warden, came and peeked in on me. I performed the same dog act for his benefit, and he reacted with epithets in Mandarin, which I took to be words of disgust. He, too, slammed the flap shut and left.

Of course I wasn't surprised when thirty minutes later the warden himself appeared at the flap. He looked in with a nasty scowl on his face. I'm sure he was very upset at being called away from his office to trek down the long hall and observe a crazy inmate who had suddenly begun indulging in dog-like behavior. He glared at me with his beady eyes for about five minutes before he finally dropped the flap. A few minutes passed, and he quickly opened the flap again.

He didn't catch me off guard. I was still in position on my hands and knees, so I immediately lapped up some more water and gave him a prolonged growl. He closed the flap quickly, and I heard Warden Ratface, Assistant Warden Babyface, and Houseboy Sam hold a short but animated conference just outside my cell. Then they all left.

I relaxed, leaned against the wall, and reveled in my successful campaign to agitate my tormentors. I had stirred up all levels, from the lowly guard to the high-powered warden, and none of them knew how to deal with it.

On the evening of August 12, 1954, Schmidt returned from the hospital. I had fun telling him about my harassing behavior during his absence, and its result. Then he told me about his experiences.

They had carried him by car to a hospital located somewhere in downtown Peking. When they arrived, they lifted him from the car, carried him inside, and placed him on a table. Almost immediately, they took him to an operating room where two Red Chinese flunkies strapped him to the operating table. The surgeon tried to make an incision, but the dull scalpel he was using failed to penetrate Schmidt's thick skin. He tried again, and this time he sliced open his belly. They gave him no anesthetic, and the pain was excruciating. Schmidt said that, even though he was strapped down, he dug his fingers into the sides of the operating table. He thought he would pass out from the extreme pain, but he never did.

Finally, after an eternity of pain, they successfully removed his appendix and sewed him up. A nurse wheeled him to a regular room and placed him in a nice, soft, comfortable bed. From that moment on, a guard stayed with him day and night.

Schmidt said that, compared to the garbage we were fed in prison, the food at the hospital was *haute cuisine.* Of course he also received a steady diet of propaganda material during his stay at what he called the "butcher shop." He admitted that the emergency surgery probably saved his life, but he was dogmatic in his belief that it could have been performed more professionally and with more compassion; a few aspirin would have been better than no anesthesia at all.

The next morning, while Schmidt and I were talking, I stood on my bed board to prop open the window. Walleye, the guard, a typical simpleton of that particular occupation, was watching us through the flap. Apparently he thought I was looking outside, which was strictly forbidden; so, he began the usual diatribe, in Mandarin, which we had come to expect from his ilk. His vituperation came out in a shrill, sing-song stream, a kind of noise that would grate on the most sedate person's nerves. I fought back by calling him a few obscene names and giving him the finger. This angered him; and, as usual, he ran for the houseboy, like a small child seeking consolation and help from his mother.

Sam rushed to our cell, berated me for my recalcitrant behavior, and ordered me to move my bed board from under the window. I refused to obey, so he moved it himself and then left.

When I heard the bolt slide on the door, I moved the board back under the window. Walleye, whose lack of brains was always quite obvious, peeped in again and saw what I had done. When he started screaming at me, I gave him the finger again and told him to go to hell.

He did what I expected: he went for Sam again. Sam came, chewed me out, moved the board, and left to do his normal duty of letting prisoners out of their cells to fetch their wash water from the water barrel. While he was thus engaged, I moved my board back under the window. Then, when he came to let Schmidt and me out to get our water, he moved it away from the outside wall again.

It was so silly, and oh so aggravating to them, that I could not help but pursue the "battle of wills" to its conclusion, whatever that might be. So, after I returned to the cell, brushed my teeth, and washed my face and hands, I put the board back in its original position under the window.

Sam came in to check on me again, found the board under the window, and tried to move it. I stood in his way and wouldn't let him. He started yelling, whether for help or out of frustration, I never knew. I suddenly had the urge to urinate, so I went to the honey bucket to do so. While I was there, Sam moved the board again. As soon as I finished, I moved it back under the window.

Sam was totally exasperated; and, although I was getting tired of the stupid game, I was determined to resist being pushed around. He clenched and unclenched his fists and rushed from the cell. Ten minutes later he returned and was followed by Babyface, the "little wheel." They ordered me to move the board, and I refused to do it. Then they threatened me with handcuffs.

I shrugged my shoulders, extended my arms, and said, "Go ahead. I don't care."

Sam removed a pair of shiny new cuffs from his back pocket and was about to clamp them on when Babyface stopped him and said something in Mandarin. Sam put the shiny cuffs back and pulled out a dirty, rusty pair of wrist clamps. The mere sight of that tortuous device brought back many painful memories.

I pulled my hands back and said, "Oh no you don't. You can put the cuffs on me, but not those rusty clamps."

They both grabbed me and tried to force the clamps on me, but I jerked free. I shoved them away and backed into a corner. They came after me and yelled for reinforcements while they chased me around the cell.

The guard heard their call for help, sounded the alarm, and then came rushing into our cell. Schmidt, who to this point had watched the episode with a big grin on his face, jumped from his board and, clutching his sore right side with his right hand, intercepted and grabbed the guard with his free hand. He managed to twist the guard's arm behind his back and force him against the wall, thus putting him out of action.

"Damn, Kiba," Schmidt said. "Look what you've gotten us into now."

About that time seven or eight more angry, gung-ho Redchink goons piled into our cell and headed for me.

"We're kind of outnumbered, Schmidt," I said.

Our fellow crew members in the other cells had heard the ruckus, and they were trying to get out of their cells to come to our assistance. It was useless, however, because the whole damned cellblock was saturated with armed guards and houseboys, and at least one was stationed at each flap and door of the "reactionary" Caucasians' cells.

I struggled for several minutes before Sam managed to get behind me, jump on my back, and clobber me with a hard judo chop to the base of my head. Other Redchinks grabbed me from all sides and forced me to the floor.

I kicked and yelled as loud as I could, and I kept repeating, "I'm from the 581ˢᵗ ARC Wing and we were brought to Red China by force. My name is Kiba!"

Babyface brought out a dirty rag and stuffed it into my mouth. I spit it out and continued to squirm, kick, and yell. I was seeing stars because they were kicking and hitting me and pounding my head against the concrete floor; the pain from several hard kicks to my sides and genitals made me nauseous. The friggin' Redchink bastards finally succeeded in forcing my arms behind my back and putting the dreadful rusty clamps on my wrists.

While they subdued me, Big Stupe, the gargantuan guard, came in. He grabbed Schmidt and the guard he was holding, one under each huge arm, and carried them both from the cell.

After the rusty clamps were locked securely around my wrists, Schmidt was returned to our cell and the attackers left.

"You okay, Schmidt?" I asked.

"Yeah, how about you?" He helped me off the floor and onto my board.

"Okay, I guess."

"How about your head? I thought the mangy bastards were going to crack the floor with it."

"It's okay," I said. "How's your side?"

"It hurts, but I was careful not to get it injured. Sorry I couldn't help you more. You knew you were fighting a losing battle, didn't you? And how'd that dirty rag taste?" He laughed after his last question.

"Tasted like hell," I said. "And yes, I knew the fight had to end sooner or later, and that I'd lose. But wasn't it grand to give these pricks a hard time, just for a while?"

Schmidt grinned. "Yeah, I guess so," he said.

When breakfast came, watery rice gruel was served. Schmidt asked Sam how I was going to eat with my hands behind my back, and Sam told him to feed me.

Schmidt said, "You'd better remove the clamps so he can eat. I'm not about to spoon feed him."

Sam just muttered some profanities, gave us a disgusting look, and left.

The rusty clamps forced and held my wrists, one against the other, in such a way that intense pressure was put on the muscles of my shoulders and upper arms. In just a few minutes after they were put on, my shoulders and arms began to ache, and the pain increased in intensity as time passed. I had worn the painful device for about an hour when Sam and Babyface returned. They removed the rusty clamps and placed a pair of ratchet-type manacles on me instead. By then my hands, arms, and shoulders were almost numb, and the pain was excruciating. Sam pointed to my uneaten half-bowl of cold rice gruel and said, "Chiva." (Eat.)

Whenever my jailers decided my behavior or attitude was "bad," they decreased my ration of swill. Needless to say, that occurred quite frequently, and it always made me even more defiant.

I looked at Sam, then at Babyface, and said, "Shove it up your bung!"

In a voice that betrayed his exasperation, Babyface said, "Maubee. Hundotta. Miyo bung!" (Swear word; swear word; Don't say ass!)

Sam picked up the bowl and carried it from the cell.

Shortly thereafter, we heard a commotion in the cellblock; from the sound, we determined it was Vaadi and Llewellyn being removed from the cellblock. A few minutes later our cell door was opened and Schmidt was moved out and taken to the cell vacated by Vaadi and Llewellyn.

After they removed Schmidt, I started talking to Benjamin and Thompson in Dog Cell and to Howard Brown in the cell on my right as I faced the hall. Either Sam heard me or the guard reported me, because Sam came to my window. He listened a few minutes, then opened the flap and glared at me. I think I was in a semi-delirious state induced by the beating, kicking, and clamps. I ignored Sam's presence at the flap and continued trying to talk to the other cells.

Sam said, "Walla walla bushing!" (Don't talk!)

I said, "To hell with you."

He came into my cell and closed both windows—the one on the outside wall and the one on the inside wall facing the hallway.

"I'll suffocate, you stupid knucklehead!" I shouted.

"Bushing!" Sam said.

"Okay, I'll lie down, then."

I unrolled my blanket and pad and lay down.

"Miyo sijo. Miyo, bushing," Sam said. (Don't sleep. No, don't.)

I ignore him and continued to lie on my board.

Sam screwed up his oriental face into a frowning gesture, one I took to indicate his indignation at my rebelliousness. He was so perplexed he said nothing more; he just turned, left my cell, and slammed the door behind him.

For the next several days I just lay on my board. The whole cell kept spinning and moving. I felt sick to my stomach, my ears rang almost constantly, and my head felt as though it would explode any minute. My whole body ached from the countless kicks and blows administered by my "lenient" captors during our brief but violent altercation. The most frightening aspects of my condition were blurred vision and diminished hearing. The only time I got off the board was for chow, drinking water, or to relieve myself. My portions of food were cut drastically; I now received barely a fourth of a bowl. That didn't bother me too much because I didn't feel like eating. When I did eat, I grew nauseated and came close to vomiting. The sadistic swine also cut my drinking water to one-third cup a day. I dreaded having to relieve myself because it hurt so very much; in that sense, the reduced water ration was a blessing.

The houseboys and guards tried to make me sit up, but I refused to. Occasionally, I staggered to the inside window, opened it, yelled brief messages to the others, and staggered back to my board. This caused an immediate reaction from Sam or the guard on duty; one or the other would rush into my cell and close the window almost before I could get back to my board. Usually they berated me and threatened to report me if I continued to misbehave and be disrespectful to them. I was really getting on their nerves.

In addition to the physical pain and discomfort I was suffering, I was engaged in a gigantic emotional and mental tug-of-war. I was deeply depressed and felt utterly wretched for giving the inhuman communist jailers an excuse to move Vaadi and Llewellyn out of the cellblock; I rightfully blamed myself for their being moved, as well as for Schmidt's and my solitary confinement. My solitary state didn't bother me. But Schmidt had not done much, so he really didn't deserve it. Why, then, did they put him in solitary rather than letting him share T/Sgt. Brown's cell? I also felt some guilt about what could have happened to Schmidt during the scuffle; he really was vulnerable to serious injury, and I had no right to expose him to that danger.

Then I thought that maybe the Red Chinese indoctrination instructors were right about my attitude. I knew it was downright foolish to taunt them, to push them beyond the limits of their patience and ability to cope; I always ended up on the losing side. They controlled my every move: how much and when I ate or drank, when I went to bed, when I got up, when I was allowed to relieve myself and empty my bowels. They had such power over me that they even controlled whether I lived or died.

I was still uncertain as to whether or not the American people and our Government knew about us. Even if they did know, what could they do? How could they get me home alive? Like it or not—and I damn well didn't like it—my fate was in the hands of ruthless, godless Red Chinese leaders and jailers. This was a fact I'd known all along, which periodically popped out into prominence among my thoughts and which I could not totally accept. When it was dominant in my thinking, I was inclined to start behaving "properly" and present them with the kind of attitude they sought—complete and humble subservience. Realistically, my survival probably depended on it. But could I do it?

A week later, Sam entered my cell and removed the manacles from my wrists. He smiled and said, "Walla walla bushing, how?" (Don't talk to the others, okay?)

"Give me something to do, and I'll behave," I said. I made gestures to show I wanted a pencil and a piece of paper.

He grabbed his head with both hands, emitted a noise that sounded like a coyote's wail, and said something that was undoubtedly meant to scorn me and my ancestors, then he left. His actions told me how incorrigible he thought I was, and I suspected he believed I was a hopeless case.

At eleven o'clock on the morning of September 8, 1954, Big Stupe escorted me to a room in the same building where I had signed the false statement many weeks before. On one side of the room, there was a desk. About 15 feet in front of the desk was a stool. The baby-faced interrogator I'd had back at the Hotel was seated behind the desk between Babyface (the assistant warden) on his left and Bluebeard (the interpreter) on his right. I was permitted to sit on the stool.

The interrogator began talking, and Bluebeard said in English, "We have been trying for quite some time to contact your parents through your government so they can write you. Your government has been most uncooperative. Now, we have finally reached an agreement whereby your government has consented to let your relatives correspond with you."

"Took you long enough," I said.

"We do not have diplomatic relations with your country. Therefore, we must act indirectly. We tried on many, many occasions to talk directly with your government, but your capitalist gangsters refused to meet with our country's representatives. Your reactionary government refuses to recognize our communist party and its glorious leaders as the official, legal governing body of our great nation. Consequently, the United States Government denies the sovereignty of the Glorious People's Republic of China. Too many of your government officials still cling to the myth that Chiang Kai-shek and his Kuomintang bandits are the legitimate representatives of the great Chinese people, and they continue to harbor dreams that he and his renegades will some day soon return victoriously to the mainland to reclaim that which they formerly controlled. That will never happen! On the contrary, we will one day take back possession of Taiwan which rightfully belongs to us. And as we have repeatedly informed you, the People's Republic of China will in the near future conquer and occupy the United States. Regarding the many American prisoners whom we have detained, it seemed to us that your rich government officials didn't really care whether or not they received correspondence from their relatives. We were left with the impression that they do not care if you and your comrades are ever repatriated. Thanks to the persistence of our most considerate representatives, we have some letters here for you. When you go back to your cell, you may read them. Do not tear them up or try to burn them. Do you understand?"

"Burn them! With what?" I asked. We were not allowed to have matches or any device that would start a fire; I couldn't pass the opportunity to be sarcastic.

He ignored the question and said, "Within a few days we will give you paper and let you write home. Here are your letters."

I got up from the stool, and the interpreter handed me some letters. I extended my trembling hand, took them, and clutched them tightly to my breast.

"Thank you," I said.

"You may go back to your cell now. You see, we Chinese are not as bad as you think we are."

As Big Stupe escorted me back to my cell, I counted the letters and read the return addresses. I continued to fumble with them, and I kept repeating, "I can't believe it, I can't believe it."

Once in my cell, I sat down and held the letters in my hand and stared at them.

"I still can't believe it," I said.

I couldn't decide which one to read first, so I shuffled them. I finally came up with a letter from my parents. I set all the others aside and tried to open the envelope neatly, but my shaking hands prevented me from doing a very good job. I finally grew impatient and ripped it open, pulled out the letter, and quickly read it.

The letter was brief and wasn't very newsy. The handwriting was unrecognizable, so I immediately became suspicious. The thought flashed through my mind that the tricky Red Chinese interrogators and indoctrination instructors might be playing a cruel joke on me.

I set the letter from my parents aside and chose an envelope with the return address of one of my sisters. I tore it open nervously and read the letter inside. It, too, was disappointing in its content, and I thought, "Why don't they say something more? What's going on in their lives? Why don't they write something besides these bland generalities?"

175

When I picked up the third letter, I noticed that it had already been opened. I checked the others. They, too, had been slit open—and undoubtedly read—by the Red Chinese. I realized then that despite the braggadocio of our captors about their great concern for us to have contact with our families, there were limitations to that contact. Surely they had been told by both American and Red Chinese officials what they could and could not write in their letters. I made myself calm down and spent the rest of the morning reading.

Before we finished our letters, the houseboy came with our midday meal. He doled out the swill, then told us to lay aside our mail and eat quickly. It was an unnecessary order because we were anxious to swallow the unappetizing stuff as soon as possible and get back to our mail.

I picked up another letter and carefully studied the envelope. I saw stamped on it, "Care of the People's Committee for World Peace." What a joke!

After I read the last letter, I stacked them up and read them again, from the first to the last.

"Finally, mail from home," I thought. "That means that they know about us. They know we're alive." That knowledge was the biggest morale booster we'd had in a long time.

We were in contact with Vaadi and Llewellyn, the two officers who had been moved back to Carnegie Hall immediately after my fracas with the guards and houseboys. We sent messages by hacking code and by writing on the underside of their honey bucket lid; when Thompson and Benjamin washed our honey buckets, they also had to wash the one from Vaadi's cell. So, by the medium of the honey bucket lid, Benjamin and Thompson conveyed messages between all of us in the various cells in both cellblocks. We called this method the "honey bucket express."

We learned that Vaadi and Llewellyn had also received mail and that they were okay. All of us were elated about getting letters from home, and we shared an optimistic belief that we would be going home very soon.

The following day the houseboy gave us paper, envelopes, a staff pen, and ink. The Red Chinese prison officials were anxious for us to write home. They wanted to tell the outside world how well we were being treated; they wanted us to confess our guilt—that we had committed a grave crime against the People's Republic of China and the peace-loving Chinese people.

I took the writing material, sat down on my board, and began to write. It was extremely difficult for me to compose a letter, because I knew that what I wanted to say and what *needed* to be said would be censored. Also, I refused to write what the political instructors wanted me to write—lies, lies, nothing but lies.

When I finished my letter, I folded it neatly, put it in an envelope, and started to address it. "Care of the Chinese People's Committee for World Peace," I said out loud, with sarcasm. I had a sudden thought to spell it "Piece" instead of "Peace" —just to be tacky—but an eagerness to get my message out of that God-forsaken, friggin' hellhole prison I was in caused me to abandon that idea quickly. I would have ample opportunity later to spell it the way it should be spelled: Piece.

The first of October is Red China's Independence Day, and we learned that on all holidays the prison officials doubled the guard throughout the entire establishment. About two o'clock in the afternoon of the first, Benjamin pounded on my wall to attract my attention. When I responded, he told me to look out the outside window. I did so and saw the guard, whom we had named Shortcrotch, parading back and forth outside our cellblock. Just as he passed beneath Benjamin's cell window, either Benjamin or Thompson hit the bars and let out an ear-piercing scream. Shortcrotch jumped back several feet, threw his rifle into the air, and took off around the corner of the building. All of us burst out laughing.

A few minutes later Shortcrotch peeped around the corner. I think he was checking to see if his superiors—or any other guards—had observed his act of cowardice. When he saw that no one was around, he walked quickly to his rifle and picked it up. He looked up at Benjamin's window, where both Benjamin and Thompson were still staring out and laughing, and cursed them out.

The next day Shortcrotch was on duty inside our cellblock. Every time he looked into Dog Cell, he gave Benjamin and Thompson a dirty, irate look. When he looked into my cell, I mimicked his

177

cowardly act, pointed at him, and laughed. On a practical level, such bedevilment was a great stress-reliever for us, even entertaining; but it did not endear us to the guards. We didn't care.

During that same time, we had a guard who understood and could speak English fairly well; we nicknamed him Squinty. I often chatted with him when he was on duty. He told me that he learned his English from an American GI during World War II. He said he was not a communist and that he would like to go to America. I asked him about the communist "volunteers" —those Red Chinese who had voluntarily accepted the communist doctrine and who had gone to Korea to battle the Yankee Imperialists—and he said that in Red China nobody is a "volunteer." Everyone did what the communist leaders required of them, or they were imprisoned or annihilated. Sometimes he talked about his personal life, especially about his girlfriend. He was good about letting us talk to each other from cell to cell, and he would warn us when other guards or houseboys entered the cellblock.

PART VIII

THE BIG FARCE

Steve E. Kiba

In early October the weather in Peking grew quite cold. In the past, we had received our winter garments by this time, but for some reason we had not received ours yet. The Chinese prisoners had already gotten their winter clothing, so we took the positive attitude that ours had not been issued because we would soon be going home. However, after we endured some very cold days in summer clothing, the houseboys brought each of us a blue padded jacket, but no winter pants.

On Saturday, October 9, 1954, we asked for material to write letters to our loved ones at home. They denied our request. However, on that same morning, Sam and a character we slangily called "Morphodite" measured each of us for a new set of clothes. We were very encouraged by that act; it reinforced our belief that we would soon be leaving that dreadful hellhole. Later in the afternoon we received a new set of winter blacks, and our letters from home were taken away from us.

Our optimism was overflowing. There could be no mistake; we were really going home. We expected to leave any second, and every little noise from the hall intensified our expectations of leaving.

At boardtime we lay down in a very keyed-up state. Most of us anxiously waited for our cell doors to open, and we thought of all the things we'd do once we got home. Those not in solitary whispered to their cellmates about home, home, HOME! Every strange footfall jarred us and intensified our impatience. It was an exceedingly long and restless night for our entire crew. But no doors opened. The next morning we found ourselves still in prison, not on a train homeward bound.

Of course we were disappointed. Nevertheless, we kept hope in our hearts; we still expected to leave soon. All through the day we anticipated leaving our cells and boarding a train. We waited and waited and waited; the time dragged by, and every minute was like an eternity; but still we remained imprisoned, and our wished-for train ride became only a fantasy.

At four o'clock we were given chow. That was an unusually early time for supper, so we were puzzled. We factored in the early meal with the other changes and came up with a reinforced conclusion that we would be leaving before the regular supper hour. We gobbled our food hastily. My haste, plus my nervous excitement, caused me to bite the insides of my cheeks so hard they bled. I was really going home, so it didn't matter.

Thirty minutes after we were fed, officers John Buck and Wallace Brown were taken from the cellblock. This was done under the close scrutiny of a host of houseboys who were stationed at each of our window flaps in order to prevent us from communicating with our fellow crew members as they passed by. Buck and Brown were only gone about five minutes. Two houseboys brought them back and then took other crew members out one at a time. They took Schmidt and shortly brought him back, and then they took Howard Brown. When Howard came back, it was my turn.

Two houseboys took me to the interrogation room, and I saw an unfamiliar face seated behind the desk.

"What is your name?" he asked.

"Kiba," I said.

He handed me a sheet of paper and said, "Read this."

I quickly scanned the paper. It stated that all of us had violated their territorial air space and that we were to be tried before a people's tribunal and punished according to the laws of the People's Republic of China.

I was bewildered. "What's this?" I asked.

He pointed to a spot on the paper and said, "Sign here."

"Why?" I asked; I was totally stunned by the order.

"To show that you received your indictment."

I signed and two houseboys escorted me back to my cell. I was dejected and perplexed when I sat down on my hard bed board, and I struggled to get matters clear in my befuddled mind.

I had built up my hopes of going home so high that when I read the indictment I didn't grasp its full meaning or its ramifications. When I got back to my cell, I read it over and over again. I just couldn't force myself to accept the reality that we would not be freed; instead we would be tried as war criminals.

While I tried to deal with what was clearly a repudiation of our hoped-for release, the houseboys took the rest of the crew in succession to the same place, broke the bad news to them, and had them sign for their "indictments."

They allowed a little time for the shock of their plans for us to subside; then they came for us, one at time, to let us see our "Defense Attorney." The one I saw was a short, gruff-looking character with large round-lensed glasses propped on his wide nose.

"What is your name?" He asked, staring down at me through the plain-looking glasses.

"Kiba," I said.

"I am your defense counsel. I'm also a Professor of Law at Peking University." His introduction was filled with arrogance.

"Really?" I said sarcastically.

"Yes, and you have only one alternative; you must confess your crimes."

"What crimes?" I was belligerent because I was pissed off as hell at such a preposterous suggestion. "I haven't committed any crimes."

He ignored my anger and said, "I have reviewed your case. I am convinced that you have committed the charges brought against you. The best thing for you to do is to confess and express your regret. The People's Republic of China has a lenient policy toward those who confess their horrendous crimes and demonstrate that they are sincerely sorry. Have you anything to say?"

"What is the punishment for the *alleged* crimes?"

"I do not know," he said. "It could be severe or light, depending on the culprit's attitude. Since you are so young and since you evidently were led astray by your superior officers, the Chinese people will be lenient; but only if you publicly confess your guilt and show true repentance. Anything else?"

"No," I said.

I'd had enough experience with my captors to know it was useless to argue or to contradict them in any way. When my "erudite," so-called "Defense Attorney" sent me back to my cell, I walked dejectedly; I felt as helpless as I'd ever felt since being imprisoned.

At six o'clock the houseboys again took us from our respective cells in the same order they had taken us to receive our indictments. We were all led out of the cellblock and to the building where we were "indicted." They stopped us in the hall there and placed manacles on each of us; then they led us farther down the long hallway to a large courtyard where a bus was waiting. There were 18 heavily armed guards at the bus. The houseboys herded us onto the bus and made us sit down in the aisle so we couldn't be seen from the outside by passers-by. Neither could we see out. The guards and the houseboys sat in the seats.

The driver drove the bus slowly out of the prison compound. The road which he took, a route to downtown Peking, we surmised, was relatively smooth. However, our uncomfortable position on the hard floor made it an unpleasant, sometimes painful, ride. When we tried to shift positions to alleviate our discomfort or to see outside, the brusque guards forced our heads back down roughly and without regard for the collateral pain they caused.

About an hour later, we arrived at our destination: the courthouse, a large nondescript stone building somewhere in the center of the city. The driver parked his bus in front of the main entrance. Our ten armed guards took me and the other four airmen off the bus and escorted us through a huge mob that had gathered in front of the building. We entered the building and wove our way through the crowded main lobby; then our rough, ill-tempered, unsympathetic guards pushed and shoved us down a long hall on the right side of the lobby and put us into a large room.

Then the eight goons assigned to our four officers brought them into the courthouse, through the crowded main lobby, pushed them down a long hall on the left side of the lobby, and put them into another large room.

Major Baumer and Colonel Arnold, both of whom had been kept apart from the rest of us during our captivity, were brought to the courthouse in separate jeep-like vehicles. They put Colonel Arnold into a room by himself on the second floor; Major Baumer was kept alone in another room on the second floor.

We sat in our separate rooms and waited and waited and waited; eternity will seem shorter to us, I'm sure, than that time in our lives. Finally, the eight guards assigned to our four officers marched them back through the noisy, crowded main lobby and up a long flight of steps on the left side. They were stopped just short of the top and made to wait. Then the ten guards assigned to the five of us marched us back through the clamorous multitude in the main lobby and up the stairs on the right side of the lobby, across from our four officers.

We, too, were stopped near the top and made to stand and wait. We stood there for about fifteen minutes; then they took all of us, officers and airmen, to a large hall at the top of the stairways. We all had long faces; our countenances were haggard and etched with misery. I looked over and saw Wally Brown. He tried to console me with a "thumbs up" gesture, but I saw in his face that he, too, was apprehensive. We all were. Any observant onlooker would have concluded that we were exhausted, dejected, and bewildered.

We sat along the side railings and waited for another ten minutes; although, it seemed like ten hours. When we heard someone coming toward us from down the hall, we all looked up simultaneously and saw Colonel Arnold. He walked proudly, and with dignity; his head was held high, and his shoulders were thrown back. They were taking him directly into the courtroom; but, as he passed by, he looked at the officers, then at us, and gave all of us a big smile. He was extremely emaciated; his face was drawn and sallow, his hands wrinkled and bony. His hair was not shaven like ours, and I surmised it was probably because he wouldn't let them. Evidence of his extreme, harsh physical abuse was readily apparent; his face and eyes revealed many months of mental anguish and emotional stress imposed upon him by our "lenient" captors.

Several minutes after they took Colonel Arnold into the courtroom, two guards escorted Major Baumer in. He was using crutches, but otherwise he didn't look too bad.

The cadre in charge ordered the other four officers to stand. He lined them up according to their position on the aircraft. Then we airmen were ordered to stand and line up behind the officers. With an armed guard at each elbow, the B-29 crew filed into the courtroom. We were stopped in front of the judges' bench, which was elevated. Facing the bench and proceeding from left to right, we were in this order: Colonel John Arnold, Major William Baumer, Captain Eugene Vaadi, 2nd Lieutenant Wallace Brown, Captain Elmer Llewellyn, 1st Lieutenant John Buck, T/Sgt. Howard Brown, A/1C Steve Kiba, A/2C Daniel Schmidt, A/2C Harry Benjamin, and A/2C John Thompson.

Directly in front of us were three sinister-looking Redchinks seated behind their elevated bench. The one in the center was the head judge, and the other two were his assistants. To the judges' right and on our level, there was a large table behind which our four "defense" attorneys were seated.   One was "defending" Colonel Arnold and Major Baumer; one was assigned to Captain Vaadi, 2nd Lieutenant Wallace Brown, and Captain Elmer Llewellyn; the third one was for 1st Lieutenant John Buck, T/Sgt. Howard Brown, and me; the last one handled the "defense" for A/2C Schmidt, A/2C Benjamin, and A/2C Thompson. To the left of the judges and on our level, there was another long table where the prosecuting attorney (Bugeyes, we called him) was seated. Also seated at that table were an interpreter, a recorder (court reporter), and several other Red Chinese officials.

Our armed guards stood directly behind us. Still further behind us were a vast number of public seats, and they were all filled. Other people stood in the back, and some were even seated in the aisles on the floor. The courtroom was huge, and I estimated that there were between five and six hundred spectators there to watch the "kangaroo" court proceedings.

Large lights glared at us from all sides of the auditorium-like courtroom and from behind the judges' bench. Cameramen were running back and forth on the floor. Directly in front of us, several huge lights zeroed in on our faces. To the judges' left and at an angle from the prosecutor's table, there was a door; just beyond the open door we could see all types of radio and recording equipment. Next to the door we had entered there was a table covered with equipment and gear that had been taken from our crew and from our aircraft. There were numerous pieces of survival gear, a URC-4 emergency radio set, our .45 caliber automatic pistols, parachutes, dinghies, Mae West flotation gear, crash axes, and other paraphernalia. All of the items on display were standard equipment and materials used by all flight crews, even those flying in non-combat zones. When we saw the trouble they'd gone to and the "evidence" that they were going to present, we knew that their great big FARCE was about to begin.

The court was called to order, and the head judge rattled off something in Mandarin. The interpreter translated: "The prosecutor will now present his case to the People's Tribunal against these brazen, foreign interlopers."

Bugeyes, the prosecutor, spoke loudly and with animation, and the interpreter translated: "The following airmen: Colonel John Arnold,

Major William Baumer, Captain Eugene Vaadi, 2nd Lieutenant Wallace Brown, Captain Elmer Llewellyn, 1st Lieutenant Paul Van Voorhis, 2nd Lieutenant Henry Weese, 1st Lieutenant John Buck, Technical Sergeant Howard Brown, Airman First Class Steve Kiba, Airman Second Class Daniel Schmidt, Airman First Class Alvin Hart, Airman Second Class Harry Benjamin, and Airman Second Class John Thompson brazenly and daringly violated the territorial air space of the People's Republic of China. Our brave, courageous fighter pilots and our valiant anti-aircraft gunners gallantly and heroically attacked and shot down their B-29 Superfortress. These ruthless airmen were apprehended by our glorious ground troops. Two were apprehended the very same night we shot them down, captured as they touched the ground. The remainder of their crew was captured throughout the next day. Three of them, 1st Lieutenant Paul Van Voorhis, 2nd Lieutenant Henry Weese, and Airman First Class Alvin Hart, were killed in their insolent endeavor to violate our border to gather information. All of these arrogant, shameless foreign devils standing before you have confessed their heinous, horrendous crimes against the peace-loving Chinese people and our Glorious People's Republic. We have documents here signed by Colonel Arnold and Major Baumer, and the rest of the crew, confessing that they had knowingly and willfully violated our territorial air space in order to carry out espionage activities."

Colonel Arnold shouted, "I did not!"

Each crew member was called to step up to a microphone and was asked to state his full name, age, rank, serial number, home state, and previous occupation. Then we were told to step back in line.

Bugeyes called us five enlisted men back to the microphone and asked if we regretted having participated in such a shameless crime against the People's Republic of China and the peace-loving Chinese people. All of us stood in silence and refused to admit guilt to any charges, nor would we say we were "sorry." Finally, Benjamin and Schmidt broke the silence and stated unequivocally that we did not violate the territorial air space of Red China unless North Korea was a part of Red China.

The prosecutor chided us for our lack of cooperation. He told the judges and the audience that we remained silent and were hesitant to express our true feelings and convictions because we were afraid of our superior officers, especially Colonel Arnold. He said that we were young, that we had been misled by the Imperialistic Warmongers, and that we were not fully to blame for our actions. He asked the judges to treat us more leniently and with more consideration because we had allegedly confessed our crimes; he reminded them of the People's Republic's "lenient" policy. He concluded his remarks, and our guards shoved us back into line.

Bugeyes then called the four officers of our crew to step forward to the mike, and they went through the same irrational nonsense.

The head judge spent more than an hour telling us how bad we were, how generously we had been treated, and how lenient the Red Chinese were. The guards escorted us five airmen back to the large room on the first floor and the four officers to theirs. We sat and waited in our rooms, and the minutes dragged by oh so slowly. At that moment, things looked hopeless for us.

While we sat in our rooms on the first floor and waited, Colonel Arnold and Major Baumer were catching hell in the courtroom on the second floor. They were abused and excoriated for nearly and hour, and then they removed Major Baumer from the courtroom. This left Colonel Arnold alone to face whatever torment the Redchink pricks wanted to inflict.

We later learned that he really "caught hell." He was reprimanded for speaking up in front of the "other criminals." The judges blamed him for our refusal to follow their script and admit our guilt publicly, for our failure to apologize and express our regret, for our failure to show our "repentance," and for our refusal to "beg for mercy." They threatened him with all sorts of punishments.

At ten o'clock that night Major Baumer, the other officers, and we (five airmen) were returned to the courtroom. The four "defense attorneys" were given time to plead for their clients, and the "Kangaroo Court" continued. The "defense attorney" for Colonel Arnold and Major Baumer said that it was evident that his "clients" had committed grave and serious crimes against the great People's Republic of China and that "they must be punished." He pleaded for leniency. The head judge said that the "defendants" must be and would be punished and that Colonel Arnold, as the "ringleader," must receive the harshest punishment.

Next, the "defense attorney" for the Aircraft Commander (Captain Vaadi), the Pilot (2nd Lieutenant Brown), and the Navigator (Captain Llewellyn) "admitted" that his clients had also committed grave crimes. He hastened to add that they were only carrying out the orders of Colonel Arnold and the Imperialistic money grabbers. He, too, begged for leniency for his clients.

Then the "defense attorney" for the Bombardier (1st Lieutenant Buck), the Flight Engineer (Technical Sergeant Brown), and the Radio Operator (A/1C Kiba) and the "defense attorney" for the Scanners (A/2C Schmidt, A/2C Benjamin, and A/2C Thompson) forced us to endure the same travesty of justice as all the others endured. Both declared that the airmen (enlisted men) were young and naïve and deserved another chance. They said because of our youth we had been swayed and misled by the Capitalistic-Imperialistic Warmongers of Wall Street and that we were merely "cannon fodder" for the Capitalist System. They both pleaded for leniency on our behalf.

In his summation, the head judge reiterated that all of us should be punished but that the airmen would be dealt with less severely because they were so young and impressionable. He said that Colonel Arnold, Major Baumer, and Captain Vaadi were the ones who should bear the heaviest punishment because command responsibility rendered their crimes more heinous. He emphasized the conclusion that the airmen and the other officers were simply carrying out their orders and that Colonel Arnold was the "main culprit." "Colonel Arnold," he said, "was directly fulfilling the desires and commands of his Capitalistic-Imperialistic Warlords by relegating the 'dirty tasks' to junior officers and lowly enlisted personnel." He concluded his summation by saying that the matter was of such a serious nature that he and his colleagues would have to engage in many long and profound deliberations before a "just" sentence could be pronounced.

Our guards escorted us from the courtroom and back to our respective rooms in the courthouse where we waited until nearly midnight. Then they led us from the building and to the vehicles in which we had come.

The ride back to the Spider Web was especially long because we were weary and heavy-hearted. So was the routine walk back to our dreary cells in our individual cellblocks. Needless to say, when we were again locked up, we collapsed on our hard bed boards in a state of total exhaustion and devastation. I thought, just before I fell asleep, about the lengths to which the vile communists went to make us miserable. When they took our mail from us, we should have known that they had a sinister surprise in store for us. The future looked mighty bleak for us, and I knew that everyone's morale was at the same level as mine: rock-bottom. The hopes we had of ever getting out of that living hell were in the process of being changed to the despair of the damned.

During the next several days, we discussed the "kangaroo" trial they had publicly given us and speculated on what our punishment would be and when the sentence would be pronounced. We already knew for certain what the verdict would be: guilty!

Colonel Arnold's emaciated appearance both shocked and infuriated us. The Redchink interrogators had broken his body but not his mind and spirit. In this and other periods of utter despair, his steadfast spirit and firm determination inspired us to "hang in there."

His behavior and attitude reminded us of who we were and what the whole rotten business was about. I personally admired him and was exceedingly proud to be associated with such a remarkable man. I sincerely regretted not being able to relieve him of some of the horrible agony that would be inflicted upon him for his unsolicited outburst in the courtroom.

Six long, dreary days after the so-called trial, Big Stupe escorted me to the front office for another tedious "bull session."

As soon as I got there, the interpreter said, "Sit down, please, and tell us what you have been thinking while you wait for the decision of the judges."

I sat down on the stool and said, "The same as usual." I really wanted to scream out my feelings of total injustice, to describe the pain and hardship I'd suffered, and to cry out against their cruelty and barbaric natures; but I knew it was no use; they were devils, and you can't reason with devils.

My Red Chinese inquisitor looked at me with his dark, beady eyes and a smirk on his face. He uttered some Mandarin gibberish, and the interpreter said, "It would help if you changed your attitude toward the peace-loving Chinese people. We know that you do not like us. You show very little respect for us, and you refuse to acknowledge that you are our prisoner and are at our mercy. Your country is our enemy. Yet, we know you are not to be blamed fully for your false beliefs, so we try to re-educate you and get you to see the truth. The sooner you realize this, the easier everything will be for you. What do you think of our justice?"

I contorted my face in a sneer and said, "There *is no justice* in Red China!"

The inquisitor was unperturbed. He said, "You insist on keeping a hostile attitude toward the great peace-loving Chinese people. You are young, and in time you will come to realize your mistake and learn to appreciate our generous and lenient policy toward our prisoners. Soon you will discern this, and then you will change your bitter attitude. Is there anything I can do to make things more comfortable for you in your cell?"

"That's a stupid question! Of course there are many, many things."

"Tell me and I will see what I can do."

I was disgusted with the familiar, baiting kind of questioning. I said, "I've told you many times already, but you never listen. My miserable conditions have never improved. Despite what I've told you, nothing ever changes."

"Now that you've been tried, we may be able to make things easier for you."

"Okay," I said. "I'll play your game. I want to be put with the rest of the crew. I want some bacon and eggs, milk, candy, and fruit. I want to be able to receive food and other articles from home, and I want to go outdoors more often."

"Anything else?"

"Yes! I want to go home!"

"Why to you wish to go home?"

"I want to be free."

"Do you have a special girl friend at home?"

"No. What's that got to do with conditions here?"

The inquisitor paused for a moment and looked away from me. I assumed he was losing the cold patience with which he conducted his questioning. When he looked back at me, he said, "Would you like to see your folks?"

The simplicity of his questions and his tenaciousness in asking them exasperated me. I wanted to reach up and choke the life out of him for asking so many questions, the answers to which were obvious—even to an ignorant fool. Nevertheless, I reached down deep inside and drew on my dwindling reserve of patience in order to give a reasonably calm response.

"Of course," I said.

"Are you homesick?"

"No, not really."

"Then why are you so anxious to go home?"

"It's not that I'm so anxious to go home; it's that I'm damned anxious to leave Red China."

He sighed and said, "It is too bad that you refuse to play ball with us. You possess all the right qualities to become a good communist. You are intelligent and very persistent. You are still young enough to be trained and molded into a top ranking cadre. With us you have a future, a very bright future. On the other hand, in your country your opportunities are limited. Your parents are indigent immigrants with many children, and they do not possess the means to send you to a quality university like the University of Peking. If our intelligence is accurate, they do not have resources to send you to any institution of higher learning. And, does your government care about your well-being now or about your future if you ever return to the United States? I will answer for you: the answer is an emphatic NO! If they really cared, they would come to terms with us so that you might be repatriated. Believe me, Kiba, your government is not concerned about your well-being. We call you and the rest of the so-called prisoners-of-war that we are holding just what you are: war criminals; and, to your own government, you are expendable.

"Accept the facts, Kiba. The truth is that they do not care if you are ever released. You must face the reality that your government does not want their prisoners-of-war to return. Are they living up to their commitment to you? No, of course not. Do they care about you? Does *anyone* care about you? No! Even your God has forsaken you.

"So, why remain loyal to a country that does not care about their fighting men who are unfortunate enough to fall into enemy hands and become captives? Why remain loyal to a government that knowingly abandons fellow countrymen? As I have said to you many times before and as my fellow political commissars have also told you, we are truly concerned about your well-being and future. Please, for your own good, seriously consider the fabulous opportunities that we are offering you. Remember that the wave of the future is communism. Do not allow ardent patriotism to blind you and cause you to lose forever a better way of life. I entreat you to join us in our battle to free the whole world from the shackles of decadent Imperialism-Capitalism. I am your friend, and I am sincerely concerned about your future. Your government cannot help you; your fellow countrymen and your family cannot help you; even your religion and your God cannot help you.

"But *we* can! We control your present life and your future. We control your very life. As you ponder your deplorable predicament, keep in mind all of what I've told you."

I said, "I will carefully weigh what you've said and give it my most thoughtful consideration. Yet, I do have a major problem."

"What is that?" he asked.

"I hate communists!"

The political inquisitor came halfway out of his seat, suddenly realized his loss of control, and sat back down. There was an awful frown on his face that very clearly showed his rage. When he spoke again, it was in a high-pitched, sing-song voice, and his delivery sounded more like a wail to me.

The interpreter relayed his message: "Your mind has been thoroughly poisoned by the Capitalists!"

"Don't you jokers ever change your lines?" I said. "If you've said that once, you've said it a thousand times. And it's still as false as when you first said it."

"You are a wiseass! You think you are smart, do you not?"

"You said I was, didn't you? I won't refute it."

The inquisitor's gritting teeth were visible in the undulations of his jaw muscles. He finally lost control over his emotions and said with pompous authority, "Enough! You go back and think and read and study. Soon you will see we are right. Some day you will see things our way."

While Big Stupe was escorting me back to my cell, I was discouraged. Yet, there was a calmness about me I couldn't explain. By the time I reached my cell, I had reached the conclusion that my political brainwashing session had the opposite effect they meant it to have: all they accomplished was to arouse my fighting spirit to a new level; I made up my mind to resist them to the very end, whatever that might be.

During the lull between our trial and the announcement of the verdicts, our prison life became routine again. We looked to those mundane daily occurrences which, although not always dramatic or terribly funny, nevertheless gave us momentary breaks in the terrible monotony. In late October 1954, Technical Sergeant Brown had problems with his eyes. He was visited by a little nurse; her nose was running, and she wasn't wearing a mask. She instructed Brown to lie on his back on his bed board. Then she bent over him and put drops in his eyes. After she left, Brown told us he thought that perhaps he had received a mixture of drops—some from the dropper and some from her runny nose.

Time passed very slowly to early November 1954. The weather was very cold in Peking, and all of the proceedings involving us had faded away. Nothing had been mentioned about the Americans—or our B-29 crew in particular—on the public address system for over two weeks. Then on the seventh, talk about us suddenly resumed. The PA system blasted away all day and half of the night, and for about two weeks our B-29 crew was the main source of talk that was aired via the system.

With the little bit of Chinese language we had learned during our long months of imprisonment, we were able to figure out that our crew and our alleged "border violation" were the topics of discussion for over 450 million Red Chinese men, women, and children. We also learned that "secret" talks were going on regarding our fate. What we finally gleaned from the way we were treated and from all that we heard was that we were the "pawns" in a gigantic international chess match between the United Nations and Red China.

We tried hard to find out more about our status. We pumped any guard or houseboy who was willing to take the risk of fraternizing with us to give us any tidbit of information they had. From some of the more friendly and sympathetic guards we learned that our October trial proceedings were broadcasted throughout Red China and most of the other communist countries. Those friendlier guards told us that public opinion was running strongly against us and that the masses believed we really did intentionally fly into their country; most believe that we were guilty of committing horrendous war crimes against the peace-loving Chinese people and that we should be—and probably would be—severely punished.

On Wednesday, November 17, 1954, Schmidt, Howard Brown, and I were moved into the third cell on the left from the hub (circle). Llewellyn and Vaadi were brought back from Carnegie Hall. Now, all nine of us were back in Skid Row.

Getting Vaadi and Llewellyn back in the same cellblock with the rest of us gave us a boost in our morale. They briefed us concerning their condition and activities during their absence. Vaadi told us that Llewellyn had angered the houseboy call Smokey over certain exercises he was doing. They exchanged verbal abuses. Smokey called for assistance, and shortly numerous houseboys and guards, including Big Stupe, appeared. Big Stupe seized Llewellyn, grabbed both ears, and twisted them violently in an attempt to rip them from his head. Needless to say, Big Stupe and the rest of his goon squad roughed Llewellyn up and quickly subdued him. They bound his wrists with a pair of ratchet-type handcuffs, but the cuffs didn't stop him from doing his exercises. His wrists swelled up so bad that the houseboys had to loosen them on several occasions.

On the afternoon of November 23, 1954, six houseboys took the nine of us from our cells and put manacles on our wrists. They then escorted us to a bus that was parked just inside the prison gate. As before, there were eighteen heavily armed guards—two for each of us—waiting by the bus. When we boarded the bus, they let us sit on seats and look out the windows. On the way to our destination: the courthouse, we saw the famous Tien An Mien Square.

As before, the bus driver pulled up and parked in front of the same "nondescript" stone building: the courthouse where our "show-case" trial had been conducted. Our eighteen heavily armed guards escorted the nine of us from the bus into the building, through the crowded main lobby, down the familiar long hallway, and into one of the large waiting rooms. The nine of us sat on the wooden floor and whispered among ourselves, and the gung-ho guards tried—in vain—to keep us quiet.

After a thirty minute wait, the cadre in charge came to the door and said something to the guards. The guards ordered us to our feet and escorted us upstairs to the courtroom; they lined us up in the same order as they had us during the "trial." Colonel Arnold and Major Baumer were already there. A "judge" called the court to order.

The first speaker was Bugeyes, the prosecutor. He spewed out a lengthy verbal barrage directed against United States policy, its leadership, and our crew in particular. Then he re-read the trumped-up charges against us.

The head "judge" followed with a vitriolic and vituperative speech that vilified America. Then he began a long and boring presentation that glorified communism before he pronounced sentence on the "hardened American war criminals." He finally read off the

196

sentences; they ranged from four years imprisonment for each of us airmen, the "cannon fodder," to 10 years imprisonment for Colonel Arnold, the "main culprit."

When the gloating "judge" of the "kangaroo court" finished reading our "sentences," our guards took us back downstairs to a waiting room. They took Colonel Arnold, "the main culprit," and Major Baumer to separate waiting rooms on the second floor. Again, we sat on a wooden floor and waited; we were indeed a morose group: heavy-hearted, somber, and downright depressed. I grew weary of just sitting and waiting, so I began doing sit-ups. For some reason this upset the guards. Several of them almost simultaneously ordered me to stop, but I ignored them. Feigning concern that I might injure myself because of the manacles I was wearing, they repeated their command. I told them to go bug themselves, and my talking upset them, too. I ignored them and continued to exercise.

Thirty minutes later they finally took us to the bus outside. We rode back to our dingy, dismal prison in silence, with each one lost in his thoughts and in considering the devastating pronouncements we had just heard. Everyone felt totally crushed by the injustice of it.

As we walked back to our cells, Schmidt said, "Four years! Four friggin' years! I wouldn't mind if I were guilty of—of *something* to justify it. But hell, we ain't done *nothing* to deserve it."

Howard Brown said, "I didn't expect more than six months, and I expected that to be suspended."

"I'd rather be in hell than in Red China," I said, in a moment of deep dejection.

"What's the difference, Kiba?" Howard asked.

Schmidt and I answered almost simultaneously, "Hell wouldn't be as bad!"

On Thursday, December 2, 1954, Big Stupe took me to the front office. The political instructor was waiting for me, and he began his "indoctrination" session the moment I arrived.

He said, "Kiba, you still have a hostile attitude. This is not good! We Chinese are good people, and we try to treat you well. Now that your investigation and trial are over, we will be able to treat you even better. We feel that you are sorry and regret the outrageous crime that you have committed against the peace-loving Chinese people and against our Glorious People's Republic; we think you are ready to be re-educated. My colleagues and I think that you now realize that your warmongering government is the cause of your deplorable dilemma and that you also realize no one in the United States Government cares what happens to you. You are an intelligent young man. You will take the right road and study hard to improve yourself. We will give you many books and do everything we can to make things more comfortable for you. Very shortly you will admit that the Chinese are good people. I know that up to now your treatment has not been the best; in our country, before a prisoner is tried, the treatment is poor. After the trial, the prisoner is no longer our enemy, but our friend, and the treatment improves. Do you understand?"

I said, "Yes, but why did you wait almost two years to try us?"

"Tongue" ignored my questions and said, "If you have no more questions, you may go back to your cell.

"I have one more question," I said.

"What is it?"

"When am I going home?"

"After you serve your time. However, there have been cases where prisoners were released early on account of their good behavior. So you behave yourself, and you might get to go home earlier."

"How much earlier?"

"Several months."

"Big deal!"

"Tongue" squinched his face and asked, "How is that?"

"Nothing," I said. "Just forget it."

"Okay. You may go now."

On Saturday afternoon, December 4, 1954, we were taken separately to the front office. There were numerous packages from home sitting on the floor. A female interpreter handed me an itemized list for each box and told me to check them against the contents of each box. My mouth watered as I checked each item in the boxes of goodies.

After I checked and double checked each box carefully and confirmed that there were no discrepancies between the lists and the contents, she gave me a receipt to sign that confirmed I had received everything.

"Will I be given everything I've received?" I asked.

She said, "You can have the clothing, towels, soap, pencils, and paper. You cannot have anything that can be taken internally."

I became very angry. Everything there was sent to me by my family and friends, and *all* of it belonged to me.

I protested and asked, "Why can't I have the food, the medicine, and the toilet articles? They're *mine!*"

"It's against prison regulations," she said. Then she shoved the receipt toward me and asked me again to sign it.

"Screw you and your prison regulations," I said. "I'm not signing unless I get *everything* that was sent to me."

She pleaded with me and vowed that the items held back would be stored for me and not consumed by someone else.

"I'll sign *only* for those items I receive, and nothing more," I said.

My adamant stance on the matter frustrated her, so she called on Warden Ratface to resolve the matter. They held a brief conference across the room, and they finally agreed that it was okay for me to sign for what I actually received and nothing more.

I signed and then I was allowed to carry non-ingestive items back to my cell. I was extremely upset by the knowledge that all that delicious food sent with such care by those back home was there in the office, and I was sitting in my cell slowly wasting away from malnutrition.

Schmidt didn't receive any packages, and his disappointment was etched deeply in his face. He couldn't understand why his wife didn't send him anything. Howard Brown and I shared ours with him, and we did our best to console him and boost his spirits.

The following Tuesday morning, December 7, 1954, Sam opened the doors to Dog and Charlie Cells and ordered us five airmen (enlisted men) to pick up our bedding and follow him. We followed Sam from Skid Row into the small (hub) circle; then we went through the double doors on the right into the cellblock we called Shower Corridor. We traversed the whole length of Shower Corridor and passed through a set of double doors into the large (hub) circle near the interrogation-indoctrination area. Here Sam led us through the next set of double doors to the left and into our new cellblock. He led us to the very end of the cellblock and into the last cell on the right. The cells in this cellblock were small, about six feet by ten feet, but they had knocked out a wall between the last two cells on each side of the hall to create two large cells. This was to be our "new home," for awhile anyway.

After we were settled in our new cell, Sam returned to Skid Row and brought our four officers from Able and Baker Cells and put them into the large cell on the left across from us. In addition, they brought Major Baumer from wherever they'd been keeping him and moved him in with our four officers.

So, after the moves were made, the five airmen: Schmidt, Benjamin, Thompson, Howard Brown, and I (Kiba) were in the large cell on the right side of the cellblock; five officers: Baumer, Vaadi, Llewellyn, Wallace Brown, and Buck were in the large cell across from us. We did not know the whereabouts of Colonel Arnold. Apparently he was still being held in solitary somewhere.

There was a small coal stove in the corner of each large cell. It was the first time during our long captivity that we were furnished with heat in our cells. The bed boards were set up on sawhorses about two feet above the concrete floor. The cell next to us airmen was used to store coal and wood. There were also several small coal stoves in the hallway.

Several hours later the houseboys brought another man into our cellblock and put him in with us. He introduced himself as Richard Fecteau, an American civilian. He said he had been captured on the night of November 29, 1952. At that moment we heard noises in the hall, and Fecteau pressed his face to a small glass window in the cell door.

He said, "It's John Downey, my partner. They're putting him in the cell across the hall."

Now we had six people in each of the large cells, and we were more cramped than we were before we were moved.

Not long after he arrived, Fecteau had to go to the latrine. The guard opened the door and let him out.

We were suspicious of the two civilian newcomers; so, while Fecteau was gone, we discussed the possibility of his being a "plant."

We weren't even sure if he were really an American. We agreed to use caution until we knew more about him.

When Fecteau returned, we talked with him and asked him a lot of questions. He demonstrated in his answers that he knew a lot about us, and he expressed great concern over the fate of their pilots.

We slept very little that night because everyone was too keyed up and excited about the changes in our treatment. We lay on our boards and talked into the wee hours of the morning.

Early the next day the houseboy opened our cell doors and let all of us out into the corridor to visit with each other. Our cell doors were left open, and we had the options of sitting in our own cell, visiting the officers' cell, or walking up and down the corridor. Of course the officers had the same options. The guards, who had almost always stood at our window flaps and glared at us, now stood in the large circle (hub) on the other side of the double doors leading into the cellblock and glared at us from there. The new development puzzled them, but we didn't care a whit. What a thrill it was to see the others and be able to actually talk to them without fear of reprisal.

One of the vacant cells in our cellblock was converted into an office for an interpreter. Two days after we were all put together in one cellblock, the warden and several other official-looking Red Chinese came into the cellblock with the interpreter and told us that as long as we behaved and obeyed prison rules things would be bright for us. They also said that if we ever had any questions that we should go to the interpreter's office and ask him. Also, they told us that we would be given some books; we had to study them or special classes would be formed for us and attendance would be mandatory.

Shortly after our visitors left, a ping-pong table was moved into the hallway, and we were given some playing cards. But they also kept their word about the books; they brought in a pile of them.

We named the new interpreter that moved into our cellblock "Bugs Bunny." He developed an "occasional" habit of leaving his "office" and coming to the airmen's cell for impromptu visits. We chatted with him and, in general, made an honest effort to get to know him. We learned that the Red Chinese officers earned barely enough to live on; nonetheless, he said that he liked the Army life. He explained that officers had to buy their own uniforms. They did have

201

a clothing allowance; but, since clothing was very expensive, the allowance was inadequate to provide for their needs. He admitted that he was a communist because, as a party member, he received extra privileges, extra rations, and special consideration in many ways.

The changes they made in our prison life gave me the opportunity to have contact with John Downey, the civilian in the officers' cell. He had gone to Yale University where he'd learned some Spanish, so he spent time teaching me everything he could remember about the language.

About eight P.M. on Christmas Eve, all of us gathered in our cell and started singing Christmas Carols and other songs. It was a much better Christmas than the previous one, but still nothing like the ones we'd had at home. In spite of our past tribulation and the promise of many more years of imprisonment, we did not forget to be thankful for our lives and the good changes in prison life we had received recently.

The next day, Christmas Day 1954, Bugs Bunny came down to our cells and handed out mail. We were all hungry for news from home, so those who received letters read them quickly. As soon as I finished my mail, I gave it to others to read. Others who received letters followed suit, and the sharing of mail was an upbeat event that somehow gave us a more Christmas-like feeling.

We had scarcely finished our mail when another surprise occurred: Bugs Bunny took those who had packages one by one to his office and let them have one or two items from them. He explained that the warden wanted us to have something special because it was a "holiday" for us. The problem with his sudden generousness was that some had not received packages. Those who did receive parcels shared with the others, providing a meager treat for everyone. We asked Bugs why they couldn't let us have more of our goodies so that each man could enjoy more than a mere taste. He said that their superiors permitted them to give us only a little at a time.

Despite their severe rationing of what was rightfully ours, each man who received something brought it back to the cell where the twelve of us shared it; each man received only a very little, but we all agreed it was better than nothing. Beyond that practical attitude, we were also humbly grateful for it. No matter how small the portions were, the fact that we got anything at all was a giant leap above what had been before. Therefore, we were thankful, and it did brighten our day.

The new phase of our imprisonment was paradise compared to the first phase (the time prior to December 7, 1954), but it was still prison. Just the though of enduring four more long, long years from America and our loved ones was sheer agony. And we wondered: would the mangy, two-faced, lying Redchink communists actually let us go home after our terms were up? We didn't know, and we didn't have much faith in their "word" about the matter.

On Tuesday morning, December 28, 1954, Bugs Bunny, Morphodite, Babyface, and Ratface came into the cellblock. They told us to assemble in the airmen's cell. Warden Ratface spoke and Bugs Bunny translated: "We must move two of you out because six in each cell is too many. You will continue to have the same privileges and lenient treatment which you presently have. This move is not for punishment."

Naturally, we were apprehensive. They were master liars, so we didn't believe them. Several of us volunteered to be the ones moved, but they rejected our offers. This proved to us that they had lied. If they actually believed that six in a cell made it too crowded, why didn't they put two of us in one of the small cells? To us, that made more sense than moving two of us out of the cellblock. But, they already knew whom they wanted to move.

Bugs Bunny said, "John Downey and Richard Fecteau will be moved. Get your things and be ready to go in five minutes."

Some of us were very upset with their bullying tactics, their sneaky ways, and the obvious false premise in their explanation. We made our displeasure known, and we made some most uncomplimentary remarks about the Redchink pricks. Some of the fellow crew members tried to calm us down because they rightly feared retaliation by our "lenient" protectors. Their cooler heads prevailed, and the "bearers of evil tidings" were allowed to leave.

"Everything I touch turns to crap," Fecteau said with disgust, as he busied himself in gathering his things.

We tried to console both him and John Downey; they were our new-found friends whom we'd grown to like and trust. With only minutes left, we gave them as much encouragement as we could in that short span of time, and we promised to try to keep in touch. Then it was time to go. We said our "so-longs" to them as the houseboys escorted them from our cellblock.

Their removal was a cause of concern for us. We wondered where they were being taken, whether they would be kept together or separated, whether they would be placed in solitary, and why they had been moved out. Why them? They had already suffered too much: solitary confinement and fetters for over two years. What really puzzled us was why they had moved these men in with us at all.

While we were considering the plight of Downey and Fecteau and the relationship of their imprisonment with ours, those of us who'd remonstrated against their removal were called to the interpreter's office. There we were castigated for our "incorrect" behavior.

Bugs Bunny said, "You should not cuss the Chinese, especially after we have been treating you so well. Here at the prison we do only what we are ordered to do. Right now we are doing all we can to make things more pleasant for you. Those two men are not from your crew, so why do you feel the way you do? Now please don't swear at us any more, or we will have to punish you."

I said, "Those guys are Americans, and we are concerned for their safety. You have already subjected them to horrible physical and mental abuses. Are you going to shoot them, or tear their bodies apart and then stomp on them until all that remains is a bloody mass of jelly that you describe in your Chinese Literature books? Yeah, I'll bet that's what you're going to do."

"No, no! We are not going to harm them," Bugs said.

"Are they together?" Schmidt asked.

"Yes, they are in a cell together and doing nicely. Do not worry about them."

During the three weeks that Downey and Fecteau were with us, we learned many things about them and their situation. Both men were young, in their twenties, and well-educated. Fecteau graduated from Boston University with a Bachelor of Arts degree in Physical Education, and Downey had a Master of Arts degree in English Literature from Yale University. Both men were recruited from their respective college campuses by a certain secret agency of the United

States Government. They were hired at a lucrative annual salary of $5,000. They spent a year in training after which they were sent to a base somewhere near Seoul, South Korea. Their duties at that base were routine and usually uneventful. However, their duties had a sudden change.

According to Fecteau, around the middle of November 1952, a C-47 airplane ferried in and dropped nine Kuomintang spies into Manchuria. Those spies had been trained and briefed by Fecteau and Downey. The Chinese communists (Chicoms) captured the nine agents and interrogated them intensively. One of the agents, the radio operator, broke down and told his captors all about the operation and the intended place, time, and date that one of the agents was to be picked up. The Chicoms forced the radio operator to remain silent and carry out the plans for the pickup as if nothing had gone wrong. The Kuomintang radio operator made radio contact with his "home base," and the pickup was arranged for the night of November 29, 1952. The planned pickup area was a level grassy strip just outside the little town of Jehol.

Since things in Seoul were dull and routine and for other reasons not entirely clear, Fecteau and Downey happened to be on the flight to Jehol. Neither was authorized to be on the flight, nor should they have been. Nevertheless, on the night of November 29th, both men were on the C-47 winging their way toward Jehol; they had no reason to suspect the disaster that awaited them.

The pilots of the C-47 were the same two who had made the original drop of the spies earlier in the month. Once they were in the designated area, the C-47 would descend to tree top level in order to lower a basket. The agent on the ground was supposed to catch the basket and pull himself into it so he could be hoisted into the aircraft. Those maneuvers were delicate and were carried out without the plane landing.

The C-47 was right on schedule. The crew was unaware that they were flying into a trap; the Chicoms, who conceived the trap, had set up machine guns in the approach area. The weather, too, was against them; it was a starry, moonlit night, and visibility was good, perfect conditions for the machine-gunners.

When the C-47 entered the pickup area, the Chicom gunners caught it in a cross fire. The plane burst into flames, but the pilots were able to crash-land it in the field. Fecteau and Downey managed to crawl out of the wreckage. When they saw the Chicom troops starting to close in on the wreckage, they chose to run. They were quickly overtaken and subdued. After they were searched, one little sawed-off runt—for no reason—hit Fecteau in the mouth with his fist. Then Downey and Fecteau were tied up and led away.

Neither Fecteau nor Downey saw or ever learned what happened to their pilots. They presumed that they were either killed in the crash or captured. Of course it was also possible that they were executed on the spot, even if they survived the crash. They just didn't know.

Fecteau and Downey were taken to the city of Mukden and placed in prison under the strictest security. Like our crew, they were kept in solitary. Their daily routine was similar to ours—interrogations, starvation, exposure to biting cold temperatures, and generally degrading treatment, except that their treatment was harsher and their interrogations much tougher.

Fecteau remained very resistant to their torture and interrogations, so he was kept in handcuffs and leg irons for the first 18 months. He was kept on a starvation diet; and even after he was placed with us, he had extreme difficulty keeping down his food. When he ate, he was like a starving, wild animal; he gobbled down his food as if he feared that it would be taken away from him.

Both Fecteau and Downey said that in many of their interrogations the Red Chinese tried to link them with us. Later I learned from Colonel Arnold and other officers that the interrogators were insisting that we were getting our directives from a particular civilian agency.

Fecteau and Downey told us that they and the nine Kuomintang agents were tried on Saturday, October 9, 1954—the day before our crew was tried. In those trials, the prosecutors insinuated that their mission and ours were connected and that we were all working together and were from the same outfit. The Red Chinese accused Downey of being the ringleader in charge of both missions. Since our B-29, Stardust Four Zero, was shot down a month and a half *after*

Downey was captured, he would have been an extraordinary man to have directed a mission from a prison cell deep in Red China.

Downey and Fecteau were sentenced the day before we were. For his atrocious crimes against the People's Republic of China, Downey was sentenced to life imprisonment. Fecteau was sentenced to 20 years. The nine Kuomintang agents received various lighter sentences; several of the more cooperative agents were awarded suspended sentences by the appreciative Redchink judges.

Fecteau and Downey were gone now, and we believed that they were probably slapped back in solitary confinement. We were depressed and heavy-hearted concerning them and their treatment and especially their horribly unjust sentences, and we continued to feel that way for many, many days.

During the last three days of December, we noticed that Bugs Bunny had not been in his office. Why?

Lubbock, Texas: November 24, 1954
Headline on the Lubbock Morning Avalanche newspaper
U.S. Fires Angry Protest To Reds
Heading over an item on page 1:
Sentencing Of 13 Americans Is Denounced
By William Theis
Washington, Nov. 23 INS—

Communist China today sentenced 13 Americans, 11 of them airmen, to prison terms from four years to life on "spy charges." The U. S. protested angrily tonight, called the charges "trumped up" and utterly false" and accused the Chinese Reds of "bad faith, insincerity and amorality."

The State Department which joined the Defense Department in issuing strongly-worded statements, declared the American Government "will continue to make every effort to effect the release of these men who have been unjustly 'sentenced' to further periods of imprisonment.

Two Are Civilians

All 13 have been in Chinese custody for nearly two years—the 11 airmen since their B-29 was shot down on a mission over North Korea on January 12, 1953, and the two others, civilian employees of the Army, since a plane on which they were passengers disappeared in November 1952, on a flight from Korea to Japan.

Congressional reaction was slow—but vigorous. Sen. Herman Welker (R-Idaho) said the U. S. should act "with the only thing the Communists fear—namely force." urged Sec. Of State John Foster Dulles to ask the United Nations to take action in the case.

Claimed Political Prisoners

The Defense Department charged the Chinese Communists have been holding the 13 "as political prisoners in violation of international law, the rules of war and the Korean Armistice agreement" and added:

"The Peiping Radio report of the conviction of these U. S. prisoners on the charge of 'spying' is all too reminiscent of numerous other false charges previously made against the UN command.

"It is now apparent from the Peiping broadcast that they were captured, and as in the case of other 'political prisoners,' they were

208

refused repatriation in violation of the armistice agreement," the department said.

On Capitol Hill, Sen. Harry F. Byrd (D-Va) declared: "It is outrageous and against all rules of military law."

Sen. Walter F. George (D-Ga), who will head the Senate Foreign Relations Committee next year, said: "I don't know what will stop it except some kind of drastic action, and I don't know at this point what that would be. I don't believe the Chinese Communists expect to get into the United Nations now."

"We may expect the usual array of 'confessions,' 'evidence,' and so-called 'investigations' to bolster the current charges."

The Pentagon statement said the Communist's announcement "illustrates again the bad faith, insincerity and amorality which have characterized that regime's conduct of its international relations."

Life Term Assessed

The Peiping Radio broadcast to which the Defense Department referred reported that John Thomas Downey, 24, of New Britain, Conn., had been sentenced to life imprisonment, and Richard G. Fecteau, 27, of Lynn, Mass., to a 20-year term.

Downey, nephew of the internationally known tenor, Morton Downey, and Fecteau were the two Army civilian employees.

The radio reported the following American airmen also sentenced, along with nine Chinese Nationalist "co-defendants," for "seriously jeopardizing the security of China."

Col. John Knox Arnold Jr., 41, of Silver Spring, Md., 10 years; and Maj. William Hurl Baumer, 32, of Lewisburg, Pa., eight years.

Lighter Terms Meted Out

The following received sentences of from four to six years:

Capt. Eugene J. Vaadi, of Clayton, N. Y.; 1st Lt. Wallace L. Brown of Banks, Ala.; 1st Lt. John W. Buck of Armathwaite, Tenn.; A. 1. C. Steve E. Kiba of Akron, Ohio; A. 2. C. John W. Thompson III of Orange, Va.; A. 2. C. Daniel C. Schmidt of Scotia, Calif.; Capt. Elmer F. Llewellyn of East Missoula, Mont.; A. 2. C. Harry M. Benjamin Jr., of Worthington, Minn.; T. Sgt. Howard Brown of St. Paul, Minn.

Bomber Shot Down

The Communist announcement said the 11 were captured when their bomber was shot down over Northeast China. Three other airmen aboard were killed.

Those three previously were identified as 1ˢᵗ Lt. Paul E. Van Voorhis of Glen Cove, N. Y.; 1ˢᵗ Lt. Henry D. Weese of Knobel, Ark.; and A. 1. C. Alvin D. Hart of Saginaw, Mich.

The Defense Department denied that the B-29 commanded by Col. Arnold was over Chinese territory, saying the imprisoned airmen "were on a routine flight near the Yalu River (separating North Korea and Manchuria)…"

The New China News Agency said Downey and Fecteau were captured on the night of Nov. 29, 1952, when their plane was shot down, also over Northeast China.

"Deliberately Concealed"

The State Department said the two "were believed to have been lost on a flight from Korea to Japan in November 1952," and added:

"How they came into the hands of the Chinese Communists is unknown to the U. S., but the fact of their detention obviously was known by the Chinese Communists and was deliberately concealed by them when the possible repatriation of Americans was discussed at Geneva in June of this year…

"The continued wrongful detention of these American citizens furnishes further proof of the Chinese Communist regime's disregard for accepted practices of international conduct."

The State Department said instructions to make the "strongest possible protests" were being dispatched tonight to the U. S. consul general in Geneva, Franklin C. Gowen, for delivery to Chinese Red consular officials in that Swiss city.

82 Believed Held

U. S. and Chinese consular officials in Geneva began rigidly-limited formal contacts last spring when it was decided during the Geneva conference to authorize them to talk about the release of prisoners and other matters related to Americans held in Red China.

In that connection the State Department estimated tonight that Communist China is holding 82 American civilians.

In addition, the Air Force lists 15 personnel, including the 11 sentenced today by the Reds, as "missing in action." The four other airmen are fighter pilots.

Nine Navy men whose disabled plane was forced down are reported as "missing in action" but only six of these are believed still alive.

The Peiping radio announcement said four of the nine Chinese co-defendants were sentenced to death, four to life imprisonment and one to 15 years in jail.

"Spy Rings" Claimed

The New China News Agency account charged that Downey trained the nine—described as former Nationalist Chinese officers—for espionage work.

The Communists claimed two separate spy rings were involved in the charges and that Col. Arnold commanded an air group which parachuted "special agents into China and the Soviet Union, supplying these agents and keeping in communication with them."

The Reds charged that Downey and Fecteau were members of the U. S. Central Intelligence Agency. A CIA spokesman in Washington declined comment.

Steve E. Kiba

PART IX

A GLIMMER OF HOPE

Steve E. Kiba

On December 31, 1954, we decided to stay up and welcome in the New Year. We spent all evening talking and waiting for midnight. The guard and the houseboy were unsuccessful in trying to make us go to sleep. Midnight and the New Year finally arrived, and we wished each other a Happy New Year; then we finally went to sleep.

The next morning we noticed that Bugs Bunny was still absent. We also noticed that a young Red Chinese man dressed in blues was frequently in and out of the cellblock. He gave no indication that he spoke or understood English, so we wondered why Bugs Bunny was still gone.

Nothing unusual happened, and New Year's Day 1955, passed just like any other day: boring, boring, boring!

Every morning as soon as we arose, Vaadi and I would open the windows in the officers' cell and yell "good morning" to Colonel Arnold, Fecteau, and Downey. The houseboy and some of our crew members would chew us out for such reckless behavior.

In early January 1955, we changed our room order a bit. Buck and Llewellyn moved in with Howard Brown, Schmidt, and me. Benjamin and Thompson moved in with the other officers. When Sam and Smokey learned what we had done, they both became angry and ordered us to return to the original room order. We ignored their command.

On Sunday morning, January 9, 1955, Bugs Bunny returned and came into our cellblock. Immediately, he asked us why we changed our room order. He told us that the houseboys were very upset because we refused to obey them. I told Bugs that some of us preferred to lie down early and sleep, while others preferred to sit up and talk. I explained that we rearranged our billeting so that those who liked to go to sleep early were in one cell and those who preferred to stay up late and talk were in another. Bugs said that he would explain that to the caretakers (houseboys).

We asked Bugs where he had been for the past two weeks. We intimated that he had been in town shacking up with some sexy chick. He was embarrassed and totally flustered, and he hastened to tell us that he had been in the city on "business."

While Bugs was still in our cell, the "one-armed" barber came into the cellblock.

"A haircut on Sunday?" all of us blurted our, almost simultaneously.

Bugs said, "Yes. We are going to have a party for you this afternoon. You will also receive a nice new uniform."

The barber gave all of us a haircut and a shave; well, everyone except me got a shave. While the barber was performing his tasks, Bugs talked with several of the crew members, but he would not elaborate on the "party" they were preparing us for. We wondered if he were really serious about it, until Babyface and Sam carried in a pile of dark blue padded clothing and fitted each one of us with a jacket and a pair of pants. Then Babyface and Sam left the cellblock, and Bugs Bunny went back to his office.

Not long after we received our haircuts and new clothes, Sam and Babyface brought in several pans containing apples, tangerines, hard candy, and packs of cigarettes. While we were enjoying the treats, Bugs came to our cell and said, "In a little while you will go outside and play volleyball. You will also have your pictures taken."

"This is it!" We thought. "We are finally going home!" Everyone was sure of it.

We were bubbling over with enthusiasm and anticipation. Actually, we were ecstatic. We debated whether or not to let them take our pictures, and the consensus was "who cares as long as we are going home."

We wondered whether or not Colonel Arnold would be released with the rest of us. Several of the crew thought that our infernal "lenient" hosts might consider it advantageous to hold on to the "main culprit" as a future bargaining chip, especially since they kept him segregated from the men of his 581st ARC Wing. The diabolical disciples of the "Living Satan" (Mao Tse-tung) might decide to keep him as a living symbol of the aggressive, decadent, Imperialistic-Capitalistic Warmongers of Wall Street and Washington, D. C. The way the Red Chinese operated to control the huge number of people they governed made it very probable—if they did not release Colonel Arnold—that they would exhibit him publicly in order to curry anti-American sentiment among the masses.

A serious point of contention among our crew was how to deal with the question of the alleged border violation if it were brought up.

Some were afraid the Red Chinese would raise the question prior to releasing us; they worried that if we denied the violation, we might not be released. Several of us maintained that we should tell the unequivocal truth, that we **did** **not** violate the Red Chinese border. All of us *knew* that we had been *shot down* over North Korea and that we had been *captured* in North Korea. After we were captured, we were *transported* into Red China by *train*, and without our knowledge as to where they were taking us. Those crewmen fearful that the wily Red Chinese might spring the border violation question on us believed that we should admit to the "violation" if it meant being released early from that friggin' hellhole we were in, but only if our release actually *hinged* on an admission from us. They argued that there was a slight possibility that we might have *intruded* into Red Chinese air space. Our Navigator Captain Llewellyn reminded them that we were flying more than *forty miles south* of the Yalu River, the border between North Korea and Red China.

The group supporting an admission of guilt was apprehensive about what Schmidt and I would say and do. We were admonished to hold our tongues around any Red Chinese officials or newsmen, especially if Colonel Arnold were not to be released with us. Schmidt and I warned them that if anyone accused us of violating their damned air space, we would both speak up and deny it. We did agree to let Major Baumer do the talking as long as he told the truth—that we had been shot down over North Korea.

The Red Chinese had proven time and again that they were lying, two-faced, sons-of-bitches, and they knew that our B-29, Stardust Four Zero, was shot down over North Korea. I knew personally that they lied about our Radar Operators Henry Weese and Paul Van Voorhis; the "prosecutor" and the "judges" at our "show-case" trial maintained that they both were killed the very night we were shot down in January 1953. Yet, I had personally seen one of them alive and well in late July and early August of 1953—seven months *after* the night of our ill-fated mission when he was allegedly "killed." Not only that, more than one of my interrogators had bragged to me that they had captured "thirteen" of us, *two as soon as they landed on the ground after bailing out*. The *eleven of us* in prison had all been picked up the *next day* at various locations; *therefore, the two who*

217

*were captured on the night we were shot down had to have been our
two Radar Operators, Weese and Van Voorhis.*

Evidently the *eminent* Red Chinese officials who were trying to
perpetrate the lie about their deaths failed to inform their field
officers, interrogators, and interpreters that they wanted our crew and
everyone else to believe that the two men had been killed in the attack
on our unarmed B-29. It was clear to us that the lower echelon Red
Chinese personnel were not immediately made aware of the plot to
either execute or secretly imprison Weese and Van Voorhis.

They committed a similar error regarding their "charge" that we
violated the Red Chinese air space; shortly after we were picked up,
one of the interrogators at the wooden shacks where I was first taken
told me that we were in North Korea and that a train would take us to
Red China.

About two o'clock in the afternoon, Bugs Bunny returned to the
cellblock with Babyface and several other houseboys. They led us to
a large, open area near the administration building. On our way there
we were joined by Colonel Arnold and the two civilians, Downey and
Fecteau. As we were walking along together, Downey came close to
me and handed me a sheet of paper with more Spanish words for me
to learn. I took the paper and thanked him for his interest in teaching
me Spanish.

When we got to the open area, many cameramen were already
there waiting for us. Bugs Bunny told us that we could exercise a
little to warm up before we started playing volleyball. We lined up
and Fecteau directed us in calisthenics while the cameramen took
movies and photos. When we divided into sides and started to play,
the photographers continued their work. Major Baumer, whose
injured leg still troubled him, sat on a stool at the edge of the court.

We were able to exchange a few words with Downey and Fecteau while we played. They said they had been separated immediately after they were moved from our cellblock. The Red Chinese claimed that Fecteau had not told them everything. An English-speaking Chinese prisoner had been assigned to them, one in each of their cells. Apparently the sneaky Red Chinese were hoping to catch the Americans off guard and thus obtain whatever they were still after.

An hour later, after hundreds of still photographs had been snapped and several reels of movies had been shot, Bugs Bunny and his cohorts escorted us back to our respective cells. On the way back to our cellblocks, Bugs told us that there would be a specially-prepared supper for us later that afternoon. I asked him if Downey, Colonel Arnold, and Fecteau could visit with us in our cellblock until suppertime, and he refused my request. Schmidt asked him if a couple of us could visit them in *their* cells. This request brought a frown to Bugs's face, and he was very firm in his refusal.

Before we were separated to return to our own cellblock, Fecteau approached me and whispered, "Kiba, when you get back, tell G-2 that the Red Chinese know all about Samurai and Jehol."

"Samurai?" I asked.

"Yes. Tell G-2 they know everything."

"Roger. Anything else?"

"No, that's all."

"I asked to visit you, but they won't let me."

"That's okay, Kiba. Keep bugging the hell out of them. Don't ever let up. You have the right attitude toward these yellow-bellied bastards."

Once we were back in our respective cells, the photographers took hundreds of pictures. They were, of course, posed propaganda pictures which they would use to show the outside civilized world just how kindly and humanely they were treating us. They snapped pictures while we played cards and ping-pong and while we wrote letters. We tried our best to avoid the cameras, because we recognized their ulterior motive was to present candid shots that supposedly depicted our daily routine, but our confinement in such a small area made it almost impossible.

They finally finished the photo session in our cells about seven o'clock and took us to a dining room where Colonel Arnold, Downey, and Fecteau joined us. They seated us at a table with crude benches for seats; it was especially reserved for the American "war criminals."

After one of our officers said grace, the houseboys placed several serving bowls of Chinese food on the table. We couldn't identify the contents of the big bowls, but they looked appetizing and tasted quite good. I think they were making the point that they truly did have something besides wormy rice and watery soup. Perhaps this was what Napoleon and Bluebeard meant when they told us things could be better if we only cooperated and allowed ourselves to be re-educated. I thought to myself: "If the meaning of the whole charade was to demonstrate one of the benefits of conversion to communism, then they could shove it up their filthy bungs."

In a way, the first "feast" we'd had since becoming captives was comical; few of us were skilled in using chopsticks. Our awkwardness in manipulating the two pieces of wood to delivery the food to the exact location on our faces brought guffaws not only from us, but also from some of our Red Chinese on-lookers. We were further distracted by the pesky photographers who returned to capture our ineptitude on film, and from every angle imaginable. Finally, someone in the Red Chinese representatives there recognized a need for more orderly propaganda pictures: they brought us some spoons.

After we ate what we wanted of the Chinese dishes, we were allowed to have canned meat and fruit from the packages we'd received from home. The Chinese food was good, and our existing on a starvation diet for so many long months probably made it even more palatable to us. **The American food was absolutely delightful.** Not only was it delicious; it was also like having a small taste of America; it brought back many fond memories of years past and triggered our anticipation of the many wonderful things to come once we regained our freedom.

We ate until we were fully satisfied: it was the first time in almost two years that any of us finished a meal without the excruciating pangs of hunger *still* gnawing at the lining of our stomachs.

The houseboys cleaned up the mess and moved the tables back so they could set up the ping-pong table in the center of the mess hall. They put some small tables off to the side where we could write letters or play cards. On each small table there was a pan containing candy, apples, tangerines, and cigarettes. Some of us played cards, some pretended to write, and some elected to just sit and talk. The unrelenting photographers still stalked us to obtain more pictures for their already over-sized album of propaganda. We tried to ignore them while we stayed on the move in order to see and talk to everyone while we had the chance, especially Downey, Fecteau, and Colonel Arnold. Occasionally a couple of us batted a ping-pong ball back and forth for a short while, but our hearts were not in it.

Several Red Chinese who spoke and understood English mingled with us, and it was quite obvious they were there not only to help "supervise" us, but also to observe, listen, and learn all they could. Their intent was probably to assess the level of their success in "re-educating" us and to make sure nothing was said or done that would jeopardize their intended propaganda effect.

I recognized one of them as the mean son-of-a-bitch who interrogated me and gave me such a rough time back at the Hotel. Once, when he was in ear-shot, I said, "These lousy, no-good Red Chinese communists ain't worth a damn." I looked directly at him when I said it. His clear understanding of my words caused his ugly face to wrinkle up in a scowl. He turned his back to me and walked away.

It had been a long day filled with good food, social interchange, and other pleasant activities. All of us tried not to let their sneaky motives reduce our level of enjoyment too much; but, truthfully, they did. And we expected it to end abruptly at our usual "boardtime." However, they had another surprise for us. At nine o'clock, they took us to another big room where doctors and nurses were waiting for us. They gave us a "mediocre" physical examination, and photos were taken all during this occurrence, too.

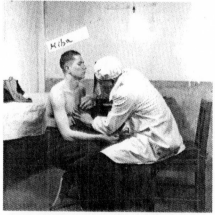

I stood in line behind Colonel Arnold while we waited to go to the next examination post, and we had the chance to talk.

I said, "Do you think we're on our way home, Colonel?"

"I don't know, Kiba," he said.

"You will do the talking for us when we cross the border, won't you?"

"America is still a democracy, Kiba. You'll have to do your own talking."

I said, "Thanks, Colonel. What if they ask me where we were shot down?"

"Tell the truth."

"What if I cross over before you?"

"Just tell the truth, no matter what," he said.

"But these inhumane bastards might hold you back. I was more or less ordered to keep my mouth shut, especially about the alleged border violation."

"You say what you want, Kiba, and don't worry about those 'orders.' Just tell what really happened."

"Thanks. I'll do that," I said.

Colonel Arnold said, "After what we've endured at the hands of these sadistic bastards, **the American people must hear the truth.** Even if they should free the ten of you and hold me, tell the truth. Tell everybody that we were forcibly taken into Red China. Tell them the details of our mistreatment. For God's sake, please don't say or do anything to help these uncivilized goons for fear of reprisal against me. That would hurt me more than anything these rotten sons-of-bitches can do to me."

I thanked him for his honesty and determination. I was glad that he and I were in agreement that the truth should be told. Anything less would be capitulation to the Red Chinese.

Buck and Downey were also conversing nearby. I overheard Downey ask Buck to contact his mother and girlfriend back in the States and let them know that he was okay. Buck said he'd do his best to find them and relay the message.

Finally, the day's "freedom and goodies" were over, and we were escorted back to our cells. We plopped down on our hard bed boards and waited anxiously for Bugs Bunny, a houseboy—or anybody—to come into our cells and take us to the train station; we had mentally accepted that the day's leniency and good treatment was a prelude to our release. So we waited and waited and waited. We were totally "wiped out": physically, mentally, and emotionally. Even so, we were just too keyed up to sleep. Occasionally some of us dozed off, but not for long; even the slightest noise would wake us. Every minute sound was magnified a thousandfold by our minds which, although weary, maintained its own "high alert" through our expectations and hopes of good news. But Bugs didn't come to announce the good news that we were so anxiously awaiting. Neither did anyone else, and the night was never-ending.

By the merciful grace of God, that horrible night finally came to an end, but it left its mark on all of us. Our failure to depart that frigid hellhole and Red China completely crushed the spirits of a few and drastically dampened the spirits of the rest of us. Some still felt that there was a very slight possibility of departing within the next few days. The others were skeptical.

On Monday morning, January 10, 1955, we discussed the party and the chances of our being freed. We felt that we had been deceived and exploited. Most of us were sorry and disgusted with ourselves for letting the wily, two-faced communists take our pictures. We knew they were for propaganda purposes; they were certain to claim that the scenes captured in the pictures depicted our daily routine. They would submit the photographs to the world as proof of their humane and lenient treatment of us. The thing that really upset us was the fact that many people would be naive enough to believe it. No matter how much we denied it, no matter what we said, there would be those who would prefer to accept the "staged evidence" as the gospel truth. Had we endured the miserable hell inflicted on us by the Red Chinese for so long, only now to have our testimony of it negated or, at the least, diminished by those damned, deceptive pictures? We wondered.

Well, we rationalized, there were two consolations: one, for the first and only time since our capture we got a full meal; two, we were able to see the others, even though our time together was very short.

The spirit and stamina of Colonel Arnold continued to amaze us. Our admiration and esteem for him grew stronger with each bit of knowledge we gained about his torture and general treatment. They had been brutal to him beyond what some people can conceive. He had been in solitary confinement since the day he was captured, and his interrogations were considerably longer and much crueler than ours. He was often physically tortured. We had learned that one thing they did to him was *clamp*, not just handcuff, his hands behind his back for hours at a time. The stress from the clamping stretched the muscles in his arms and shoulders in such a way that it slowly and painfully pulled his shoulders out of place. His hands and fingers swelled up, and one of the sadistic Redchink guards—a real prick—milked his fingers as if he were milking a cow: the pain he inflicted with that procedure was excruciating. At other times they forced him to his knees and took turns at beating him over the head with a thick stick. The beating would go on for hours, with a well placed blow occurring every thirty seconds.

During one particularly sadistic session, they forced him to stand at attention continuously for seven days and nights. They allowed him to go to the toilet once every twenty-four hours. Blood pooled in his legs and caused them to swell so big he couldn't distinguish between his legs and his feet. His feet were recognizable only by his toes; they barely protruded from the swelled stumps, like irritated blisters about to pop. The cruel torturers permitted him only one meager meal a day, and he was forced to eat it hastily and in a standing position; at all other times he was not allowed to budge from his "attention" stance. If he started to doze off from complete exhaustion or to seek refuge from his torment in a dream world, the guards jarred him back to the cruel reality of his **living hell** with a well placed blow or a kick.

After Downey and Fecteau were moved out and after we had our big "let down" on the ninth of January, several of our crew came very close to "cracking up." One went into a state of extreme depression so deep he only sat on his bed board and stared off into space. Intermittently, he recited the Lord's Prayer over and over. Without exception, all of us became moody and grouchy. Luckily, with encouragement from the rest of the crew, our fellow crew member soon snapped out of his depression and re-entered the world of reality.

225

On Thursday morning, January 20, 1955, Warden Ratface, Bugs Bunny, Assistant Warden Babyface, and Morphodite came into the cellblock and called us together.

Ratface spoke, and Bugs translated.

"We have some exciting news for you," Bugs said. "Our government has invited your loved ones to come to the People's Republic of China to visit you, but unfortunately your State Department has refused to let them come. The People's Republic of China offered to pay all expenses. We ask you to request your loved ones to come visit you. We will appreciate it if you write immediately and invite them over. That is all. Thank you."

After they left, we discussed their proposal. Most of us believed this was another one of their propaganda moves. Some thought that once our loved ones got here they would be locked up. As we discussed the matter further, we had a clear vision of their crafty intentions: once they got here, and after a very touching, well-publicized re-union, they would release us into the custody of our loved ones. It didn't take much imagination to understand what ideal propaganda material such tender and emotional scenes would make. Such a "humanitarian" move by the communists had the potential of accomplishing three things for them: refute their cruel reputation, soften world opinion, and discredit our denials of their allegation that we crossed their border and violated their air space.

Our recognition of the negative possibilities in their grand scheme caused us to agree unanimously that we would rather rot in Red China than to do *anything* that would destroy our credibility or help the enemy in any way. We wanted the world to know how rotten the communists really are; we wanted everybody to *know* that we were "shanghaied" and brought into Red China by force. We were still determined to fight the Red Chinese and their ludicrous propaganda any way we could, and non-cooperation was our greatest weapon. It was certain that, if their plans worked and we went home with our folks, the truth of our horrendous years in hell would basically be invalidated; who would believe the terrible truth about such compassionate, humane people?

On January 22nd, I wrote home. Not because they "invited" us to, but because I wanted to, and I *did not* ask my relatives to visit Red

China. To the contrary, I urged them to stay away. Just to be tacky, I changed the word "peace" in the address to "piece," something I'd been doing and getting by with.

During January, one or two airmen at a time were taken to the interpreter's office for lectures on Red Chinese generosity. Initially, Bugs Bunny conducted the sessions. Later in the month he was joined by the young Red Chinaman who'd been in and out of our cellblock just after Downey and Fecteau were moved out. We called him Young Wong, and now he was Bugs Bunny's apprentice. Very soon Bugs was "sent to the city" again, and Young Wong took over as interpreter.

The boredom of imprisonment continued, and during the last week of January we noticed a white man in the patio. We watched him closely and noticed that he was brought out about the same time every day. He was about 50, wore glasses, had grayish hair and whiskers, and wore the same blue-colored padded clothing as we wore.

Several days after he showed up, a second white man appeared. He was a tall chap, six feet two, or better. His nose was crooked and his hair was dark. The black padded clothing he wore was the same as we had worn just before our trial. He looked like an Englishman to us.

Watching the two men became a pastime for us. One day we succeeded in attracting the attention of the older, bearded man, whom we had named "Abuelo." Abuelo looked up at our window and smiled. Then he went through the motions of a man boxing. We didn't know what he was trying to tell us. He was being watched too closely to be able to walk over and talk to us, so we didn't press him. We hoped that someday we'd get a chance to exchange information.

We continued to watch Abuelo and the Englishman, and we saw them quite often. Abuelo looked up at our window and smiled whenever he had the chance. We waved at him and made signs trying to tell him who we were. When he walked around the patio in a circle, he came to a point that was close to our window. When he reached that point, we talked louder to each other so he could hear us. He responded to our talk by nodding "yes." Our subterfuge of loud talk among us and sign language was usually tolerated by the guards, but to speak out directly to someone else was not permitted. We were sure, by his careful avoidance of talk with us, that the rules for Abuelo were the same as ours.

We tried the same technique on the Englishman, but we never got any recognizable response from him. When we attempted to communicate, he just continued to walk with his chin lowered almost to his chest and paid no attention to us. There was a time or two that we thought we saw a slight smile on his lips, but we were uncertain whether or not we were getting through to him. We thought it was possible that he really didn't hear us.

February came, and we ran out of tooth powder. Whenever we asked Smokey for more, he told us to wait. Finally, after four or five days of asking for and not getting the tooth powder, I got pissed off; so I went to the interpreter's office and told him that we had been out of tooth powder for a long time. I explained to him that every time we asked Houseboy Smokey for more, he just ignored us. I exhibited a high level of anger and told him that, if they didn't want to supply us with their tooth powder, they could at least let us have some of our own from our packages.

Young Wong promised to take care of the matter and to find out why the houseboy took it upon himself to withhold an item necessary to our hygiene. He apologized and asked me not to be so bitter.

I took advantage of his congenial mood and asked him about the health and welfare of Downey, Fecteau, and Colonel Arnold.

"They're doing just fine," he said. "Your concern for their welfare is unwarranted."

I tried to persuade him to let me visit them, but he gave me the usual answer with the over-used phrase that "their cases are different from yours." Then I asked him about Hart, Weese, and Van Voorhis (the three they said were dead). I told him that the "prosecutor" at our kangaroo trial lied about their being killed the night we were shot down.

He said that he knew only what his superiors told him and that, even if he *did* know something, he couldn't tell me without jeopardizing his career, his position in the party, and maybe even his life. He begged me to believe the official "story" and never bring up the subject again. Then he admonished me to be concerned only about myself.

The next morning Smokey came to our cell carrying an armful of tooth powder. He glared hatred at me, threw all the packages of tooth powder at me, and said angrily to my cellmates, "Kiba puho!" (Kiba is no damn good!) He pointed to all the others and told them they were "How." (Good; okay.) He left the cell muttering that I was "puho," and I took it as a compliment. Evidently he had received a scolding for not giving us tooth powder when we asked for it.

On Thursday afternoon, February 10, 1955, I wrote a few letters in which I implied that the pictures they took of us were phony, except for our obviously poor physical condition. In some of my previous letters I had indicated that there were ten of us together and not 13, as the propaganda pictures might lead people to believe, and that we absolutely were not getting the food from our packages, except rarely. In some of my letters I hinted that we were not guilty of the Red Chinese allegation that we violated their border and implied that we had been transported across the Yalu River into Red China on a train.

Our lives were still miserable, but the food had changed slightly. Every two or three weeks we were getting a thick, "hopped-up" soup and hard-crusted bread or a jar of jam and a loaf of hard bread or toasted buns covered with some type of oil. The improved fare was really a treat; we just didn't get it often enough.

The "special" chow increased our optimism. We believed that if they were going to make us serve our full terms they wouldn't bother giving us anything special. We thought that perhaps they were making a feeble attempt to "soften" our bitter feelings toward them. On the whole, the food didn't improve that much, but we were getting more, which helped to alleviate somewhat our feelings of constant hunger.

One day in early March 1955, Young Wong called me into his office; I expected a chewing out and a repetitious lecture.

Before he could get started, I said, "Say, Young Wong, how about giving us some of our canned goods from our packages." My intent was to put him on the defensive and avoid a long, unpleasant session.

He said, "We cannot do that."

"Why not? They're ours, aren't they?"

Steve E. Kiba

"Yes, but it's against prison rules to let you have canned goods from home."

"Why?"

"They might be poisoned."

I gasped, "Poisoned? Man, you're crazy. Why would food from loved ones be poisoned?"

"Perhaps your government might put poison in them."

I believed he was expressing the extreme suspicion of the communist nature; it was a sickness they all had.

"Why would our *own* government poison food and medicine destined for us, their own American sons and brothers, held captive by a hostile enemy?"

"I do not know," he said. "My superiors tell me that your government does not give a damn about its missing servicemen. They say that your government officials do not want you to be repatriated, so perhaps they prefer that you die in captivity. This is likely why my superiors believe your government might tamper with—even add something to—the ingestive items sent to you."

"That's a crock of bull," I said. "You heartless barbarians just don't want us to have something good in our lives."

"I'm sorry you feel that way, but let's change the subject. What are you going to do when you are released after serving your four-year term?"

"I'm going home. I'll enter the University of Akron and become an atomic physicist."

"That is a lofty goal. Then what will you do?"

I said, "I'm going to develop a powerful bomb, drop it on Red China, and blow you lousy communists right off the map."

"No, no, Kiba. You must not do that! You must put your knowledge to a peaceful use. We Chinese are good people. We are generous and we've been very lenient with you. Why are you so bitter toward us?"

I let out a cynical chuckle and said, "You're generous and lenient? What a laugh! Is that why for the first *two* years of our captivity you treated us like dogs. For the first two months, you almost starved us to death. Since then, we've had barely enough food to keep us alive, and hunger pangs continuously gnaw away at our empty stomachs.

Do you call withholding a man's drinking water humane treatment? Do you call being manacled and chained day and night for many months 'lenient?' Is putting rusty clamps on a man's wrists with his hands behind his back a humane act? Is dislocating a man's shoulders kind treatment? Do you call standing at attention for hours and hours and being interrogated almost every day and night for over eight months a part of your 'leniency'?" Our officers had to stand for days, and all of us went without a bath for eight months. Now you have the audacity to call all of that cruelty and abuse 'lenient and generous.' I'd sure hate to endure your not-so-lenient treatment."

Young Wong said, "I did not know anything about what you just told me. All I know about is the period after your trial."

"Well, you damn sure know now," I said.

He smiled and said, "But *now* we are generous and lenient, so why do you not forget all that happened before? If you like, we can arrange to send you to the University of Peking. It is a very good university."

"I'll never forget those first two years, even if I live to a hundred. You can stick the Peking University up your ying-yang."

Young Wong said, "In time you will see that we are right. In several years the People's Republic of China will be a great power. Soon we will liberate Taiwan, and within ten years we will destroy the Capitalistic-Imperialistic Warmongering Government of the United States."

"You communists sure have high goals," I said. "The United States of America is now, and it always will be the best and most powerful nation in the world, so don't go counting your chickens before they hatch."

He squinched his face in puzzlement and said, "What? I don't understand 'chickens.'"

"Forget it," I said. "It's beyond your ability to grasp."

"Maybe the United States is presently the strongest nation, but the American Government is corrupt to its core. All of your leaders are selfish and self-serving. They care nothing about the common working people. The only thing your president, your senators, and your congressmen are concerned about is lining their own pockets. On the other hand, our glorious leaders consider and endeavor to fulfill the needs of the working class. Chinese men, women, and children are all working and pulling together to make life better for all—not just a rich ruling class. In the People's Republic there is no class distinction, no prejudice, and no discrimination, as there is in your country. The People's Republic, the Soviet Union, and the other People's Democracies will employ those weaknesses to incite the exploited classes to rise up against the Capitalistic-Imperialistic ruling classes. We will turn the 'have-nots' against the rich, the blacks against the whites, the young against the established 'older' generation, minorities against other minorities, sons and daughters against their parents, and husbands against wives. The use of alcohol and drugs will become the normal, debilitating life style, and we will encourage their use. As America becomes weaker and weaker, the People's Republic of China will grow stronger and more powerful. Soon the whole world shall be communist, and we will conquer the great United States without having to fire a single shot; the United States will crumble from within."

I didn't snicker at his predictions. It was too scary to think about. Besides, I was growing weary of all their communist grand-standing I had been exposed to. I simply said, "Dream on, fella. Dream on."

"You do not believe it?"

"No, I don't. The Monkey (Mao Tse-tung) is too dumb to rule anyone but a stupid bunch of half-baked apes like you. Communism is the worst form of government ever conceived. Stalin is nothing but a common bandit, and Mao Tse-tung is no better."

Young Wong became so angry he bit his tongue and gritted his teeth. Finally, completely losing his cool he shouted, "Some day I will get my chance! Too bad you were not shot the day we captured you. If another war breaks out, I will personally kill you!"

"Now, now," I said. "That's no way to talk. Remember that you have orders to treat us nice and to try to change our bitter feelings toward you."

He reverted quickly to his placating manner and asked, "Why are you so hostile toward us?"

"Because you brought us to Red China illegally and then falsely claimed that we violated your border."

"But you *did* violate our border. My superiors told me so."

"Your superiors are a bunch of liars," I said.

So went the conversation, and another "indoctrination session," which was intended to "re-educate" me in the direction they wanted me to go, ended. I was glad to finally get back to my cell.

A week later Young Wong had me brought to his office again. I took the initiative again and said, "Young Wong, you're absolutely right. I shouldn't harbor such evil and hostile thoughts about you kind, lenient Red Chinese. (I always used Red in front of China or Chinese because I knew that it infuriated them.) I've thought it over, and I agree that I shouldn't be bitter for all the horrible things you Red Chinese have done to me. After all, war is war. The more I think about it, the clearer it becomes. I should remember *only* the nice and kind things. I've made up my mind. I'm not going to become an atomic physicist, and I'm not going to drop a bomb on Peking."

He gave me a gleaming smile and said, "Good, good. What are you going to study?"

"I'm going to study Chinese. I'm going to Michigan State and learn Chinese."

"Why don't you stay here and attend the University of Peking? What better place to learn Chinese than here?"

"No, no. I've made up my mind. I'm going to Michigan State."

"Well, what will you do after you graduate?"

"I'm going to become an interrogator and interrogate you and your comrades in the next war." I laughed, and he couldn't stand it.

He said, "No! No! No! Kiba, you have the wrong attitude. What are we to do to get you to realize this? You must study and learn and become re-educated."

Young Wong pleaded with me for several more hours during which time he endeavored to cleanse my mind of all the **evil thoughts** and **ideas** that he claimed had been put there by the Capitalistic-Imperialistic Warmongers of Wall Street. I pretended to listen and responded sporadically, but I think he knew in his heart that he could never change me. He finally sent me back to my cell.

On Monday afternoon, March 14, 1955, we received mail. As soon as I finished reading mine, I gave it to Schmidt to read. Most of the other fellows did the same.

Steve E. Kiba

Schmidt still had not received any mail from his wife, and he was really feeling low. Everyone else had heard from their wives, as well as family, but poor Schmidt had received only a couple of letters from his sister. He appreciated his sister's mail, but he longed to hear from his wife. Inwardly, he was worried about his wife's faithfulness, but he tried hard to keep from showing it. He kept telling himself that his wife Tippie was a good, honest, faithful, loving wife, but the rotten Red Chinese interrogators and indoctrinators worked hard at instilling doubt in his mind. They constantly suggested to him that she was "sleeping around" and that she was not behaving the way a wife should. So, he became confused and unsure. Still, he reasoned that since he had not heard differently, she was okay; and, if she were okay, she certainly could write.

We were aware of his torment, and we, too, wondered what kind of woman would torture her husband the way she was tormenting him. We believed that she could write to him herself or have someone else get word to him if she weren't able. Her omission in the matter was troubling.

Schmidt talked continuously about the fine attributes of his wife, and we all listened courteously and empathetically. Daily we heard him describe her luscious lips, sexy eyes, fantastic figure, and raving beauty; and, in his mind, every day she became more and more ravishing. He had met her at a dance in Coeur d'Alene, Idaho, while we were still stationed at Mountain Home Air Force Base in Idaho; he fell in love with her immediately, but she pretended that she wasn't interested in dating him. He was persistent and continued to pursue her. At that time, she was only 17, and she was "running around" with an older man. Nonetheless, Schmidt continued to pursue her and carry on his courtship during weekends when he had liberty. One weekend he made up his mind to propose to her; but, after running all over town looking for her, he learned she was out with her older suitor. He was undeterred, however, and later was successful in seeing her and proposing. She immediately accepted. John Buck and Howard Brown tried to persuade him not to get married or, at least, to wait until we returned from overseas, but he was young and obsessed with the love he had for her. They were married and spent only a few months together before we went overseas.

Most of us strongly suspected that Tippie was not writing because she was probably too busy having a good time on the allotment money she was getting from Schmidt. However, we never let it be known to him that we suspected Tippie of being unfaithful. We sympathized with him and did our best to console and comfort him because we knew it was necessary for his survival. As long as he could hold on to his dream, he would be stronger and more emotionally stable and, therefore, better able to survive the rigid, cruel treatment we received. There was no doubt that the lack of contact with her weighed heavily on his mind and that it affected his thoughts and actions. Nevertheless, he had borne the burden successfully thus far. Actually, I believed he was holding up better than some of us who had less to worry about.

Schmidt's uncanny ability to cope under such trying circumstances was no accident. In addition to having faith in his wife, he also had a strong faith in God. All of us were somewhat less than angels prior to being shot down and imprisoned. Yet, our faith had grown substantially since then, and all of us prayed a great deal. We were continually asking for God's counsel and guidance. I believe the great faith in God that Schmidt had and his willingness to submit all of his problems to God were the keystone of his strength. Without that faith and the personal relationship he had with God, he probably would have succumbed to the tremendous stress and pressure he felt by his wife's failure to write. That stress was intensified to an almost unbearable level by the incessant needling of the sadistic Redchink instructors trying to indoctrinate us; they used the absence of letters from his wife as a psychological wedge to pry him away from his own beliefs and push him into accepting their communist doctrine. The conversion of at least one of our crew would have been a great victory for the Red Chinese. But Schmidt stood strong against their constant pressure. He held fast his belief in God, yielded to His guidance, and believed in His mercy, and thus confounded his tormentors by coping successfully with the doubt and self-pity that otherwise would have slowly destroyed him.

On Tuesday morning, March 22, 1955, the small stoves were removed from our cells, and we gave both cells a thorough cleaning. We also cleaned out the coal cell and the two cells next to it. As soon as we were finished with those jobs, the interpreter told us that they were going to change our rooming arrangements some in order to provide us with one large cell in which to eat and study.

Benjamin and Thompson were billeted in what was formerly the coal cell; Buck and Howard Brown were assigned to the cell next to them; Llewellyn and Vaadi moved to the cell next to Buck and Howard Brown; Baumer, Wallace Brown, Schmidt, and I were in the large cell on the left side of the corridor, formerly the officers' cell.

The big cell on the right side of the corridor, formerly the airmen's cell, was converted into the new "study" room which the communists wanted us to have. After they moved a ping-pong table and several crude, wooden benches into it, the interpreter told us to assemble there for an hour of hard, concentrated study.

Young Wong said enthusiastically, "You must study diligently during this class. You must learn all about communism and how good and efficient we are. You will learn the truth. We shall give you a newspaper so you can keep abreast of what is happening. I will sit at the study table with you each day." Young Wong was grinning from ear to ear as he talked. He *really* believed that we would be gullible enough to capitulate to their brainwashing. His simple ignorance was almost laughable.

After the hour was over and Young Wong had left, we had a heated discussion concerning this new "supervised" study program. Some of us didn't want to participate, and we believed that we shouldn't sit there meekly and allow the communists to cram their filthy garbage down our throats. Others believed that all of us were obligated to participate and cooperate in the distasteful project. That conclusion was explained by the logic that we would all be put back into solitary confinement if we didn't cooperate. They suggested that we could just sit at the table and *pretend* we were studying while mentally rejecting the content of whatever they made us study. The lengthy and animated discussion of our different viewpoints led us to take a vote. The few of us who didn't like the idea of participating in the "forced study" made up a minority, so we reluctantly agreed to go along with the majority; we rationalized that if the Red Chinese could put on a "showcase" trial we could put on "showcase" study sessions. We would sit at the table in order not to give them an excuse to separate us. The compromise was reached after we considered the wrath we had experienced from our sadistic "hosts." The "sensible" thing to do, we realized, was to placate their sense of progress in converting us to communism without actually being affected by their hogwash. The daily sessions would be hard for us to stomach, but we agreed to cooperate with them and silently resist their re-education tactics.

The next day we started receiving a newspaper for use in our study sessions. It was never much good to us, as far as revealing anything we wanted to know. It contained little besides farm and production reports of the different provinces in Red China and news accusing the United States of acts of aggression. It also boasted of how the glorious People's Republic was going to liberate the island of Taiwan. We were also inundated with political books, pamphlets, and pictorials dealing with Red China, the Soviet Union, Hungary, Bulgaria, and the other satellite countries.

Our classes were conducted daily, and Young Wong always sat at the head of the table. We did our best to shirk studying without being obvious about it. We frequently went to the latrine two at a time and talked as long as possible. When we stayed away too long, Young Wong would send someone after us. Generally, the person sent to check on us would linger in the latrine, too.

Young Wong grew more impatient and perturbed each day. He finally lost his control and accused us of trying to upset him and wreck the study program. I assured him that destruction of the program was not our intention, and I apologized for my untimely bowel movements. He expressed great concern and suspicion over the fact that I always had to go precisely during the study period. I explained to him that my bowel movements were quite erratic and told him that I had to run to the latrine several times a day and sometimes during the night. I even agreed with him that it looked a bit suspicious and made it appear that the communist propaganda made me sick to my stomach. I became convinced that he did not believe my explanation and that he felt I was taking advantage of him.

Young Wong didn't like to leave the class unsupervised. However, on rare occasions, he did check up on us himself. He soon learned that policing the latrine was not a productive endeavor; he was never able to prove anything, so we were able to goof off a great deal.

Of course there were more ways to avoid study than going to the latrine. One of the things I did was slip Spanish notes between the pages of the communist books and study Spanish instead of their propaganda. To Young Wong's consternation, all of us did a whole lot of whispering and very little studying. We never quite understood why we got by with that, but apparently Young Wong's naivete made him think that our whispering communications were related to our studies and that we were genuinely involved in "discussing" the communist dogma among ourselves.

My inability to concentrate on the boring material they gave us to study and my stubborn refusal to exert my mind to try to comprehend the political doctrines and drivel they forced on us must have caused the political commissars great distress and concern. Many times after a "re-education" session, Young Wong summoned me to his office for private tutoring and counseling. He scolded me for my "incorrect" attitude and accused me of sabotaging the training program. He reminded me that I was always going to the latrine at the start of our study period and spent too much time away from the study table. He pointed out that the others were behaving and trying to learn, whereas I was continually wasting time and making derogatory remarks about the Red Chinese and the study material. He told me I was a bad influence on the others, and especially on Schmidt.

He said, "Schmidt has enough problems without your adding to them. You lead him astray and corrupt his mind with your decadent mind."

In other words, Young Wong believed I was rotten to the core; my mind was totally dominated by the Capitalistic-Imperialistic Warmongers. He said my only hope for salvation was to allow my mind to be cleansed, acknowledge the errors of my sordid past, open my mind to the truth as found in the teachings of the Great and Glorious Mao Tse-tung, and assume a "correct" attitude. In short, my only salvation lay in being "re-educated."

On numerous occasions Young Wong told me that since both of my parents had been born and raised in Hungary I wasn't really an American. He pointed out that since Hungary was a People's

Democracy I should seriously consider becoming a proletariat. He tried to convince me to forget about going home to the United States and to stay in Peking where I could undergo intensive training in the doctrines of Marx, Lenin, Stalin, and Mao Tse-tung. If I chose to stay and join their "cause," arrangements would be made to transfer me from the prison to the University of Peking. Perhaps to help me in my decision to stay, he informed me that there were several Americans from the Korean War studying there presently and that two enlisted men from the Akron, Ohio, area wisely chose to stay in the People's Republic rather than be repatriated and returned to the United States. He asked me to think over their proposition very carefully.

There was nothing to think about, so I quickly told him that I had no intention of turning against my country and people and that he could shove Peking University up his filthy bung. He patiently explained that staying and attending the University was in no way betraying, or even letting down, my countrymen. As for my government, he tried to convince me it was my worst enemy.

He said, "You must show courage and denounce the Capitalistic-Imperialistic dragon which is oppressing not only you, but all people. If you will do that, you will be a hero to all the peace-loving people back in the United States."

Before I could answer his stupid suggestion, he added, "Rejecting the United States Government and pledging allegiance to the People's Republic of China would not be traitorous of you. On the contrary, it would be a highly honorable and selfless act that would endear you to the common people of the entire world."

At that point in his ludicrous attempt to brainwash me, I more or less tuned him out. He rambled on and on and on; finally he ran out of communist nonsense or got tired of seeing my lack of enthusiasm and the bored look on my face. Whatever his reason, I could tell he was disgusted with his failure to produce the results he wanted. He ordered me to return to my cell; and, when I stood up to leave, he urged me to think seriously about my future.

On Easter Sunday 1955, Vaadi, Howard Brown, Schmidt, and a couple of others decided to hold an Easter Mass. They assembled in Howard Brown's cell and began the service. In the meantime, Buck and I were walking up and down the corridor. Sam, the three-thumbed Chinaman, came down the hall. He stopped and looked into the cell where they were having Mass and saw all of them on their knees praying. He laughed.

Shortly Buck and I came by, and he pointed to the praying men. He laughed again. He expected us to laugh, too, but we scolded him instead.

"Don't laugh!" we said, seriously and without equivocation.

He muttered something in Mandarin which we didn't understand, but it sounded crude and disrespectful. I told him that it was disrespectful to laugh at anyone worshiping God and that he was no friggin' good. He recognized our indignation, stopped laughing, and explained that he and the communists did not pray; neither did they believe in God.

Later in the afternoon we saw Abuelo sitting under a tree directly across from the window of the small cell next to our large cell. Thompson and I went to the window in the small cell for a better look and to try to talk to the old man. Schmidt stood watch for us at the door, and we hissed to attract Abuelo's attention. He looked up at our window and smiled. Then he told us he had been very sick. He also said he was from New Zealand and had been arrested in 1950. He had been tried and sentenced to one year by the People's Tribunal. We told him who we were and asked him if he had heard anything about us.

He told us that he had read about our trial; he also knew about Downey and Fecteau. On the chance that he would be released before us, we asked him to inform the United States and all the Free World that we were not guilty of the alleged border violation we were accused of. The truth, we said, was that the Red Chinese had *taken* us across the Yalu River after our capture in North Korea; they had brought us to Red China forcefully and against our will. He told us that his treatment was very harsh and inhumane; he agreed to pass on the information we gave him when he was released.

On Saturday morning, April 23, 1955, we were transferred to another cellblock where we were assigned two crewmen to a cell. We surmised that they moved us because they learned about our conversations with Abuelo and the Englishman.

Even though we were back in semi-solitary, they left our cell doors unlocked and permitted us to visit the men in the other cells. We also retained the privilege of walking in the hallway. The Catholics among us continued to hold their Mass, while the Protestants held their prayer meetings.

Young Wong continued to hold supervised study classes, still without success. He always left our sessions visibly dejected and frustrated. During the week he often called us younger airmen, one or two at a time, for sessions in his office. He berated us for not learning and lectured us on the virtues of communism and the **evils** of Capitalism. The individual attention he gave us bore no more fruit than did the supervised study we were forced to attend. We didn't understand why he and his superiors could not accept their failure to turn us into communists; we only wanted to be left alone until the time when we could be freed.

Steve E. Kiba

PART X

HOPE BECOMES A REALITY

PSALM 86:13

For great is thy mercy toward me: and thou hast delivered my soul from the lowest hell.

Scofield Reverence Bible

Steve E. Kiba

In early June 1955, during the supervised study hour, we discovered something interesting in the trash sheet: four American fighter pilots had been released in April 1955. This was extremely promising news for our crew; it renewed our hopes that we, too, would soon be released.

On Sunday morning, June 12, 1955, several of us were called individually to a cell, which had been converted to a temporary office, near the small (circle) hub. When I entered the office, I noticed immediately that the man behind the desk was a complete stranger. He was very short, probably no more than five feet tall, and he had an extremely large head. His dark eyes bulged outward from a fleshy face. After he stared at me for several minutes before asking me to sit down, I decided I was in the company of a communist nut.

After I was seated, he said, "I just want to have a friendly talk with you and ask you a few questions." I was not given the choice to agree or object.

He started out by asking me where our plane was shot down. From the moment I had entered, his boring stare had never left me. As he talked, he continued to stare; he was visually examining me from head to toe and from inside to outside. His demeanor gave me the creeps.

"North Korea," I said, without any hesitation.

My answer wasn't the one he expected or wanted to hear. For a moment he appeared stunned, and there was a brief period of silence before he recovered his composure and said, "You were shot down in the People's Republic of China. Why do you not acknowledge that?"

I vehemently denied his accusations and protested their illegal detention of us, but he ignored my words. I was totally discouraged with trying to make any of them understand the truth. They had fabricated a story to support their actions, and they were going to stand by it forever, no matter how much we rejected it.

He reminded me of their "lenient policy" and told me that the Chinese people would forgive me if I would only admit my guilt. He just couldn't understand why I was so bitter.

I knew it was a waste of time, but I still tried to make him understand that we were forcibly brought into Red China against our will and that we were being held illegally against our will. I reminded him that the Korean War was over and that it had been over for a long time; so, their refusal to release us was illegal, wrong morally, and was grossly inhumane.

He hinted that, if I were to behave myself and study diligently, they might review my case and, quite possibly, release me early.

Then he said, "Your behavior in your cell is unsatisfactory, even strange. Why don't you change your attitude and behavior?"

I just listened while he talked in a monotonous, even-pitched voice and told me, for what seemed like the millionth time, that the Capitalistic Warmongers had done a superb job on me and that my mind was completely saturated with poisonous misconceptions about the freedom-loving communist people. He said it was I who held the key to whether or not I would *ever* be released or would spend the remainder of my wretched life in some communist prison. As long as I harbored hatred and bitterness against the great Chinese people and the government of the People's Republic, I would remain incarcerated and be subjected to "re-education" sessions until they either completely cleansed my mind or deemed me incorrigible. Should the latter be my case, my future would indeed be a bleak one. When he finally dismissed me, he once more begged me to admit my guilt, to repent, to cooperate in my "re-education" process, and to behave.

Some of us were interviewed and some were not; so, all of us got together afterward, compared notes, and analyzed the situation. We learned that the new interrogator, whom we named "Evileyes," had asked each of us basically the same questions. What really puzzled us was the fact that they had selected some to question and not others. What was their purpose? How did they "select" whom to interview? Those *not* interviewed insisted that it was because the Red Chinese knew that *they* were sane but weren't quite sure about me and the others. Those interviewed believed that Evileyes was a psychiatrist because of his mannerisms, particularly the way he studied his "subjects" with his huge, evil-looking eyes which seemed to penetrate our souls. However, we all agreed that the interviews were *probably* held to determine whether we were emotionally and politically ready to be released. Several crew members were very much concerned as to whether or not I gave the man a rough time. I put their minds at ease; I told them I was a perfect gentleman during the interview. I neglected to mention our political debate.

Early Monday morning, July 4, 1955, the houseboys and Young Wong came into the cellblock. Young Wong told us we were being moved to a more comfortable area. He ordered us to collect our belongings and follow the houseboys.

We gathered what little we had and followed Sam and Smokey from the cellblock. We went outside, past a basketball court, and to a patio where a pump and a large cement tub were located. They led us past the base of a new round house (hub) and into a side door of the new cellblock. The cells in this cellblock were large. Five of us were put into the last cell on the left of the entrance, and the other five were put into the last cell on the opposite side. After we stowed our personal belongings, we made several return trips to bring our water barrel, chow buckets, and ping-pong table.

A vacant cell, next to the last cell on the right side, was used as a dining room, a recreation room, and the supervised study room. The first cell on the left, nearest to the double doors that opened into the hub, was set up as an office for the houseboys.

At the far end of the cellblock, there was a door that opened into a walled-in, unroofed area with a stone floor. On the right of this area was a one-slit trench toilet. The door to the area was left open, and we were allowed to sit out there if we wished. We quickly made use of the extra space as a "sun room" by moving our bed boards outside and lying in the nice, warm sun. We also used the area to wash our clothes and take sponge baths.

I was billeted in the cell on the left side of the corridor with Llewellyn, Buck, Howard Brown, and Schmidt. Thompson, Benjamin, Wallace Brown, Vaadi, and Baumer were in the cell across the corridor from us. Both new cells were large enough to accommodate our numbers, and we were pleased with the extra space.

That same morning we were given our mail and a few cans from our packages. According to Young Wong, it was so we could celebrate our Independence Day.

For most of us, our hopes continued to mount each day. When we compared the treatment we were presently receiving to that of a year ago, the difference was so vast we couldn't help but be encouraged.

But some refused to admit that they were optimistic, mostly because they were afraid to get their hopes up only to have them crushed again; the terrible blow of our showcase trial and the sentences they gave us still stuck in our minds like a grass bur in the throat. Because we'd had so many let-downs before, we were suspicious of any good treatment we got, and we wondered what the sorry bastards were up to now. For all we knew, these added perks and privileges we were now enjoying just might be a setup, a prelude to our execution during a trumped-up escape attempt from our less secure quarters. As a matter of self-preservation, we refused to let our hopes of being released by our brutal captors grow beyond what was reasonable and logical.

A few days after the Fourth, the interpreter we called Young Wong was reassigned. We surmised that he was demoted and sent to a re-education camp because his endeavor to re-educate us was a failure. A day or so later a new tongue showed up in our cellblock and introduced himself as Wong. His name was really Wong; therefore, we called him New Wong. He was older, more mature and experienced, and better educated than was Young Wong.

Our supervised classes continued, and the political literature increased in volume. We were still getting their filthy, one-sided newspaper. It would have been nice to at least be able to read the comics; but the paper, which was nothing more than a daily propaganda sheet, was devoid of such simple-minded diversions. Yet, when I thought about it from a practical viewpoint, the entire paper was one big, hilarious comic strip.

In our new quarters, Llewellyn, Buck, Howard Brown, and I carried our food to our cell and ate there instead of in the "dining room" with the others. There was no apparent reason for this, except that the four of us had similar ideas and interests. Also, it was a little more comfortable and much less noisy than at the large table. The others thought that we were mad at them for some reason, but that wasn't true with any of us. I gave it some thought and decided that the time all of us had spent in solitary confinement must have affected us in some way and made us into individuals who liked, maybe even needed, some privacy.

Our actions puzzled Sam, our houseboy. He continually asked us why we weren't eating with the others. Finally, New Wong asked me the same question. I told him it was more comfortable in our cell. He wasn't satisfied with my answer; he told me that we would *have* to eat in the large room set aside for that purpose.

Then I said to New Wong, "The *real* reason I prefer to eat apart is that I am an *atheist.*"

"Really?" he said. He had a satisfied smile on his face. He was obviously thinking that at last the Red Chinese had a great victory: they had at least changed stubborn old me that much.

"How about the others?" New Wong asked, smiling like a 'possum in a dung heap. "Are they atheists too?"

I said, "I don't know. You'll have to ask them."

After my brief conversation with New Wong, Sam and the other houseboys became friendlier with me, even cordial, and nothing more was ever said about our eating in our cell.

At that particular point in my life I was not much of a Christian, but neither was I an atheist. I didn't know *why* I told the interpreter that I was; it was a spur-of-the-moment thing, a reaction that was typical of my stubborn, resistive behavior. I was brought up in a Christian home and attended church quite regularly until I entered high school. The summer before entering the ninth grade, I started working at Fairlawn Country Club golf course as a caddy. After I graduated and entered the service, it was easy to skip church services. Yet, although I had strayed, I had not forgotten how to pray. I used to pray every night before retiring. I continued that practice in my captivity and daily asked God's counsel and guidance. I prayed for help in being a good airman and for the willingness and ability always to do the right thing. When I was weak and feverish from the incessant interrogations and fearful of divulging information that might be of some value to the enemy, I begged God to give me strength to resist and to survive. At other times, I grew weak and asked for the "easy" way out. I confessed my sins and asked for help to be better. I felt the guilt one feels in not being a "perfect" Christian, but the Red Chinese torturers never killed my faith in the Divine Power.

So my conscience would not let me forget the lie I told New Wong about being an "atheist." My guilt compelled me to tell my fellow crew members what I had done. I expected their understanding and forgiveness; instead some of them panicked and berated me for opening my big mouth. This hurt at first, until I realized that my off-hand remark had in a small way made the Redchinks feel a moment of victory. When I got the matter into proper perspective, I did what I should have done at first: I prayed to God for forgiveness and put the matter to rest.

Some days I passed my time in the cellblock by walking up and down the hall with Buck, Llewellyn, and anyone else who felt like walking. Now and then I played a game or two of ping-pong, and I always lost. I usually studied Spanish and Hungarian while the others played bridge or sat in the open area by the latrine and talked. After dark and just before boardtime, we stood in the open area and looked up at the stars. Our Navigator Llewellyn pointed out some of the more important stars and identified some of the constellations visible in the night sky in that area of the world.

In the middle of July the amount of food they gave us increased considerably. They started serving us a thick, viscous tomato soup and raw tomatoes daily. The quality of the food also greatly improved. Occasionally, we got green beans as the main dish. Near the end of the month, the houseboy brought in a bucket of hot, pea-like juice. New Wong said it was full of vitamins that were very good for our malnourished bodies. It seemed to us that an effort was being made to fatten us up before releasing us. At least that's what we "hoped." We were still suspicious of their motives.

On Thursday afternoon, July 28, 1955, Sam brought in two large blocks of ice, one for each cell. He put the ice into wooden tubs. Then he gave each of us a pack of Sen Sen and told us the ice was brought because it was "very hot" and the Sen Sen was to keep our breath fresh.

Later, while we were eating supper, Bugeyes, New Wong, and several other official-looking Red Chinese came into the cellblock. First, they went into the "dining" room where part of the crew was eating and looked around. Then they came into our cell, watched us eat for several minutes, looked around, and left.

As soon as they left, several of the others rushed over to our cell from the dining room and asked us if we had recognized the prosecutor. How could any of us not recognize that bug-eyed, Redchink son-of-a-bitch who falsely accused and prosecuted us? On the other hand, none of us remembered ever seeing any of the other visitors whose curious behavior—they obviously were on some kind of inspection tour—caused us to speculate some more about all the changes in our prison life. We tried to make some sense of the unexpected visit, the extra, nutritious food we were receiving, and the friendly attitude of the houseboys. When we put it all together, we construed a definite change of attitude in the Red Chinese that gave us some hope. Some of us were filled with optimism; we became absolutely sure that we were going home soon. A few were undecided, and a few believed that something truly was happening; but, whatever it was, it had nothing to do with our release. Yet, little by little our spirits rose, and I looked forward to each new day with fervent hope that this day would be the day. I was so keyed up that I could scarcely sleep at night. I tossed and turned on my bed board and visualized the things I would do once we left that hellhole of a prison.

On Saturday afternoon, July 30, 1955, we were again given a small amount of the food from our packages and also some mail. While I was in the office receiving mine, New Wong asked me some questions.

He said, "What do you think of the Chinese now, Kiba?"

I said, "The same as before, but thank you for our food items. What you are letting us have is scarcely enough for a good taste after we divide it ten ways."

"We have been doing all we can to make things more comfortable for you. We know you want your canned foods, so we are giving them to you a little at a time. Pretty soon you will think better of us."

"Perhaps," I said. "But why won't you give us all, or at least more, of the food items? After all, they do belong to us."

New Wong ignored my question and said, "Your folks write to you quite often, and we try to get your mail to you as quickly as possible."

251

His evasiveness irritated me, but I let it pass. I had something important I wanted to ask.

"Why doesn't Schmidt get any mail from his wife? Are you holding it back for some reason?" I asked.

New Wong said, "I really don't know why he doesn't get mail from his wife, and no, we're not holding it back. We have no reason to."

"I don't get all the mail written to me," I said. "Neither does anyone else. You could very well be withholding Schmidt's mail, too."

"We have held back some letters that contained certain forbidden things in them."

"We've figured that out, but I'm glad to hear you admit it. I also believe that not all the letters we've written have been sent."

New Wong lost his patience and wouldn't comment further. He said, "Kiba, you need to study harder! And try to behave yourself! Go back to your cell now."

I fired a parting shot. "I know perfectly well that I can't behave myself for another three-and-a-half years. I won't even try it."

I carried my articles back and deposited them with the rest that the others received so they could be divided. Then I went to my cell, sat on my board, and read my mail.

About four o'clock on Sunday afternoon, July 31, 1955, the barber came into our cellblock. I felt sure that the time for our release had come. Because I wanted to look sharp for that train ride to freedom, I permitted the barber to shave me, also. The barber gave everyone a shave and a haircut before he left, and we made note that such efficiency in regard to our personal hygiene was indeed unusual when compared to past performance. So we sat in the open area and talked about it. While we were out there, we noticed that the houseboys and the interpreter kept running in and out of our cellblock.

New Wong came down the corridor to our area and told us that a little later we would be given a special supper; then he hurriedly left the cellblock.

At seven o'clock, New Wong and several houseboys returned to our cellblock and led us across the prison to a building somewhere near the administration building. We were made to wait outside for about five minutes during which time we were joined by Colonel Arnold. Then they took us inside and lined us up in the same order as we assumed at the trial. We were led single file into a room where we had to remain standing in front of a desk behind which two Red Chinese officials were seated. They looked familiar, but truthfully I was too excited to recognize them. It was hot in the room, and the two were fanning themselves and fidgeting with some papers.

Finally, one of them spoke. He said, "We have reviewed your case. Since the People's Republic of China is lenient toward those who have confessed their crimes, we have decided to free you because of your good behavior. But you must never again return to the People's Republic."

We shouted simultaneously, "We're free!!!!"

An avalanche of words poured forth from our long-abused crew: "Hotdog!" "Thank God!" "The sooner we get outta here, the better!!!" "Who'd want to come back to this place!"

After they calmed us down, the official continued, "First you will be taken to the dining hall for a good Chinese dinner. After you eat, you will be taken back to pick up your belongings and then to the train. You may go now."

Words cannot express how happy all of us were. I, personally, was overflowing with so much joy all I could think about was getting on the train. The excitement was so great I could hardly eat when we got to the dining hall. Actually, the food was delicious, but all of us were so anxious to leave that **damned hellhole** and start our journey back to freedom that our appetites were greatly diminished. Our Red Chinese "hosts" kept urging us to eat more, but their prodding was useless; at that moment even sumptuous food couldn't rekindle our persistently deprived appetites.

After we had eaten all we wanted and our Red Chinese "hosts" had eaten their fill, the houseboys took us back to the cellblock. We hastily gathered our personal belongings and put them in net-like bags which one of the houseboys had given to us. I put my small, green tin cup and a Chinese hand towel in with my personal stuff. I also hid the book EL CANAL VOLGA-DON among my letters and other books.

Sam, the three-thumbed chinaman, was excited, too. He was running back and forth among us and smiling like a 'possum in an outhouse. Everyone was laughing and carrying on, even Sam.

"Llewellyn, it looks like you guys were right this time."

Buck said, "I told you I felt it in my bones."

Someone else said, "That's just rheumatism, Buck."

Our noisy, unregulated chatter filled the room: "Man, I can hardly wait to get on that train;" "I must be dreaming!" "Are we really going home?" "When I cross the border, *then* I'll really be happy."

At nine o'clock that night, carrying our bundles, we left that horrible cellblock for the last time. Sam rushed back and forth among us offering to help carry our sacks. He was smiling and seemed genuinely happy for us to be going. He even patted me on the back and said, "Kiba dinghow!" (Kiba is okay!) He was probably thinking that after 932 miserable days of putting up with us big, bad Capitalistic-Imperialistic Warmongers his life would be a lot easier now. As we walked past the guards on the way out, they also appeared to be truly happy about getting rid of us.

They led us back to the administration building, took us inside one at a time, and searched us. Several of the fellows realized what was going on; and before they went inside, they threw away the tin cups they had hidden in their bags. The inspectors found the house plans that both Llewellyn and Wallace Brown had spent months working on; they confiscated both sets. Red Chinese "flunkies" loitering close by took our prison uniforms and ordered us to put on some of the civilian clothes that had been sent to us from home. A few of the articles that had been taken from us at the time of our capture were returned to us. They returned my U. S. Air Force hack watch, about one-half of my M.P.C.'s (Military Pay Certificates), and my empty wallet. They kept my identification card and other papers that had been in my wallet. They also kept our flight clothing, our .45 caliber automatic pistols, and all of our other military gear, all of which were most certainly put on display in some museum in Peking.

At ten o'clock they took us to a bus. About twenty minutes after we left, we passed Tien An Mien Square. Fifteen minutes later we arrived at the railroad station. The station, the area around it, and the streets were teeming with people and security guards dressed in yellow. Babyface, New Wong, and several others left the bus to find out if they were ready for us to board the train.

Several minutes later they returned and hustled us from the bus to the train and into a Pullman-type coach. A small percentage of the contents of our packages from home—canned goods, clothing, books, magazines, hygiene products, and other items—were also placed on the train. (We never saw the majority of the packages that had been sent to us; it was obvious that the Red Chinese officials had confiscated them for their own personal use.) It would be safe to say that we were given less than ten percent of the food and health items our families had sent to us.

The railroad car we rode in was similar to an American Pullman car; the seats could be made into a bed, and another bed folded down from the ceiling. The seats were very hard, but they didn't seem nearly as hard as the seats on our first two train rides after we were shot down. Perhaps it was because we knew we were headed for freedom and not into the deep, dark, dismal hell of interior Red China.

We left the station in Peking at exactly eleven thirty on Sunday night, July 31, 1955. Interpreter New Wong and "Little Wheel" Babyface accompanied us, and we were totally surrounded by a plethora of security guards.

We sat up for awhile, talking to each other and looking out the windows. Then we were ordered to lie down and rest; so, we tried out the hard beds provided in the coach. Schmidt took the lower bunk, and I took the upper bunk in our little compartment. After we got settled in, we couldn't sleep; we were just too keyed up with the excitement of going home; so, we spent most of the night just whispering to each other.

Early the next morning (Monday, August 1, 1955), we crawled out of our beds, washed up in the washroom located at the rear of the car, and resumed sitting on the hard seats and looking out the windows. The Red Chinese brought us a fairly decent breakfast, which we consumed routinely because we were still possessed with overwhelming thoughts of freedom and home.

After breakfast some of the fellows started a bridge game. I sat and looked out the window at the scenery. The Red Chinese countryside was by no means a paradise or a place I would want to

255

spend very much time. It was filled with dilapidated shanties on both sides of the tracks, and the hordes of peasants who occupied them were shabbily and simply dressed. On our long journey, we passed through many towns along the railway. I saw multitudes of dirty houses, closely packed, and crowded streets covered with litter and trash. Many people slept outside on the ground, and everyone looked dirty. I did not see any of the "beauty" described in the propaganda books they forced us to read; all I saw was filth and poverty.

The farm lands we passed through were no different. The poverty and low standard of living the peasants had to endure were evident in their poor, shabby abodes and on the small plots they worked merely to "eke out a living." In the books the political commissars forced us to read, the authors boasted that the Red Chinese farmers had many, many tractors and other types of farm machinery, but I didn't see a single tractor on the whole journey. Instead, I saw that the farmers were using donkeys or working by hand with ancient, inefficient hand tools. The soil itself had the appearance of poor, overworked, infertile ground.

The food on the train was good, and throughout the day we ate fruit, meat, and candy from our packages. Whenever we saw children along the way, we threw candy and chewing gum to them. This infuriated the security guards, and they frequently warned us not to throw things from the train. The children were undoubtedly taught to hate Americans, but they sure liked our American candy and chewing gum.

Just after dark, the train pulled into the station in a small town and stopped. We saw a group of young men playing cards on a stack of old railroad ties near the tracks. We watched them for awhile. Their cards were old and tattered, so Benjamin opened the window and tossed them a brand new deck of playing cards. They acted as if they had received the Worker's Hero Medal from Chairman Mao himself; they were overcome with joy, and they gave a demonstration of their gratefulness with a long series of nods and bows.

At ten thirty on Tuesday morning, August 2, 1955, the train pulled into the city of Hankow on the north side of the Yangtze River. Our "chaperones" hustled us off the train and into a bus. The bus snaked through heavy bicycle and cart traffic for about thirty minutes and pulled to a stop in front of a large building in the center of town. We were escorted off the bus to a large lounge on the second floor of the building. While we waited for whatever business we had there, we watched the people walking hurriedly in the streets below. The street was filled with carts and bicycles; we saw very few cars or motor vehicles of any kind.

They served lunch to us there; then they took us back to the bus. The driver battled the heavy cart and bicycle traffic by making a zigzag pattern through the narrow streets until we arrived at a primitive embarkation center on the north bank of the Yangtze River. We were led from the bus to a makeshift dock where a small motorized boat was waiting to ferry us across the big river. When we got out on the south side, we were escorted to the train station through dirty, rough streets filled with potholes. As I walked along the tracks to our coach, I noticed a white man sitting in one of the coaches. I waved to him, but he did not respond.

We boarded our assigned car, and the train pulled out heading south toward the city of Canton. All along the way we continued throwing candy and other goodies to the children.

On Wednesday morning August 3, 1955, we were still on what seemed like an endless train ride, but at least we knew we were rolling closer and closer to freedom. Everyone was still ecstatic. We were more excited than ever, and our excitement increased in proportion to our distance away from that hellhole we'd lived in for over two years.

The train pulled into the Canton railway station at three o'clock that afternoon. We were escorted from the train and put on a bus that took us to a rundown hotel somewhere in downtown Canton. They put us in several very dirty rooms on the third floor. The entire hotel was in utter disrepair and downright filthy, but we accepted the situation as best we could with the rationale that our discomfort would be for only one night, hopefully. The food they served us at supper was typical of the hotel; it was no good, either. However, we still had canned goods, so we ate our own food—meats, fruit, and other delicacies from home.

During the early evening we passed the time by throwing candy, chewing gum, cans of peanuts, and fruit to youngsters in the alley

Steve E. Kiba

below. An old woman in the building across the alley saw what we were doing. She clapped her hands and yelled to attract our attention; then she smiled and motioned for us to throw some of our goodies to her, too.

Our "chaperones" searched us at seven o'clock. They did this every day, and to us it was a pretty stupid thing to do. The only people we had contact with were Red Chinese, so the message we got from their searches was that they didn't even trust their own people. After they finished, we sat around and talked until bedtime.

We left for the Canton train station at nine o'clock the next morning. We arrived at the station just in time to board the train before it pulled out. Our destination was Hong Kong, and this would be the last leg of our long journey. I was eager for it to end, to finally taste again the sweet freedom that we had been robbed of by the Red Chinese; so I had to curtail my excitement by continuing to sit on the hard seat and watch the passing countryside. The area we were in was swampy in many places, and I could see pineapples growing almost everywhere along both sides of the tracks.

The weather was hot and sticky. The closer we came to the border, the slower time seemed to pass, and the slower the train seemed to move. I looked at my hack watch every few minutes, but that didn't speed things up at all.

Finally, at approximately twelve thirty, the train rolled into a station on the Red Chinese side of the border. Babyface and his comrades escorted us off the train and over to the border check point where they searched us again. After they were satisfied that we big, bad "war criminals" weren't smuggling out their "crown jewels" or some other valuable contraband, they cleared us to be "deported." Then they led us down a covered walkway to the actual border where they handed us over to several congenial-looking British Military Policemen. It was exactly thirty six minutes after one on the afternoon of Thursday, August 4, 1955, when we stepped across the dividing line into the most welcome arms of those British Military Policemen. We had spent 936 endless and utterly miserable days in Red China's dismal, god-forsaken hell. It was with great pleasure to me that I saw the last of Babyface, New Wong, and all those other ugly, mangy, rotten, no-good, sadistic Redchink bastards. I truly felt

258

no pain or remorse in parting company with them or in leaving their DAMNED RED CHINA!

The British MPs gave us a warm welcome, and then they led us down the tracks toward Hong Kong proper. Within a few minutes we were met by American Air Force personnel led by Colonel Delk Simpson. Photographers were swarming all around us and taking our pictures as we walked along the tracks toward a group of buildings.

Colonel Simpson and his men took us to an office building and gave each of us a Coca Cola; believe me, that Coke *really* tasted good. Colonel Simpson and several of the others gave us autographed Hong Kong dollar bills to keep as souvenirs.

We went from the office building to the swank Jockey Club which was crawling with reporters and photographers. They took many, many pictures of our crew in front of the Jockey Club.

Then they took us upstairs in the Club to rooms they had reserved for us. There we found brand new khaki uniforms and a shaving kit provided to us by the American Red Cross. We were allowed a minimum time to freshen up; but, even while we were bathing and cleaning up, photographers and other people were running around in our rooms. We found that to be irritating and inconsiderate.

After we shaved and bathed, we were subjected to a "hasty" pre-physical checkup. Then we were allowed to put on our new khaki uniforms. Man, it really felt great to be back in uniform again!

We then went downstairs to the dining room and sat down to a sumptuous steak dinner.

During the meal we talked, and more photographs were taken. Colonel Arnold led us in a song to the tune of "It's a Long Way Back Home." The song ended something like this: "So goodbye to Peking and to HELL with your DAMNED RED CHINA!"

During the meal we were given $150 in cash and a check for the balance due us up to July 31, 1955.

Of course the United States Treasury neglected to pay us any interest on our money which they so dutifully "safeguarded" for us. Prior to being shot down, I had signed a document requesting the Air Force to send my pay home so my father could bank or invest it for me, but someone screwed up and ignored the aforementioned document. Consequently, I was bilked out of, or to put it in more genteel words, I was **denied** the opportunity to earn interest and dividends on thirty-two months of my pay which was supposed to have been banked or invested for me.

After we finished eating our fill of the fantastic dinner, we were taken to another building for a brief press conference in which the reporters were instructed to confine their questions to the subject of our health. But, as anyone might imagine, they immediately violated that instruction. The place was crowded, wall-to-wall with reporters and photographers. The Air Force did its best to hold back the news-hungry reporters, but even so it was a very stressful and tiring experience for us.

After they questioned us intensively, we returned to the Jockey Club to pick up our gear. From there Air Force personnel rushed us to the airport where we boarded a plane.

At six o'clock in the afternoon, the plane took off for Clark Field in the Philippines. It had been a long, exciting day, and I personally was totally exhausted. I stretched out in my seat and tried to rest, but I couldn't: my high state of excitement still prevented me from relaxing enough to get any sleep.

At nine-thirty we landed at Clark Field. We stepped from the plane in front of Base Operations where Clark Field personnel gave us a heart-warming welcome. General Lee, Colonel Arnold's old friend, and Ambassador Ferguson came out to the plane to shake our hands and welcome us home.

After the warm greeting, our American guards rushed us to the base hospital and billeted us in a nice air-conditioned ward. We attempted to talk our guards into letting us go off base and into the town of Angeles for a little fun and excitement, but our request was denied.

Several corpsmen and two lovely nurses were on duty in the ward, and there was an Air Policeman stationed at each entrance to the ward. Their objectives were to keep out the curious and to keep us in.

We were given all the food we wanted, but we had appetites for other things besides food. Around eleven o'clock, some of us decided to slip out, go to town, and have a party; but the guards were watching us too closely. We even tried to bribe the guards, but they refused our offer. Therefore, we abandoned the idea of slipping out, but not

263

before we tried to convince the corpsmen to aid us in our plot. We had no luck with them, either.

We were somewhat dispirited because we had exchanged our Red Chinese guards for American guards, and we were still restricted. After 936 horrendous days and nights—22,464 never-ending hours— we were still being guarded! In the "land of the free and the home of the brave," we were not yet free; our lives were still being "controlled and watched."

A short time after our failed attempts to go into town, someone brought in some whiskey. It wasn't long before some of the fellows started getting very happy. I stayed up with them for awhile, but I was really exhausted. I tried to get some sleep, but my mind kept thinking of home and what was awaiting me there. I got very little sleep that night.

The next morning, Friday, August 5, 1955, we got up early; I think most of us were afraid we'd miss out on something. Around eight o'clock, Schmidt learned that his wife Tippie had remarried while he was in that dismal hellhole in Red China. The news was like a hammer blow to his head, and he went into one of his "black" moods. We felt sorry for him, but the news only confirmed the suspicions the rest of us had secretly maintained for a long time. I really believed that Schmidt suspected it, too, but refused to accept the reality of it.

About thirty minutes later, Schmidt came to me. He was very upset and confused. The emotional strain caused by Tippie's betrayal showed its effects.

He said, "She must've thought I was dead, Kiba." He struggled to hold back his tears.

"I reckon so," I said. What more could I say? I really felt sorry for him, but I truly didn't know any comforting words.

"What would you do?" he asked.

"You know what I'd do. But listen, Schmidt, I can't tell you what to do. Neither can anyone else. This is something you'll have to decide for yourself."

"I just don't know—I really don't know what to do."

"Do you still love her?" I asked.

He had a woebegone look on his face, and his voice quivered when he answered, "Yes."

"Enough to take her back after this—this hell she's put you through?"

"If she'll come back to me."

"Schmidt, you're a man now, so don't let anyone tell you what to do. Think it over. One way or another you'll come up with an answer."

"Thanks, Kiba. It looks like you and me are going to have a lot of fun at college," he said. His voice was steady, and he acted as if he had regained his composure.

The story-hungry reporters attempted all the tricks in the book to get to poor Schmidt, because the news of Tippie's remarriage had already broken in the United States media. Thanks to the Air Force, they didn't get to him at Clark Field.

During the morning we had our pictures taken with the nurses, corpsmen, and the rest of the hospital staff.

Buck received his orders promoting him to Captain, and Colonel Arnold pinned the silver bars on him.

At noon we were taken back to Base Operations and put on another plane. Shortly we were winging our way toward Japan.

That afternoon we landed at Tachikawa Air Force Base in Japan, where we were instantly taken to the base hospital at FEAM COM. The officers were put in one part of the hospital and the enlisted men in another. Again they told us we were restricted to the ward, and much to our dismay, American Air Policemen were assigned to guard us. We were growing more anxious to leave the base and go into town; the fact that we were still being "cooped up" and guarded angered us very much.

The next day, August 6, 1955, Air Force doctors gave us a cursory physical examination. A dentist also checked and cleaned our teeth. Then the Air Force conducted a preliminary debriefing, and I turned over the book EL CANAL VOLGA-DON to them. We also talked to a team from Washington, D.C., that was in charge of studying prisoner-of-war treatment. In most of the sessions during our brief stay in Japan, our interviewers from Washington tape-recorded everything we said. They told us they would study and analyze the tapes later. One of the main areas of their questioning centered on the false statement that we had signed. I told them that in our January 12, 1953, briefing our team had instructed us to sign anything if it became a matter of life or death and as long as we were being coerced. In that same briefing, they advised us to lie as much as possible in any dealings with our captors. The debriefing officers and the Washington team seemed to doubt that we had been given such instructions and advice, and they gave me the impression that they thought I was lying to them. It appeared they wished to shift the blame, if there were any, away from the briefing personnel and onto our flight crew.

Saturday night the Red Cross arranged for us to talk with our folks. We appreciated that, and it was really great to hear Mom's and Dad's voices.

Also, during our stay at the hospital, the Red Cross gave each man a fine piece of luggage. The American Red Cross really did its best to see that we were given everything we needed.

At four o'clock on Sunday afternoon, August 7, 1955, we endured a long press conference. The reporters asked us all kinds of questions, including whether or not we had ever signed any statements. Colonel Arnold told them that he had signed the false statement first and the rest of us were not culpable because we had signed only after he had. But the rest of us believed that we were personally responsible for our own actions. The reporters also asked us if we were over Red China when we were shot down.

"Hell no!" Colonel Arnold shouted. "We were *taken* into Red China."

Llewellyn, our Navigator, showed the reporters on a map of Korea just where our flight had taken us, where the searchlights had first picked us up, our position at the time of the attack, and where we had been forced to abandon the aircraft.

Llewellyn said emphatically, "No, we didn't fly into their damned Red China! We were a good forty miles *south* of the Yalu River!"

Then the reporters asked about our treatment. Colonel Arnold told how he had been tortured and kept in solitary confinement the entire time of his imprisonment.

It was a long, tiring press conference, and it seemed as if the news-hounds would never run out of questions; but it finally ended, and we went back to our wards.

On Monday afternoon, August 8, 1955, our debriefing was temporarily discontinued. They told us it would be resumed in

Washington, D. C. They allowed us the remainder of Monday and all day Tuesday to spend as free time.

On Wednesday August 10, 1955, we were escorted to our plane at one o'clock. A large crowd of Tachikawa personnel gathered at Base Operations to see us and give us a rousing send-off. Prior to boarding our plane, a lovely Japanese girl presented each member of our crew with a picture of Mount Fujiyama and said to us, "The Japanese people think of Fujisan as a symbol of greatness, purity, and tranquility. We want you to have this picture as a symbol of two great countries marching toward world peace."

Finally, our plane departed and we were homeward bound. After a brief refueling stop at Midway Island, we continued on to Hickam Air Force Base in Hawaii. We were allowed to spend two glorious days there before flying on to Travis Air Force Base in California. There we parted and boarded planes that would take us to our respective hometowns.

When I arrived in Akron, Ohio, it was raining. However, the weather did not deter thousands of my fellow Akronites from meeting the plane to welcome me home. Rain or not, there were no words to express my feelings and gratitude on finally getting home—and free at last!

After a hectic, but very delightful, 60 days at home, I drove to Bolling Air Force Base in Washington, D. C. I reported to the 1100 Perp. Squadron and signed in. I was assigned to a ramshackle barracks, which, according to the custom of my past imprisonment, I examined carefully. It was deserted and had an uninviting appearance, and it appeared I was the sole occupant. The whole sorry environment imposed on me caused me to feel as if they had slapped me back into solitary confinement.

I immediately became morose, and a profound feeling of depression invaded my still fragile psyche. After enduring a couple of miserable days in the dismal quarters, I received orders transferring me to the Visiting Airmen's Quarters. The VAQ was a hundred percent nicer than the initial dump they put me in. It had a lounge downstairs with a television set and a Coke machine. The move improved my disposition and outlook tremendously.

To add to my moroseness, Schmidt told me that while he was on leave he contacted Tippie and discussed the dilemma posed by her marriage to the "other man" while he was in prison. Her claim that she thought he was dead gave her the legal option of nullifying the second marriage and going back to him. She decided to do just that, and I thought the choice was unfortunate for him. I personally believed that she returned to him to get the rest of his money and to share in what she perceived to be the "limelight" of publicity our crew had received upon release. Nevertheless, she did come back to him, and he seemed happy enough about it.

Several days after we arrived in Washington, D. C., our debriefing was resumed. Air Force Intelligence and two civilian intelligence agencies conducted the debriefing sessions, which were held almost daily from eight to five. Sometimes they were held on the base and sometimes downtown. They asked me hundreds of questions pertaining to our mission, our capture, our interrogations, our treatment at the hands of our captors, our meeting with Downey and Fecteau, and our seeing other Caucasians, including Van Voorhis. They quizzed me at great lengths about the three weeks we had spent with Downey and Fecteau. Almost everything we said was recorded on tape and in writing.

During the sessions I passed on the message which Fecteau had given me concerning both Jehol and Samurai. The Air Force, the CIA, and the State Department warned me to keep my mouth shut about seeing Downey and Fecteau and about what the two had told us. Schmidt and some of the other crew members told me that they had also received the same instructions. (Even though Red Chinese Intelligence already knew the full scope of CIA operations in Manchuria through its gestapo methods with Downey and Fecteau and the captured Kuomintang agents, we Americans who had endured similar methods of horror were now being told to keep our mouths shut.)

They told us that both Downey and Fecteau had known what they were getting into before they signed on the dotted line and that the United States Government and the agency for which they worked would not acknowledge them or even admit that these two were American citizens. As far as the U. S. Government and the CIA were concerned, Downey and Fecteau did not exist. They admonished us to forget these two men and the whole touchy mess.

We were also told to forget all the other Caucasians we had seen. Some of the debriefers suggested that perhaps I had not seen Van Voorhis and the other white men I told them about. They endeavored to convince me that I was probably hallucinating and just *thought* I saw him and the others. In an effort to confuse me and to discredit my reported sightings of Van Voorhis and the other Caucasians, they asked me over and over in different ways about my "alleged" sightings. I repeatedly told them that I saw Van Voorhis and the others. I told them that it was either Van Voorhis or his twin brother. They looked at me skeptically and gave the impression that I was lying to them and making all of it up. Yet, they emphatically admonished me to remain silent about seeing Van Voorhis and the two CIA agents, Downey and Fecteau—and all the other Caucasians. They said I was *never* to write about or talk about my sightings or my contact with any of my aforementioned fellow countrymen.

This warning upset me immensely because I had grown to like and admire both Downey and Fecteau, and I knew from personal experience that imprisonment in Red China or any other communist hellhole for any length of time would completely destroy even the strongest man. It really disturbed me to know that there were still thousands of my fellow American countrymen sitting in Red Chinese political prisons, their minds and bodies slowly but surely wasting away. It equally disturbed me to find out that our own government was going to sit by and allow this unthinkable act to happen. This knowledge caused me to wonder whether the United States Government really and truly tried its best to secure the release of our crew. Considering the willingness of certain government officials to "write off," abandon, and then forget all those who were not fortunate enough to have been repatriated (and taking into account their indifference regarding those who were left behind) almost convinced me that our own government had very little to do with our release. I began to believe that we were released simply because the Red Chinese thought we were no longer of any value to them, politically or otherwise. That being the case, they could still profit from our release politically through the "world sympathy" generated by such a "compassionate" act.

Despite the unpleasant circumstances surrounding our government's attitude toward our missing servicemen, the debriefings themselves were a snap compared to the interrogations in Mukden and Peking. At least we could sit and drink coffee or tea if we became thirsty. Nonetheless, they became tiresome and boring before they were finished.

Occasionally we went to the Pentagon for various reasons; we had to ride the launch across the Potomac to get there from where we stayed. While there, we visited the Casualties Department and looked through old letters and telegrams which dealt with our incident and imprisonment. We saw letters written by our families inquiring about our status, and we saw the Air Force's reply to those letters. I told the personnel in Casualties about the white men, including Van Voorhis, whom I had seen at the Spider Web prison in Peking. They told me and the other crew members that there were still hundreds of American servicemen unaccounted for and that those poor, unfortunate souls were being carried on the "missing" list. They also showed us photographs of the missing servicemen to see if we could recognize any of them.

Toward the end of October 1955, our debriefing in Washington, D. C., came to an end, and we received orders transferring us to Maxwell Air Force Base, Alabama, for more interviews and evaluations. We had almost two weeks free time before we had to report there. Buck invited me to spend the time at his home in Armathwaite, Tennessee, so I went with him and spent ten very enjoyable days there.

Early Thursday morning on November 10, 1955, I left for Maxwell Air Force Base. I arrived there about seven that evening and signed in at the rundown transient barracks; it, too, was almost empty, and again I started to feel lost and depressed. I should've counted my blessings though, because the next day I was moved to another barracks that was completely deserted. My immediate thought was that the Air Force certainly had strange ideas about making its repatriated POWs feel at home. After 936 unbearable days in a communist hellhole, most of which were spent in solitary confinement, this was just what I needed: having a whole damned barracks to myself. I truly was not ungrateful for being home and having those freedoms and advantages that went with it. At another time, and under other circumstances, being the lone occupant of a large barracks building probably would have been an enjoyable experience. But at that particular time, and considering the trauma of my imprisonment, the vacant, lonely space unconsciously elicited bad memories and at the same time challenged me to overcome them.

At Maxwell we underwent more debriefing. Several psychologists, or psychiatrists—maybe even both—examined us and prepared evaluations based on their examinations. While this was going on, I tried to stay away from the empty barracks as much as possible because it triggered in my mind those frightful days of solitary in Mukden and Peking. Every chance I had, I visited the other members of our crew. At other times, despite intense pain in my legs—which I tried to ignore—I practiced basketball at the base gymnasium. At night I had difficulty falling asleep; but once I went to sleep, I was plagued by the same horrible nightmare that frequently jarred me awake in Red China.

On the second weekend we were at Maxwell Air Force Base, Schmidt, Tippie, and I went to New Orleans, Louisiana. We visited some of the well-known night spots and had a good time, but something was missing in the camaraderie we shared, and I sensed it; although they *appeared* happy, it was obvious that things simply were not as they seemed. As for me, I just couldn't embrace the festive spirit so common in New Orleans. I kept thinking about Downey, Fecteau, Van Voorhis, and all the others left in that sorry hellhole. Also, I kept thinking about their loved ones in the United States who kept hoping, praying—and waiting patiently for the return of their loved ones. My heart told me I should contact and visit those courageous people, but my mind kept posing the question, "What will you say to them? That their own government has left them behind?" Not only was a struggle taking place between my heart and my mind, but also I was burdened by the debriefers' admonishment not to make contact with them. What stress and pressure to lay on us returned POWs!

Our debriefing and tests ended just before Thanksgiving, and I asked for a few days of furlough. Some of the crew went straight to their next assignment; and before we left, we were given a party at the

Officers' Club. It was a nice party, but it didn't dispel the loneliness and solitary feelings I still had and couldn't seem to overcome. On my way home to Akron, Ohio, I drove as far as Armathwaite, Tennessee, and spent the night there with Buck's parents. Next day, I finished the trip home where I spent over a week visiting with relatives and friends. Thanksgiving Day 1955, was absolutely superb.

On Thursday, December 1, 1955, I drove back to Bolling Air Force Base and signed in at the Visiting Airmen's Quarters (VAQ). My enlistment was actually over on July 31, 1954, while I was still imprisoned; so the Air Force was anxious to know whether I was going to re-enlist or take a discharge. For the next few days after I arrived, they urged me to re-enlist. Actually, I wanted to stay in the Air Force, but I also had a very strong desire to go to college. Somehow my experiences in the last four years had revealed to me my own limitations, and that lack stimulated in me a great desire to learn more. I was affected by a certain amount of conflict about my future because, on the way home from Japan, the Air Force had promised us *any assignment* we wanted if we re-enlisted. I told them I would sign up for another tour of duty if they would send me to college or to South America. They said that since I was only an *airman*, and not an officer, I did not qualify to be sent to college. They also said that I would have to remain in the States for a year before I could be sent overseas again; and, even then, I would have to wait for an opening. A vague promise was made to send me to Central America "in a year or so." In the meantime I would have to stay at Bolling AFB, or be assigned to some other stateside base and do—what? The nebulous offers were never put in writing; in fact, my request to have them put in writing was denied.

During my last days at Bolling, each member of the crew was given a reel of the propaganda film made by the wily Red Chinese at the one and only "party" they gave us. Then, on December 16, 1955, Schmidt and I received our discharge papers from the "grateful" United States Air Force. We said our farewells to each other and to all the other crew members who had decided to make the Air Force their career.

Schmidt, his wife, and their son headed west back to Idaho. I was sad to see them go because I was apprehensive about their chances for a happy marriage. But Schmidt was an adult, and he was entitled to lead his life, to make his own decisions and mistakes.

I headed north toward Akron, Ohio, again. Leaving the Air Force and all my friends was an emotional experience somewhat akin to leaving family and a long-time job all at once. However, I realized I could no longer endure either the petty rank-pulling atmosphere that existed in the Air Force or the Air Force's ambiguous statements in the matter of public relations vis-a-vis the daily realities of its members.

Also, I thought as I drove, there was the matter of Fecteau and Downey; Fecteau was serving a 20 year sentence, and Downey was in for life. It really bothered me that those two poor men were living in that god-forsaken prison in Red China with little or no hope of ever seeing their homeland and family again. On numerous occasions during our debriefings, I told our government officials what the Red Chinese told me it would take to secure their freedom: first, our government had to admit that the two of them were CIA agents and that they did illegally and covertly enter the People's Republic of China in order to establish a network of Kuomintang espionage agents in Manchuria; second, our President had to make a public apology for that provocation against the "peace-loving" Chinese people. Of course, I was told point blank that those things would never happen, and I didn't really expect that they would.

Then there was the sorrowful knowledge I had of Van Voorhis and all the other Caucasians whom I had seen at the Spider Web. Both the Air Force and the CIA told me to "forget about them" and to "put them out of my mind." But how could I? As a Christian and a human being with feelings and emotions, how could I go on with my normal daily life knowing that my fellow countrymen were being left behind—abandoned, actually—by the very same government that sent them off to do battle against a vicious and cruel enemy of freedom, peace, and democracy? How could I erase from my mind the vivid images of our Instructor Radar Operator Paul Van Voorhis, walking around the courtyard just outside Cell #15 at the infamous Spider Web? It was too much to assimilate with any degree of reconciliation at that moment in my life.

Far removed from the action on the battlefield and from the life-draining idleness of being chained up in a stifling, miserable six-by-ten cubbyhole in some remote, dismal communist hellhole, it was quite easy for the "desk jockeys" sitting in plush offices somewhere in downtown Washington, D. C., and in the Pentagon, to suggest to us—to *advise* us—and yes, even to go as far as to *admonish* us to *forget about* our fellow countrymen whom we had seen in Red Chinese political prisons enduring the same **living hell** we were forced to endure, and who—unlike us—were never repatriated, and likely never will be.

Did the Air Force and the CIA realize the tremendous stress and feelings of guilt they were inflicting upon those of us who were fortunate enough to be freed by asking us to *forget* that fellow Americans were yet languishing away and suffering never-ending agony in those hellish communist prisons? Could they not foresee that our knowledge of those poor, wretched souls would result in adverse effects on our health and well-being? The big question is did they even care? Their callousness regarding our missing captives and their concerned loved ones left me with only one conclusion: they didn't give a damn about us repatriates either.

It was a long, tiring drive back home to Akron, Ohio, and it was late evening when I finally pulled into my parents' driveway on Robin Street. I spent a hectic, restless ten days there, most of it visiting relatives and close friends. The nights were devastating. I had great difficulty falling asleep; and, when I did, the dreadful, horrifying nightmares kept interrupting my sleep. I kept dreaming that I was being forced to return to the Spider Web in Peking, and the result was always the same—I sprang up in bed, wide awake, and in a cold sweat.

On Tuesday morning, December 27, 1955, I got into my 1955 Chevrolet and headed west. My destination was Missoula, Montana, where I would start my four years of higher education.

Steve E. Kiba

September, 15, 2000
Air Force Museum in Dayton, Ohio

It was the last night of the ARC Services Reunion in Dayton. Former members of all ARC Wings—the 580th, 581st, and 582nd— were gathered in a hangar at the Air Force Museum for a banquet. The tables had been arranged in a clear area just inside the entrance to the hangar. Wings, engines, and stabilizers of surrounding aircraft formed the background of our gathering. After a great meal and a lot of good visitation, former Air Force Officer Eugene Vaadi stepped up to the podium. He had been a prisoner of war in both WW II and the Korean War. Since at that time it was also POW Week—a time set aside for national recognition of POWs—he was asked to make a relevant speech for the occasion.

The crowd became quiet and attentive. All faces were turned toward the podium. Eugene Vaadi adjusted the microphone, silently looked out across the huge gathering before him, and began to speak.

He said, "In recognition of this being POW Week and in remembrance of all of those returned POWs and those still missing and deceased, I would personally ask everyone to remember the MIAs and POWs who never returned. In today's times it is very difficult for people to understand the meaning of the ordeals and hardships that they endured and which still remains with them today. There were so many who were captured and died in captivity in the hands of the enemy and so many who did not receive care and were left to perish under their control.

"I was one of the unfortunate people who was shot down in World War II and again in the Korea War, both times way behind enemy lines without much hope of being rescued or of escaping. I was fortunate to survive several moves from place to place in Germany and to survive the strafing by our own people in the closing days of the war. Lack of food played havoc on our bodies, but somehow I survived.

"After being shot down in North Korea, I was shipped to Peking, China, where I suffered quite a bit during the nine months of around the clock interrogations; I was kept chained up, suffered severe beatings, had little or no food, and lived under conditions that are

280

difficult for people to understand. Again, there was little or no food, and the conditions were most primitive. On the ninth month they dragged me back to my cell because I was unable to move myself. I was still in the same clothes that I had been shot down in, had not been allowed to bathe or shave, or allowed any sanitary necessities.

"Following the ninth month ordeal, I was given my first haircut and beardcut with clippers, overall. They brought in a wooden washtub to my cell and ordered me to bathe. I was given my first set of prison clothes while still in solitary confinement.

"I remained in solitary until the late fall of 1954, when we were being prepared for the trial there; the entire crew was taken and sentenced for up to 15 years. Not until the last part of the year when negotiations were started in '54 and '55 by the United Nations and Dag Hammarskjold did any changes come about and we saw all of the crew that remained. From that time on, we were allowed freedom in the corridor during the day, the food started improving, and our living conditions also improved until our release in Hong Kong on August 4, 1955.

"I can tell you this, when I walked across to freedom and when I first saw the American flag..."

He became very choked up and stopped speaking. Finally he continued.

"Having been blown out of the air in Germany and Korea by fighters, I am one of the more fortunate ones to be here tonight."

(He pointed to the American flag nearby and said in a choked voice), "I can tell you **that (Our American Flag)** is the most beautiful sight you will see in your entire lifetime. So many people gave their lives so that those who live under it might be free. It is with great sorrow that I remember my three crew members and good friends who lost their lives."

At this point he was so overcome with emotion, he just stopped speaking; he turned away and left the podium. The crowd was so greatly moved by his words and his overwhelming emotion that there was a long period of silence. Finally someone began clapping. Then another joined in, and then another, until everyone was standing and clapping in tribute to him and to all of those on whose behalf he spoke.

281

THE FLAG

"...The flag represents a living country and is itself considered a living thing..."

The Federal Flag Code, Section 4, paragraph J.

Yes, it *is* a "living thing" that has grown in stature, strength, and meaning since its creation on June 14, 1777. It is an integral part of the legacy each American generation receives freely, maintains zealously, and passes on to the next generation through love of country, dedication to national duty, courage—and sacrifice when necessary.

There have been many versions of the Stars and Stripes flag, and the one we are most familiar with is the Star Spangled Banner. Its history began in June 1813, when Major George Armistead, the Commander of Fort McHenry in charge of defending Baltimore Harbor, ordered a huge flag made that the British could spot while they were still at sea and a long way from the Fort. The great flag was made by Mary Pickersgill, a Baltimore widow, and delivered to the Fort in August 1813. It was immediately mounted on a 90-foot flagpole inside the Fort.

In September 1814, after their soldiers began occupying Washington, D. C.—a circumstance that forced President James Madison and his wife to abandon the city and escape to Virginia—the British became interested in capturing Baltimore. Records show that 16 British ships were sent to attack Fort McHenry, and they got close enough to exchange shots with the defenders there. On September 13, the ships withdrew to positions about two to three miles from shore where they were safely out of range of the Fort's cannons. Then they began to bombard the Fort; it was a sustained siege that lasted through the night.

An American lawyer, Francis Scott Key, had been "detained" by the British and kept aboard the Admiral's flagship. At sunrise the next morning, Key managed to observe Fort McHenry through a telescope on the ship and assess the damage inflicted by the British. Amid the scars and rubble of the damaged Fort, he saw the huge flag fluttering in long, flowing waves on its 90-foot pole, and he was instantly inspired to write a poem about it. The only paper available to him was a letter he had in his pocket, and he used the back side of it on which to begin the famous poem he called "The Defense of Fort McHenry." After he was released by the British, he stayed in a hotel in Baltimore where he finished the poem. Later, he set it to the music of another song, "To Anacreon In Heaven," but the printers changed the title to "The Star Spangled Banner." It wasn't until 1931 that it became our National Anthem.

Like the defenders of Fort McHenry, our veterans, former prisoners of war, and families of MIAs all understand how precious our freedom is; they are the essence of what we are as a nation. Since our beginning, they are the few who have suffered and died for the many, even though dissidents often confronted them with a contempt born of cowardice, or ignorance—or both. Those many patriots and their faithful supporters on the home front have protected and preserved our nation and our sovereignty by refusing to yield to any of our enemies.

Through the years the Star Spangled Banner has been flown in many places around the world and also on the moon. Its image has been transported to outer space, far beyond where man has ever been. It has witnessed the hell of Montezuma and the Argonne Offensive, the streams of blood on Iwo Jima and Pork Chop Hill, and countless other battles in which our sons and daughters have bled and died to preserve our nation. The well-known emblem has been an observant, watchful friend in every war we've fought and a constant discouragement to the enemies that would enslave or destroy us. Our flag is the enduring symbol of all the things we cherish—freedom, liberty, justice, and the opportunity to pursue our own happiness, in our own way, without destroying the happiness of others.

It would be a terrible tragedy if our children and grandchildren did not receive from us that which we were given—a free America. Another tragedy, just as great, would be the failure of this generation—*or any generation*—to practice and teach patriotism, that quality of character from which grows a genuine respect for the flag and the meaning it embodies for **every** generation.

Truman Dayon Godwin

EPILOG

A few years after Schmidt and I were discharged from the Air Force, I received a letter from him telling me that Tippie had run off with another man. I was sorry to learn of his misfortune, but I really wasn't surprised. He got a divorce from her, and not long after that he met a nice girl whom he soon married. She was good for him, and they were genuinely happy. Then in January 1962, I received the shocking news that he had to have open heart surgery. On May 9, 1962, he died on the operating table at Fort Miley Veterans' Hospital. Poor Schmidt! He had just found real happiness and had only a short time to enjoy it. I was very much saddened by his death. I knew him extremely well, and he was a true friend.

His death made me think of Hart and the others who were gone. I sometimes considered visiting the relatives of Van Voorhis, Weese, and Hart, but I still could think of nothing to say. I was just too emotionally involved in their remembrance myself to be of much comfort to anyone else; so I avoided the possibility of re-opening old wounds that might be difficult for them to deal with. I also continued to feel guilt because I was free and enjoying life to the extent I could, while their loved ones were either imprisoned somewhere in a small dismal cell, or they were dead.

After leaving the Air Force, I tried numerous times to write to Downey and Fecteau and to send them magazines and packages, but I was unsuccessful in that endeavor; the mail never went through to them. Either the CIA wouldn't let it out of the country, or the "benevolent" Red Chinese officials refused to allow it into Red China. In either case, Downey and Fecteau were deprived of the letters, magazines, and goodies which I attempted to send them.

Many times I started letters to their relatives, but each time I ended up tearing them to pieces and throwing them into the wastebasket. Occasionally I contemplated visiting the New England area where they lived, but ultimately I just couldn't do it. I still suffered from the "nothing to say" syndrome, and I couldn't get beyond it. Also, I still remembered that the CIA warned us not to see or contact their relatives or try to contact Downey and Fecteau.

However, the warning wasn't what restrained me from doing it. I just didn't know how to "break the ice" with them or what to say afterward. How could I tell them that their sons would probably never come home and that our government even refused to acknowledge the fact that they were working for the CIA?

What really infuriated me was that the same United States Government and the same CIA that refused to admit that they were working for our country wasted no time in publicly admitting that captured U-2 pilot Gary Powers was a CIA agent and was on a spying mission for the United States when he was shot down over the Soviet Union. The U-2 incident was a greater blunder than was the Jehol incident, and the United States Government lost face to a greater degree than it would have by admitting that Downey and Fecteau were CIA agents and American citizens. Had the U. S. Government admitted to the Jehol blunder, Downey and Fecteau would have been spared many years of harsh treatment at the hands of the Red Chinese devils. In the special disciplinary "re-education" sessions during our final months in Red China, I persistently inquired about their condition and their fate. I was told repeatedly that their case was "different" and that the only way they would ever be freed would be for our government to acknowledge publicly that they were CIA operatives. Those who tried to indoctrinate us also said that our President would have to make a public apology for the daring act of aggression perpetrated against the People's Republic of China by these two men.

Richard Fecteau was finally released on December 13, 1971, after 6,954 miserable days in that damned communist hellhole. Most of that time was spent in solitary confinement.

Finally, on January 21, 1973, President Nixon admitted publicly that John Downey worked for the CIA. As expected, during Henry Kissinger's mid-February visit to Red China, the Red Chinese told him that Downey's behavior "had been exemplary" and that within the year his case would be reviewed. In the meantime his aged mother suffered a stroke. Feigning compassion and humanitarian concern, and upon a personal request by President Nixon, the Red Chinese consented to Downey's "early" release; they did this in recognition that the "humanitarian" act would enhance their image in the eyes of the world community. So, after over 20 years of hell-on-earth, he was released in early March 1973. Had the Red Chinese *really* been concerned and compassionate, they would have released him in the fall of 1971, when his ailing mother paid him a visit in Peking.

Through the years, since my return to the civilized world, I have often wondered about the other white men whom I had seen walking in the patio at the Spider Web. Could they be some of the thousands of American servicemen still missing and who have not yet been accounted for? Have they, too, been callously abandoned by the individual governments of whatever country they are citizens and, perhaps, forgotten by most of their fellow countrymen? It is difficult to believe that such a cruel and heartless act can be perpetrated in our "modern" world, but it has happened before and probably will continue to happen because war is "hell." For those who are unfortunate enough to be captured by the communists, their barbaric jailers carry out the sentences imposed upon their victims with a peculiar, sadistic glee. Yet, our own United States Government has contributed to that brutality by refusing to get tough with any nation suspected of holding American prisoners and by not demanding and not obtaining a complete and accurate accounting from them for ALL AMERICANS missing-in-action (MIAs).

It is my belief that the cruelest and most horrible fate a man can possibly suffer is to be made an anonymous captive against his will and without notification to his loved ones by his captors that he is alive and being held. It is heinous enough to fetter a man's body and to attempt to control his mind; but to do it over a prolonged period of time and to remove any hope of ever escaping the tedium of solitary confinement in a tiny, stifling hole is just too appalling for the average Westerner to comprehend; it really strains our credibility. But, fellow Americans, there are indeed people that cruel.

Presently there are hundreds of American servicemen unaccounted for from the Vietnam War. None of these men appear, nor have they ever appeared, on any communist list of POWs. Yet, since 1975, there have been 751 firsthand live sightings reported to our Defense Department. The communists persist in claiming that they have no knowledge of any of the men reported seen, yet evidence exists that some of them were captured alive by the communists. Granted, many MIAs are likely dead, but not all of them. It is not believable that so many of our missing servicemen could simply disappear off the face of the earth, especially in a tightly controlled totalitarian society such as that of communist North Vietnam. The truth is, these men have been abandoned. All that remains now is to forget them, and it appears that our government is ready and willing to do exactly that. Although "token appeals" to North Vietnam have been made by the United States Government regarding the fate of our MIAs, it has done more to hinder the efforts of the League of Families and other POW/MIA organizations. Attempts have been made to keep the missing prisoners' families from speaking out too loudly. Adverse and detrimental statements have been made—and are still being made—by so-called governmental "experts." In January 1974, an advisor to the Department of Defense callously and coldly told family members of missing prisoners and MIAs that the missing men "weren't worth the trouble" and that the MIA issue was definitely not a "vital" item for the U. S. Government.

My parents and relatives were afforded the same "comforting" sentiments while I was on "missing" status. They were advised to remain silent and bear their grief and burden in silence and not to speak up because it was not in the best interest of the United States "foreign policy." My father and mother were verbally threatened with dire consequences if they continued to insist that I was alive and if they didn't "go along" with the way the government was handling the matter. Incredible? Yes, but true. It is safe to assume that the relatives of the Southeast Asia MIAs met with the same stubborn resistance as did my parents.

It is a fact that Red China and North Korea did indeed hold over American servicemen after the end of the Korean War. It is also a fact that the American Government did **abandon** those men to a life of never-ending misery and agony in an isolated communist hellhole somewhere. My story testifies to that fact. So does the story of Downey and Fecteau. There are still over 8,000 men—our fellow Americans—missing from the Korean War.

It is also a fact that North Vietnam did not and still has not properly accounted for the prisoners they captured in Southeast Asia.

They did "agree" to "provide us with information" and to "aid us in recovering bodies"; instead, they have done every thing possible to hinder our search teams. They have even resorted to the cold-blooded murder of a member of the United States search team. Could it be they have something to hide? Perhaps live prisoners?

The communists were able (and still are) to subject American captives to years and years of indescribable hell and to inflict untold suffering and anguish on their innocent loved ones because—for some reason—the U. S. Government prefers to abandon its own fighting men to "ruffling" the communists and jeopardizing our "shaky" diplomatic relationship with the godless disciples of the devil. They also were able (and still are) to get away with it because the majority of the American people either refuse to believe that *our own government* can do such a cruel thing or they themselves are just too insensitive and indifferent to become involved in a concerted effort to prevent it. Yes, the godless communists starve, torture, and abuse their captives, but the U. S. State Department sanctions it and allows it to happen. The American public, too, must share in the guilt for failing to voice their anger and disgust to our government over this deplorable practice of making our POWs "expendable" on the basis of political expediency. By our silence, we tighten the manacles and leg irons of untold numbers of "forgotten" prisoners, whether military or political, and we guarantee that their insecure and uncertain fate shall forever be unchanged. Each and every American owes it to our "less fortunate" fighting men—the missing prisoners—and to their families to join in a concerted effort to secure the release of any still living and to obtain a complete and accurate accounting for the deceased. The patient, courageous MIA families have a right to know the truth: the fate of their loved ones.

Many people claim that they don't get involved because no "definite and conclusive" proof exist that there are any of our servicemen still alive, much less alive and in the hands of the communists. At the same time, they don't ask or expect concrete evidence from the double-dealing communists that the missing men are dead and are not being "detained" by them. Even if ALL the MIAs were dead, the families have a right to have the remains returned for burial at home.

It is the height of naiveté to believe that ALL MIAs are still alive. It is just as naive to believe that they are ALL dead. The American people must face the truth that the former Soviet Union, Red China, and North Korea did indeed hold back American servicemen after the Korean Armistice was signed. In addition, the American people must also face the ugly truth that after Little Switch and Big Switch (the exchange of prisoners between them and us) not all of our men were repatriated and that the U. S. Government abandoned those who were not. During the Vietnam War, I asked my government and my fellow Americans, "Can it happen again? Will it happen again?" My answer to them was, "Not only can it happen again, but it is happening right now."

I tried diligently and persistently to get the United States Government and the American people to see and to understand that the communists were not giving us a complete and accurate list of captured American servicemen that they were holding. As was the case during and after the Korean War, the communists in Hanoi were listing only about 25% of those they captured as prisoners.

It has been over 29 years since the signing of the Paris Peace Treaty (January 27, 1973) which resulted in the release of some of our POWs, and it has been over 27 years since American servicemen were pulled out of South Vietnam in 1975. Up to this point, all we have gotten from the North Vietnamese are a few sets of remains, bits and pieces of human bones. True, the communist government in North Vietnam did turn over thousands of photographs and pieces of apparel and equipment of American servicemen whom they captured, but the vast majority of that material "evidence" belonged to POWs who had been confirmed as killed-in-action or to POWs who had been repatriated in 1973. So, the so-called "humanitarian" gesture by the Vietnamese communists was nothing more than a cruel ploy to loosen the purse strings of the U. S. Government and to attract the "blood money" of certain unscrupulous American businessmen.

In 1992, a "special" Senate Select Committee on POW-MIA Affairs held scores of meetings and conducted hundreds of interviews with so-called POW-MIA "experts," former POWs, government agencies and officials, etc. Of course, the Vietnamese communists only showed the members of that Committee what they wanted them to see. Did our "illustrious" senators really expect the wily communists to take them to the prisons where they were detaining our brave, courageous fellow American countrymen who were already abandoned and mostly forgotten?

And what about the unfortunate POWs from World War II, the Korean War, the Cold War, and the Vietnam War who were transported to both Red China and the Soviet Union? A former Soviet Intelligence officer released a document written by a high-ranking North Vietnamese official stating that North Vietnam was still holding hundreds of American POWs. Some of the prisoners with high technical knowledge were sent to the Soviet Union to be interrogated, and none of them have yet been released. Likewise, those held by Vietnam have not been released either.

During the Senate Select Committee's hearings, the members heard testimony from a member of the National Security Council Staff during the Eisenhower Administration stating that American and United Nations POWs had been shipped in boxcars—about 450 per boxcar—to the Soviet Union. He told the Committee that then President Eisenhower knew that this incredible act was being perpetrated, but he elected to ignore it and to abandon his fellow American fighting men to an agonizing existence in that "frozen hell" called Siberia, perhaps never to escape their "private" hell-on-earth.

For me and the thousands of former POWs and the thousands of MIA families, it came as no surprise that the "prestigious" Senate Select Committee determined that no evidence exists that *any missing and unaccounted American servicemen remain alive.* This was not a unanimous decision, for we believe that Senator Robert Smith shared our views about live POWs. However, the way we read it is this: the Senate Select Committee, the United States Government, and the vast majority of the American people believe that, since the MIAs' families are unable to produce any "evidence" and are unable to "prove beyond a shadow of a doubt" that their missing loved ones are alive, then they must all be dead. This is the same **sorry** attitude that our government officials have taken for the past 47 years. Another reasonable question is this: on the subject of MIAs, why does our government take the word of **proven liars**—the communists—as the gospel truth? The communists are *professional liars; they even lie to* *their own people.* Communism (socialism) is predicated on the "Big Lie" theory. Marx, Engels, Lenin, Stalin, Mao, and all the communist (socialist) elite maintained that if you tell a lie over and over long enough, the people will eventually believe it. Could it be possible that a number of our elected and appointed government officials (America's "ruling elite") foster ideas of a Soviet Socialist Republic of America with themselves as the Central Committee? That's a stretch, of course, but whatever the case may be, they *have* catered to and believed the words of the communist enemy to the exclusion of the American MIA families and the former American POWs. By that action, they have added a few more nails to the coffins of the voiceless, abandoned, missing but still living American servicemen. I say "living" MIAs because the human being's will to survive, even in the most difficult and adverse conditions, is absolutely tenacious. Therefore, it is very possible that a number of our brave, courageous, steadfast MIAs might still be alive in some filthy enemy hellhole, still struggling and still fighting their captors and jailers in order to simply survive. Those brave American warriors, wherever they might be, undoubtedly place their hopes and faith in the United States of America for their ultimate rescue. They surely still believe and are intelligent enough to know that, even though America has its faults and is not perfect, it is the best country on God's Earth. They also understand that our democratic form of government is by far superior to any other existing form of government.

Because of my personal experience as an MIA and as a sojourner in various foreign lands, I have a profound sense of remorse and anguish by the revelation that many of our elected leaders and appointed officials, for various reasons, don't share the same strong faith in our country and its present form of government as do the MIAs and their families. They have this lack of faith even with their high living standards and conditions that are a virtual paradise compared to that of the MIAs and the vast majority of the world's population. Our elected leaders don't seem to have the courage, the experience, or the desire to stand up against foreign encroachment; it is easier to *appease* our enemies than to confront them. Publicly they claim that they sympathize with and understand the dilemma of MIA families, and they boast that they are doing everything humanly possible to bring the MIAs home or to account for them. Privately, they think, "So what if we leave a few thousand of them behind? What's the big deal?" And they choose the coward's way by concluding that risking war over a few thousand MIAs just isn't feasible. Or they make the excuse that they "must think of the whole country first, and MIAs are expendable." Consequently, America still does not have a complete and accurate accounting of our missing fellow countrymen.

It is indeed a disgrace when our government sends our young men off to war to risk life and limb and then turns its back on them if they are so unfortunate as to be captured by the enemy. Oh God, please open the eyes and touch the hearts of ALL AMERICANS! Help them cast off their shackles of apathy and indifference. Help us all to recognize the enemy within and to ferret out those that seek to betray and to destroy our Great **GOD-BLESSED AMERICA**. As our "Pledge of Allegiance" so aptly states... **"one nation under God"**...

Hebrews 13:3
"Remember them that are in bonds, as bound with them; and them who suffer adversity, as being yourselves also in the body."
Scofield Reference Bible

STEVE KIBA: TESTIMONY
Transcript of 10 November 1992 Testimony
to Senate Select Committee in Washington, D. C.

.

Transcript of 10 November 1992 Testimony
ALDERSON REPORTING COMPANY, INC.
1111 FOURTEENTH STREET, N.W.
SUITE 400
WASHINGTON, D. C. 20005

Vice Chairman Smith: Mr. Kiba, let me move to you. Is that pronounced correctly? Mr. Kiba?

Mr. Kiba: Kiba.

Vice Chairman Smith: Excuse me. You were a prisoner of war in the Korean War, correct?

Mr. Kiba: During the Korean War, yes.

Vice Chairman Smith: Proceed with your statement.

Mr. Kiba: I just want to say something before I start. I appreciate your inviting me here. But what I don't understand is, you are supposed to have a committee of 12.

[Applause.]

Mr. Kiba: I have waited a long time. I have been trying to inform you for years and years and years, and I am not trying to be disrespectful or anything.

Vice Chairman Smith: You are entitled to make your statement. I hear you.

Mr. Kiba: I will go ahead with this. I would appreciate it — and I have waited a long time. I would appreciate it if you would let me read this, and then I want you to question me.

Vice Chairman Smith: Proceed, sir.

TESTIMONY OF STEVE KIBA, FORMER KOREAN WAR U. S. POW HELD IN RED CHINA

Mr. Kiba: In appearing before you—before the committee. I say you, now, because almost all the committee—well, except for you, they're gone. Well, it's intimidating to me because I'm an ex-airman. I didn't have much education, and so forth, and I'm a country boy from West Virginia, and I now live in South Carolina.

But it really is not half as intimidating or anywhere near as intimidating as being cut off from your world, being isolated, and being forced to stand 18 to 24 hours a day in front of Red Chinese interrogators with a Red Chinese guard holding a machine pistol to your temple, caressing your temple. Now, that was intimidating.

And they were sadistic and barbaric. And because I know you're not going to threaten to shoot me—the committee's not, right? But they did every day, every hour, every few minutes, and then threatened me with all kinds of horrendous tortures, and they even did some of them.

And you're not going to put me on a starvation diet. They did. And you're not going to withhold my water because I don't answer your questions. They did. I would go days and days and days without a drink of water. And I would go days and even weeks without a bite of food.

And you are not going to threaten not to send me home, and they did every day. They told me I would never go home unless I cooperated. And they threatened to keep me for life. And they kept some of my friends for life. They're still there.

Now, in my testimony I'm going to tell you about American POWs who were abandoned after the 1953 cease-fire, and I know what I'm talking about, because I was left over there after the 1953 cease-fire.

Now, our essentially unarmed B-29—I say essentially unarmed because we were flying a B-29 with only two tail guns, and we were flying way up high, at 24,000 feet in the jet stream, and they caught us. And we were attacked and shot down. And this happened on January 12, 1953, about 10:45 P.M. And we were captured. And we were held over 2 years after the war was over.

Now, if the United States Government had accepted and lived up to its responsibilities to the men it sent off to fight, fight our battles during World War II, the Korean War, and the Vietnam War, we wouldn't have to be here, would we? It is a known fact that we abandoned American servicemen after these wars and let their families down. I know we abandoned some because I saw some of them.

President Harry Truman was the first President to leave Americans behind. Then President Eisenhower abandoned American POWs after the Korean War in North Korea, Red China, and the Soviet Union. In a press conference on April 29, 1959, President

Eisenhower acknowledged that not all American POWs were repatriated after the Korean War cease-fire. And Richard Nixon was Vice President then.

Then in March of 1973, President Nixon went on national TV and proclaimed that all POWs were home. He knew this was not true, and Henry Kissinger knew that this was not true, and North Vietnam knew that this was not true; and even I, an insignificant ex-POW, knew that it was not true.

Surely, President Nixon must have known about the Korean War POWs who were left behind. I'm positive that he knew because I wrote him numerous letters reminding him of this fact and pleaded with him not to allow it to happen again if and when we had peace with North Vietnam.

And during Lyndon Johnson's administration, I wrote to President Johnson and informed him about American POWs abandoned in North Korea, Red China, and Siberia after the Korean War cease-fire. And I pleaded with him not to let it happen again.

And during President Nixon's first administration, I wrote more than one letter—I don't know how many, but I wrote quite a few letters to every single Congressman and every single Senator about the POW/MIA issue. And, well, I don't know whether you were a Senator then or not. I don't remember.

I was going to say maybe some of you got some of my letters. Some of these fellows probably were Senators then, right? And maybe they got some of my letters, but they didn't answer me. In fact, I received very few replies.

I received replies from the Ohio Senators, because at that time, I was living in Ohio. In addition, I wrote to every middle school, junior high school, high school in Ohio. And I say, at that time I was living in Ohio.

I wrote to almost every, if not every, daily paper in the State of Ohio, to many of the larger papers throughout the Nation, like New York Times and all the others.

And I wrote to TV stations, radio stations, talk show hosts, national offices of the VFW, American Legion, and every civic and service organization I could think of. And I got very few replies.

I wrote to anyone that I thought might be willing to speak up for the MIAs. Response, or shall I say lack of response, was disheartening. It seemed that no one or very few people really cared about our abandoned POWs, except, of course, for their immediate families and a few friends.

Very few people even believed me that the POWs were left behind in Red China, Red North Korea, and the Soviet Union, and no one wanted to believe that it could happen again in Southeast Asia.

I tried to warn them that it was going to happen again. Presidents Ford, Carter, Reagan, and Bush were all informed about our Government's leaving POWs behind in communist hellholes in North Korea, Red China, the U.S.S.R., and Red Vietnam.

I wrote to every President from Johnson to Bush about our abandoning our fighting men. The response, if they even bothered to respond, was always the standard form letter by some underling telling me that everything humanly possible was being done to resolve the matter.

It seems that we live in a throwaway society. Like everything else we use, we "used" these brave, courageous, loyal men to fight our battles and then when they were captured, we just threw them away, abandoned them and forgot them. What about their families? We take away their husbands or fathers or brothers or sons and then tell them to be patient.

Well, they have been patient for years and years, some even for decades. Like Robert Dumas, for example. He has been trying for 42 years to learn the fate of his brother, who is an MIA in North Korea. And Robert has much pertinent information and pictures and documents proving that his brother was seen as late as 1957, alive. And I think this committee ought to hear what Robert and some of the other family members have to say.

I have a question for you? Why does our Government expect the POW/MIA families to come up with concrete, conclusive evidence to prove that their missing loved ones are alive and not ask the enemy for any proof that they're dead? You always ask the MIA family to prove that they're alive and to give you some concrete evidence. Now, how in the world are they going to go over there and get you concrete evidence?

Why does our government take as gospel the word of the communists who are expert, professional liars over the word of its own loyal, patriotic servicemen. And what about the MIA children? If we can't bring the parents home—their fathers home—then we should provide each one of them with a good college education, all the way up to a doctor's degree if they can handle it.

The draft dodgers and war protesters are afforded more consideration than our MIAs and their families. I know because I was an MIA; I was a POW, and my family was an MIA family. And you would be surprised at some of the things they tried to pull on them just because they were dumb Hunkies.

Why is the Government afraid that some of our MIAs/POWs might still be alive? Why was the Government in such a hurry to decide that all MIAs should be declared KIA? In my testimony, for purpose of brevity, I limit it to specific sightings, statements concerning the capture of Weese and Van Voorhis—those were the two men on my crew. They were captured alive as they touched the ground in North Korea.

And I also limit it to specific threats never to release me.

Vice Chairman Smith: What was the year of that incident?

Mr. Kiba: We were shot down on January 12th, 1953.

Vice Chairman Smith: And when were you released?

Mr. Kiba: August 4th, 1955. And this was 2 years after the cease-fire.

Vice Chairman Smith: Did you see your two crew mates in captivity after the armistice?

Mr. Kiba: I saw Van Voorhis.

Vice Chairman Smith: He was alive with you?

Mr. Kiba: He was alive.

Vice Chairman Smith: Did he come back?

Mr. Kiba: He did not come back. Let me finish this. There are things you should ask me about.

I did not include the horrible conditions and treatment at the hands of the sadistic communist captors, even though it might help you to understand better the type of warped minds with which we're dealing. I hear so many people say, well, why would they keep them? They have no reason to keep them. They do! The reason is, they don't

300

need a reason. They are mean, sadistic. They're different than we are. A communist is different.

I know. I had to live with them for 32 months. For almost 40 years, I've been trying to inform the American people and the news media of the heinous crime of enslaving the bodies and minds of our courageous fighting men by the godless communists. And they are. They don't believe in God. They're atheists.

For almost 40 years, our own Government has known of it and for almost 40 years kept it from the POW families and the American people. They've kept this a secret. They have known a lot of things, but they don't tell us.

Isn't it high time to correct this grave injustice perpetrated by the communist enemy and covered up by the MIA's own Government? What I have said to you and to the American people is important. This is doggone important. The information in the 30-page testimony which I presented to the Select Committee is extremely pertinent. The American people have a right, and especially the POW/MIA families, to know that living, missing American POWs were left behind. They damn well were left behind! This information must not be hidden any longer.

Government officials used to, and perhaps still do, tell the families that to release information on the status and circumstances of a POW might jeopardize his well-being. Keeping the families informed with the truth couldn't jeopardize the unfortunate POW any more than what leaving him to rot in a far-off hellhole could jeopardize him. Which is worse?

The families can take it. I've waited decades to tell you these incredible facts. I've attempted to tell you many times. So don't treat them lightly. What the Red Chinese did to our crew and what they forced us to endure, I can understand. I understand it completely. But what I don't understand is why our Government—I can't understand it and it really hurts—is why our Government, when I came back, when our crew came back, they ordered us to remain silent about the others whom we had seen.

I couldn't understand, and I still don't, why they chose to abandon fellow countrymen.

Vice Chairman Smith: Sir, could I interrupt you just for a second right there? How many others did you see after the armistice, other than your crewmates?

Mr. Kiba: Okay, let me see.

Vice Chairman Smith: Roughly, a number.

Mr. Kiba: Roughly, 10 to 15.

Vice Chairman Smith: You saw them. You were imprisoned with them or you saw them, you talked with them.

Mr. Kiba: I didn't talk to them, no. You have to realize, as I told you, these Chinese are mean. And they kept us under very close guard. I could see them. It was very difficult to communicate, even with Van Voorhis. He was 6 feet from me.

Vice Chairman Smith: But you knew there were other Americans other than Van Voorhis?

Mr. Kiba: Yes.

Vice Chairman Smith: And you saw them?

Mr. Kiba: We saw them and some of my crew saw them. Now, I have to tell you this, none of the crew saw Van Voorhis. I was the only one that saw Van Voorhis. And this makes it difficult because when I came back, they tried to discredit me and tried to make me believe that I had imagined it.

Vice Chairman Smith: Well, now, let me ask you about that. When you came back, you were debriefed—

Mr. Kiba: Debriefed, yes.

Vice Chairman Smith:—and you told the debriefers what you just told us.

Mr. Kiba: Yes.

Vice Chairman Smith: And what was their response to that?

Mr. Kiba: Well, it depends on which debriefer, now. We were debriefed by at least three groups, Air Force, CIA, and I think it was either the Defense Department or State Department. I'm not sure which it was.

And in some cases they tape recorded most of what we said. In some cases they would shut the tape recorder off and then would talk to us.

I love this country, and I wouldn't hesitate to volunteer again. If my country needed me, I would go tomorrow. And I didn't dodge the draft or protest the war. No Kiba ever dodged the draft or protested his country's policy while it was in conflict with a foreign power.

Our parents instilled in us family values, strong patriotism. They loved this country and sent four sons off to war. I had three brothers who also fought in World War II. They didn't run away.

Are there any MIAs still alive? I believe so. Because deep down a man wants to live, and this strong will to live helps him to endure the worst kind of treatment and conditions. And I'll tell you one thing. For the first 3 or 4 months, I wanted them to kill me. I was hoping they would kill me. I was praying that they would kill me to put me out of my misery.

My diet at the Peanut Palace—did you read this? Okay, at the Peanut Palace, my diet was fifteen half peanuts. You know what a peanut in a shell looks like? Okay. There are two in there, right? And so I got 15, but if you put them together back in the shell, they would be 7 ½, and a small bun about that size.

And for lunch, I got 15 peanuts and two small buns. For supper, I got 15 peanuts and two small buns. Now there was a catch, though. Oh, they also allowed me a cup of water a day. The only problem was, if you weren't in your room, in the cell, and you were upstairs being interrogated, you didn't eat. If you were out of the cell at the time they delivered the food, you didn't get any.

And that happened many times, because as I told you, the interrogations ran anywhere from 6 hours to 18 hours to 24 hours. And when they were through doing this, they would take you back to the cell. Maybe a half hour later, you'd be taken right back up.

So you were going sometimes days and days and days without getting any sleep. And you were going days and days and days without food or water. And they would sit in front of you, and they would slurp their tea and their brandy and their water, and they'd ask you, would you like a drink? Yes, I'd like a drink. Cooperate and we'll give you a drink.

And I won't tell you what I told them. Okay, are my friends Weese and Van Voorhis still alive? I don't know. But I do know one thing. That they bailed out of the B-29 because airmen in the back of the B-29 saw them leave. And, as I told you, I saw Van Voorhis 6 to 7 months later. In fact, the exact dates were around July 20th or 21st through about the end of July, first of August of 1953, was when I saw him.

And if there's even the slightest chance that even only one POW is alive, we—and by we I mean you and me, the Government, the news media, everybody, every single American—owes it to that POW and to that family to get him home.

And I'm telling you, don't let down our missing men from World War II, the Korean War, and the Vietnam War. Also, Senator, don't endanger our future men by cutting the defense budget too much. You cut that defense budget too much and we still have enemies. We have 1 billion Chinese over there, and they're not our friends. They told me that they were going to destroy us. And they told me it didn't matter if it takes 1 year, 5 years, 10 years, 100 years; they're going to destroy us. And they mean it.

If you send the boys off to fight again, let them fight to win, not like in Korea and Vietnam! You tied our hands. And we want no more no-win wars like Korea and Vietnam! And if they are so unfortunate as to be captured, don't leave them behind and don't abandon them and don't forget them.

Now that's all the statement I have here. Now, I'm sure you have some questions here. You're probably wondering why the CIA interrogated me, I mean, debriefed me. It seemed more like interrogation, but it was really a debriefing.

Vice Chairman Smith: Why don't you answer your own question of why?

Mr. Kiba: See, we were shot down in North Korea. In fact, it was 4 days. On the 16th, a mean son of a gun came in, and he asked me where I was shot down. I told him North Korea. And he started screaming, and he said, no, you're in Red China. Well, he didn't say Red China, he said the People's Republic of China. Now I refuse to say that.

Then a friendly interrogator came in, interpreter, came in, he told me I was going to take a trip. I said, you're sending me to a POW camp. He said, no, you're not going to camp. You're going somewhere better.

I said, where are we going, Red China I told him, you know. He said, you're going to the People's Republic of China. And that night they put us on a train and shipped us off to Mukden up in Manchuria.

And a few months later, in the interrogations—at first they started accusing us of germ warfare, dropping germs on the leaflets that we were dropping. And then they changed, and they accused us of espionage. They claimed that we were CIA agents working for the CIA.

And I don't remember whether I put it in the testimony or not, but we were put on trial, and we were tried and convicted of being espionage agents working for the CIA. And a few months later, they moved two CIA agents in with us for a 3-week period. That would be John Downey and Richard Fecteau.

And at the end of the 3 weeks, they moved them out with no explanation. They moved them in with us with no explanation. They moved them out. So that's why the CIA wanted to question us.

I saw others, too.

Chairman Kerry: Mr. Kiba, let me, if I can, intercede here for just a moment. First of all, I want to thank you for your testimony and I know you were concerned that not all Senators are here or something, but I want you to know I was watching you on television. This is being televised internally in the circuit in the Senate. And we have this technology today that somehow connects us even when we're not here.

So I did hear your testimony. I listened to you talk about—

Mr. Kiba: It does make it look a little bad though, doesn't it?

Chairman Kerry: No, no, no. I understand. I just wanted you to know that, because I found your testimony riveting obviously and—

Mr. Kiba: I mean to me, personally, to me. I come all the way from South Carolina to testify before a committee, and all I have is the co-chairman.

Chairman Kerry: I know, but unfortunately, sir, that—the nature of the lives of most people here is such is that they get pulled back to their office for one thing or another. It doesn't mean that they're not listening to you.

Mr. Kiba: Oh, one or two.

Chairman Kerry: No, no, no. I'm saying, I can't vouch for everybody, but I'm telling you that people really are, you know, listening. I heard you and I've also read your entire testimony.

Mr. Kiba: Okay.

Chairman Kerry: And it is not just us you're talking to, it's also the American people.

Mr. Kiba: Right.

Chairman Kerry: And there is a record here and yours is very much a part of that.

But I want to ask you a couple of questions based on what you're saying. First of all, in your testimony, you mentioned a number of names of people who were there with you, different people who were there, Colonel Arnold and different folks that you saw at one time or another.

When you say that there were 15—is that the group you're referring to?

Mr. Kiba: No, no.

Chairman Kerry: It's a separate 15.

Mr. Kiba: This would be in addition to my crew.

Chairman Kerry: Okay. So, in addition to your crew, there were maybe 15 people.

Mr. Kiba: Between 10 or 15, I'll say, yeah. I'd have to stop and count them up, but between 10 and 15.

Chairman Kerry: Often in your testimony, you referred to somebody who was, you could see, a white man who was walking around the patio or somebody who was enclosed or something.

Mr. Kiba: Yes.

Chairman Kerry: Were you able to tell that they were, in fact, American? Did you know that or did you just—

Mr. Kiba: I could tell they were Caucasians.

Chairman Kerry: Okay, but you weren't certain they were Americans?

Mr. Kiba: There would be no way, because, see, during that war, we had UN involvement, so they possibly could have been British or French or—

Chairman Kerry: But at any rate, there were 15 Caucasian?

Mr. Kiba: Caucasians, yes.

Chairman Kerry: And, was that the total number of people in the course of the period beyond the armistice that you were there? You were there until 1955?

Mr. Kiba: 1955, right.

Chairman Kerry: Almost 2 years beyond, is that right? Now, they ultimately release you?

Mr. Kiba: Yes.

Chairman Kerry: Can you explain or help the committee to understand why they might have released you, but not released the others?

Mr. Kiba: Okay, I think the reason they released us and I got this from the Chinese interrogators and interpreters. One thing they kept telling us, that our Government has abandoned us. They don't care about you. If they did, they'd bring you home.

And they say, we're trying to get you free. We're trying to release you. And what we want from your Government is a seat in the United Nations and the island of Taiwan. And of course, our Government wasn't dealing.

And if our Government had dealt, I'd have been disappointed, because I would rather have sat there and rotted in hell for the rest of my life than to give them anything.

Chairman Kerry: I understand that. But why did they let you go?

Mr. Kiba: Well, I think this was a ploy. They released us because they could claim that they were humane and they could claim that they were kind and so forth. In fact, on—

Chairman Kerry: Were the others alive when you were released?

Mr. Kiba: Some of them were, but I can't tell you about all, because some of these—the most of them I saw in July of 1953, the big part of them, when I was in cell number 15.

Chairman Kerry: In the aftermath of 1953, did you see any people, after 1953?

Mr. Kiba: Oh, yes, yeah. We saw some in '54 and in '55.

Chairman Kerry: And these people that you referred to just as Caucasians? This is where your testimony was referring to people you saw in that prison?

Mr. Kiba: That's right.

Chairman Kerry: Now, what does our Government say was the location of your flight?

Mr. Kiba: We were south of the Yalu River.

Chairman Kerry: Our Government concurs that you were shot down 40 miles—

Mr. Kiba: Our radar tracked us.

Chairman Kerry: So no one from our Government ever tried to assert that you might have strayed over Chinese soil?

Mr. Kiba: Oh, no, no.

Chairman Kerry: That's not even at issue?

Mr. Kiba: No.

Chairman Kerry: Okay.

Mr. Kiba: See that black dot there? See the P on Pyongyang? Okay. We were coming across this way toward where that little bay goes in there. We were coming right through there, and we were approximately 40 miles south.

Chairman Kerry: Okay.

Mr. Kiba: And we were flying high, 24,000 feet. And along there's a set of railroad tracks with searchlights, radar-controlled searchlights and radar controlled ack-ack. And so they hit us with the radar-controlled ack-ack, plus a bunch of MIGs.

Chairman Kerry: Now, when you were on your journey north very shortly, it was about 72 hours later, right? You were transported north almost immediately?

Mr. Kiba: Right.

Chairman Kerry: Did you see any other people being transported north at that time?

Mr. Kiba: No.

Chairman Kerry: During the course of your captivity, other than the people you saw, did you learn from others in the prison or from guards or anybody, about other Americans being brought?

Mr. Kiba: See, after we were moved to China, we were in solitary confinement most of the time. And, most of the guards wouldn't talk to you because if they did, they were punished. And if we talked to the guards, we were punished, too. But a few—

Chairman Kerry: You learned nothing from the guards or anything?

Mr. Kiba: Oh, I learned a little bit from the guards. I learned enough Chinese to know when the war ended. And I knew when Big Switch took place and Little Switch took place.

Chairman Kerry: The most people that you saw in this prison who were Americans, was it what period, in 1973?

Mr. Kiba: '53, yeah.

Chairman Kerry: In 1953, excuse me.

Mr. Kiba: July '53.

Chairman Kerry: And that was in China?

Mr. Kiba: In China, in Peking. See, we spent about 3 weeks in Mukden, and they put us on another train, and we took a long train ride and ended up in Peking.

Chairman Kerry: Now, when you were debriefed and told not to tell anybody about this; that was in 1955 after you came back?

Mr. Kiba: 1955, right.

Chairman Kerry: Did you ever go to anybody and begin to kind of say, I am troubled by this?

Mr. Kiba: I was troubled by it a great deal, but I didn't do too much until 2, 3 years later, then I started trying to contact people and trying to get people to listen.

See, right after I got—

Chairman Kerry: As you contacted people, did you find other people who confirmed what you were saying from other places or experiences?

Mr. Kiba: No. The people I was trying to contact were Government officials and newspapers, you know, people—

Chairman Kerry: And they just gave you the cold shoulder basically?

Mr. Kiba: Yes.

Chairman Kerry: What do you attribute that to?

Mr. Kiba: I don't know. I think it is hard for the American people to even think that we would do such a thing, would do something. I mean, it's unbelievable, incredible. And it's hard for you to believe.

Chairman Kerry: It is hard for anybody. Sure it is. I wanted— well, I guess it is not hard for us to believe any more after the course of last year's hearings.

309

Senator Smith has a question. I just want to finish up, but go ahead.

Vice Chairman Smith: Well, just on your point there. Were you aware, were you made aware by the Chinese of the exchange of prisoners at the armistice? Because you came in just before the armistice, you obviously extended beyond the armistice.

Were you told, did they try to rub your nose in it or—you are not going to go home? What did you know?

Mr. Kiba: The Chinese kept saying—I know the war is over.

Vice Chairman Smith: You did know that.

Mr. Kiba: I knew exactly when it was over, and I knew when they were exchanging POWs, and I would tell my interrogators, the interpreters, that the war is over, let me go home. And they would keep telling me the war is not over.

And then, a little bit later, about a year or so later, they would tell me that my case is different. And they would tell me, you're not a POW. Nobody knows you're alive. If you don't do as we expect of you, we're going to keep you here forever.

Chairman Kerry: Well, I would like to—yes, Colonel Simpson?

The only concern I have is Mr. Oprica has a plane to get to and we have one more panel.

Colonel Simpson: I just want to say one more thing. When he came home, I met him at the border.

Chairman Kerry: You met him at the border?

Mr. Kiba: Yeah, he gave my first Coca-Cola. I remember it.

Colonel Simpson: This may help you understand. I was ordered to go up to the border to meet him when they were coming in, but I didn't know exactly when they were coming in. And so I went and told the consul general, who had the rank of minister, that I was going up to the border to meet the possible return of the POWs.

And he said, no, you mustn't go. And I said, I'm sorry, I'm going. I said, I've been ordered by Washington to go up there.

He said, well, I don't want you to go and I said, well, I'm going anyhow. He said, I don't give a damn if they never come back. That gives you a clue to the prevailing attitude from the American ambassador.

Chairman Kerry: Mr. Kiba, let me just say to you that—first of all, I want to ask one last question. Was there any effort made to recruit you? Did they try to—

Mr. Kiba: Yeah, they did. I was very young at that time and after the interrogators—another thing. You, know, we were interrogated for almost 8 months. And you know that's not necessary. You're going to get all the information you need within a few days. But they interrogated our crew for around 8 months.

And they would work in shifts. I think what they were doing was training interrogators and so forth.

Okay, now, starting in the latter part of April, May, they started the political indoctrination. And I think I mentioned that in here—

Chairman Kerry: Yes, you did. Yes, you did.

Mr. Kiba: We called that communist bull.

Chairman Kerry: Yes, sir.

Mr. Kiba: And they offered me several times to stay and you know, they even told me, you're not American. You're a Hungarian. Your mother and dad are Hungarian. You're not American. Why don't you stay? We'll train you. We'll send you through the university.

Chairman Kerry: Well, let me just say to you that I dare say there aren't many people much more American than you. And I personally want to extend to you my profound respect and admiration and gratitude for coming forward today, but particularly my respect and I think the respect of Senator Smith and the entire committee.

I must tell you, you know, I spent 24 hours in a fake captivity in the SERE training and decided that nothing could be worse in human existence than losing one's liberty and was petrified of the notion of ever being captured. So, I tell you, for anybody who spent 24 hours in real captivity, let alone years as you did, you have my just undying respect and admiration and I thank you for—

Mr. Kiba: Let me say one thing. Young men had it rough, the airmen. But the officers had it 10 times as rough as we did. They really gave the officers a real going over, especially Colonel Arnold.

They made him stand one time 7 days and 7 nights in interrogation. They fed him one time a day, and they took him out to the bathroom one time a day. If he started to fall, they'd hit him with the rifle. And they would put clamps on him and dislocate his shoulders.

Then they'd take his fingers—his hands would swell up, and they would milk his fingers. See, so they were really nasty with him.

Chairman Kerry: Well, some of the most extraordinary tales of human spirit have come out of prisoners of war.

Mr. Kiba: Oh, another thing, Colonel Arnold was in solitary confinement the complete time.

Chairman Kerry: I saw in your testimony, you mentioned that there was one point where the door opened and you saw him but they immediately shut it.

Mr. Kiba: Right.

Chairman Kerry: Well, let me thank you. We do have to move on to the next panel.

Vice Chairman Smith: Let me also, just in closing, just thank you, Mr. Kiba, for what you did for your country and what you endured. You are one hell of a brave man and I am proud that you came up and your country has every reason to be proud of you and thank God there are people like you who are willing to—

Mr. Kiba: I apologize for losing—

Vice Chairman Smith: No, that is all right. I also thank all the witnesses.

Chairman Kerry: I would like to thank you all. Colonel Corso, thank you. Colonel Simpson, thank you very much.

ALDERSON REPORTING COMPANY, INC.
1111 FOURTEENTH STREET, N.W.
SUITE 400
WASHINGTON, D. C. 20005
(202) 289-2260
(800) FOR DEPO

CALENDARS

1953

January						
S	M	T	W	T	F	S
					1	2	3
4	5	6	7	8	9	10
11	12	13	14	15	16	17
18	19	20	21	22	23	24
25	26	27	28	29	30	31

February						
S	M	T	W	T	F	S
1	2	3	4	5	6	7
8	9	10	11	12	13	14
15	16	17	18	19	20	21
22	23	24	25	26	27	28

March						
S	M	T	W	T	F	S
1	2	3	4	5	6	7
8	9	10	11	12	13	14
15	16	17	18	19	20	21
22	23	24	25	26	27	28
29	30	31				

April						
S	M	T	W	T	F	S
		1	2	3	4
5	6	7	8	9	10	11
12	13	14	15	16	17	18
19	20	21	22	23	24	25
26	27	28	29	30		

May						
S	M	T	W	T	F	S
					1	2
3	4	5	6	7	8	9
10	11	12	13	14	15	16
17	18	19	20	21	22	23
24 31	25	26	27	28	29	30

June						
S	M	T	W	T	F	S
	1	2	3	4	5	6
7	8	9	10	11	12	13
14	15	16	17	18	19	20
21	22	23	24	25	26	27
28	29	30				

July						
S	M	T	W	T	F	S
			1	2	3	4
5	6	7	8	9	10	11
12	13	14	15	16	17	18
19	20	21	22	23	24	25
26	27	28	29	30	31	

August						
S	M	T	W	T	F	S
						1
2	3	4	5	6	7	8
9	10	11	12	13	14	15
16	17	18	19	20	21	22
23 30	24 31	25	26	27	28	29

September						
S	M	T	W	T	F	S
		1	2	3	4	5
6	7	8	9	10	11	12
13	14	15	16	17	18	19
20	21	22	23	24	25	26
27	28	29	30			

October						
S	M	T	W	T	F	S
				1	2	3
4	5	6	7	8	9	10
11	12	13	14	15	16	17
18	19	20	21	22	23	24
25	26	27	28	29	30	31

November						
S	M	T	W	T	F	S
1	2	3	4	5	6	7
8	9	10	11	12	13	14
15	16	17	18	19	20	21
22	23	24	25	26	27	28
29	30					

December						
S	M	T	W	T	F	S
		1	2	3	4	5
6	7	8	9	10	11	12
13	14	15	16	17	18	19
20	21	22	23	24	25	26
27	28	29	30	31		

1954

January

S	M	T	W	T	F	S
					1	2
3	4	5	6	7	8	9
10	11	12	13	14	15	16
17	18	19	20	21	22	23
24 31	25	26	27	28	29	30

February

S	M	T	W	T	F	S
	1	2	3	4	5	6
7	8	9	10	11	12	13
14	15	16	17	18	19	20
21	22	23	24	25	26	27
28						

March

S	M	T	W	T	F	S
	1	2	3	4	5	6
7	8	9	10	11	12	13
14	15	16	17	18	19	20
21	22	23	24	25	26	27
28	29	30	31			

April

S	M	T	W	T	F	S
				1	2	3
4	5	6	7	8	9	10
11	12	13	14	15	16	17
18	19	20	21	22	23	24
25	26	27	28	29	30	

May

S	M	T	W	T	F	S
						1
2	3	4	5	6	7	8
9	10	11	12	13	14	15
16	17	18	19	20	21	22
23 30	24 31	25	26	27	28	29

June

S	M	T	W	T	F	S
		1	2	3	4	5
6	7	8	9	10	11	12
13	14	15	16	17	18	19
20	21	22	23	24	25	26
27	28	29	30			

July

S	M	T	W	T	F	S
				1	2	3
4	5	6	7	8	9	10
11	12	13	14	15	16	17
18	19	20	21	22	23	24
25	26	27	28	29	30	31

August

S	M	T	W	T	F	S
1	2	3	4	5	6	7
8	9	10	11	12	13	14
15	16	17	18	19	20	21
22	23	24	25	26	27	28
29	30	31				

September

S	M	T	W	T	F	S
			1	2	3	4
5	6	7	**8**	9	10	11
12	13	14	15	16	17	18
19	20	21	22	23	24	25
26	27	28	29	30		

October

S	M	T	W	T	F	S
					1	2
3	4	5	6	7	8	9
10	11	12	13	14	15	16
17	18	19	20	21	22	23
24 31	25	26	27	28	29	30

November

S	M	T	W	T	F	S
	1	2	3	4	5	6
7	8	9	10	11	12	13
14	15	16	17	18	19	20
21	22	**23**	24	25	26	27
28	29	30				

December

S	M	T	W	T	F	S
			1	2	3	4
5	6	**7**	8	9	10	11
12	13	14	15	16	17	18
19	20	21	22	23	24	25
26	27	**28**	29	30	31	

1955

January						
S	M	T	W	T	F	S
						1
2	3	4	5	6	7	8
9	10	11	12	13	14	15
16	17	18	19	20	21	22
23 30	24 31	25	26	27	28	29

February						
S	M	T	W	T	F	S
	1	2	3	4	5	
6	7	8	9	10	11	12
13	14	15	16	17	18	19
20	21	22	23	24	25	26
27	28					

March						
S	M	T	W	T	F	S
		1	2	3	4	5
6	7	8	9	10	11	12
13	14	15	16	17	18	19
20	21	22	23	24	25	26
27	28	29	30	31		

April						
S	M	T	W	T	F	S
					1	2
3	4	5	6	7	8	9
10	11	12	13	14	15	16
17	18	19	20	21	22	23
24	25	26	27	28	29	30

May						
S	M	T	W	T	F	S
1	2	3	4	5	6	7
8	9	10	11	12	13	14
15	16	17	18	19	20	21
22	23	24	25	26	27	28
29	30	31				

June						
S	M	T	W	T	F	S
			1	2	3	4
5	6	7	8	9	10	11
12	13	14	15	16	17	18
19	20	21	22	23	24	25
26	27	28	29	30		

July						
S	M	T	W	T	F	S
					1	2
3	4	5	6	7	8	9
10	11	12	13	14	15	16
17	18	19	20	21	22	23
24 31	25	26	27	28	29	30

August						
S	M	T	W	T	F	S
	1	2	3	4	5	6
7	8	9	10	11	12	13
14	15	16	17	18	19	20
21	22	23	24	25	26	27
28	29	30	31			

September						
S	M	T	W	T	F	S
				1	2	3
4	5	6	7	8	9	10
11	12	13	14	15	16	17
18	19	20	21	22	23	24
25	26	27	28	29	30	

October						
S	M	T	W	T	F	S
						1
2	3	4	5	6	7	8
9	10	11	12	13	14	15
16	17	18	19	20	21	22
23 30	24 31	25	26	27	28	29

November						
S	M	T	W	T	F	S
	1	2	3	4	5	
6	7	8	9	10	11	12
13	14	15	16	17	18	19
20	21	22	23	24	25	26
27	28	29	30			

December						
S	M	T	W	T	F	S
				1	2	3
4	5	6	7	8	9	10
11	12	13	14	15	16	17
18	19	20	21	22	23	24
25	26	27	28	29	30	31

ABOUT THE AUTHOR

Steve Kiba was born February 5, 1932, in Lundale, West Virginia. His parents were Hungarian immigrants who worked hard to rear their eleven children. Seeking opportunities for better education and employment, the family moved to Akron, Ohio, in 1945. Steve graduated from Kenmore High School in 1950, and in July he joined the Air Force. He proudly served his country for 5 ½ years, almost 32 months as a political prisoner in Red China. He was deported from Red China on August 4, 1955. After he left the Air Force, he went to college and earned a BA from the University of Akron in 1959 and an MA in Spanish from Kent State University in 1967. He and his wife Darlene now reside in South Carolina.

DATE			

03 329059